Machine Learning

CHAPMAN AND HALL COMPUTING SERIES

Computer Operating Systems
For micros, minis and mainframes
2nd edition
David Barron

Microcomputer Graphics
Michael Batty

The Pick Operating System
Malcolm Bull

Programming in FORTRAN
3rd edition
V.J. Calderbank

Expert Systems
Principles and case studies
2nd edition
Edited by Richard Forsyth

Expert Systems
Knowledge, uncertainty and decision
Ian Graham and Peter Llewelyn Jones

Artificial Intelligence and Human Learning
Intelligent computer-aided instruction
Edited by John Self

Artificial Intelligence
Principles and applications
Edited by Masoud Yazdani

Machine Learning

Principles and techniques

Edited by

Richard Forsyth

LONDON   NEW YORK

Chapman and Hall

First published in 1989 by
Chapman and Hall Ltd
11 New Fetter Lane, London EC4P 4EE
Published in the USA by
Chapman and Hall
29 West 35th Street, New York NY 10001

© 1989 Chapman and Hall Ltd

Chapter 8, The acquisition of natural language by machine,
© 1989 Chris Naylor.
Chapter 9, A computational model of creativity,
© 1989 Masoud Yazdani.

Typeset in 10/12 pt Photina by Cotswold Typesetting Ltd
Printed in Great Britain by
St Edmundsbury Press Ltd,
Bury St Edmunds, Suffolk

ISBN 0 412 30570 4 (hardback)
ISBN 0 412 30580 1 (paperback)

British Library Cataloguing in Publication Data

Machine learning.
1. Machine learning.
I. Forsyth, Richard, 1948
006.3′1
ISBN 0–412–30570–4
ISBN 0–412–30580–1 Pbk

Library of Congress Cataloging in Publication Data

Machine learning/edited by Richard Forsyth.
    p.   cm.
    Bibliography: p.
    Includes index.
    ISBN 0–412–30570–4.   ISBN 0–412–30580–1 (pbk.)
    1. Machine learning.   I. Forsyth, Richard.
Q325.F64 1989
006.3′1—dc19   88–22872
                                                         CIP

Contents

Preface

Machine learning is moving from being an esoteric postgraduate speciality to a topic taught to undergraduates as a core field within artificial intelligence (AI). It is not hard to foresee it moving further out to computer science in general and to other disciplines such as linguistics, philosophy and psychology. Current texts are rather expensive and highly technical. This book aims to present the key findings of machine learning research, explained by experts in the field, in an accessible manner for both students and computer professionals. The authors attempt to convey some of the excitement of working in this dynamic area at the frontier of computer science. They also show how the techniques described can lead to impressive practical results.

The book is intended first and foremost as a guide for those setting out to write or use a computer system which, in some sense, learns to improve its performance. College and university students, however, will also find it a useful survey of a highly active research field, whose results are beginning to have important practical applications.

The chapter authors show that machine learning can be viewed from a number of perspectives – as optimization, as concept attainment, as scientific discovery, as automatic programming and many more – but that these perspectives can be unified. The common theme is: generate + test – also known as trial + error (in psychology), as conjecture + refutation (in philosophy), as hill climbing (in engineering) and under other labels.

By abstracting this unifying principle from the plethora of self-improving computer systems it is possible to put forward a provisional taxonomy of machine learning algorithms. To start with, the generate + test approach suggests two central questions about any learning system:

1. How are new knowledge structures generated from old ones?
2. How are candidate knowledge structures evaluated?

The answers to these questions help to organize a field which, up to now, has been characterized by somewhat anarchic eclecticism.

Richard Forsyth   March 1988

Notes on contributors

The contributors to this work are all leading researchers and practitioners in AI, with special interest in the question of machine learning. In addition, they are all good technical writers who know how to present technical details in a comprehensible style without excessive use of jargon.

IGOR ALEKSANDER

Igor Aleksander was educated in South Africa and London in electrical engineering, computer science and mathematics. He has been on the faculties of the Universities of London, Kent and Brunel (where he was Head of the Electrical Engineering Department). He is presently Head of the Department of Electrical Engineering at Imperial College, London, and he carries the title of Professor of Neural Systems Engineering. His interests lie in AI, specifically the topics of machine learning and neural computing. He has published over one hundred papers and twelve books in these areas. In addition, he has given distinguished lectures as the Silvanus P. Thompson lecturer and the Kelvin lecturer for the IEE. He is currently Chairman of the Association for Information Technology and the British Pattern Recognition Association.

TOMASZ ARCISZEWSKI

Tomasz Arciszewski is an Associate Professor of Civil Engineering at Wayne State University in Detroit. His major research area is design methodology and applications of artificial intelligence in engineering. He has authored and co-authored more than 40 publications in the areas of structural engineering, design methodology and expert systems. His research is supported by grants from the National Science Foundation, the State of Michigan, and Wayne State University. He founded the Intelligent Computers Center at WSU in 1987. The mission of the Center is the development and implementation of new types of expert systems for engineering purposes, including model-based and learning expert systems, and research on the methodologies of expert systems development and knowledge acquisition, including machine learning. The Center has a network of computers based on the TI Explorer LX. A number of commercial and experimental inductive systems are being tested. An international group of twelve PhD students is involved in research at the Center.

DIMITRIS CHORAFAS

Professor Chorafas has an international reputation as an independent consultant, specializing in strategic planning, evaluation and design of information systems – established over twenty-five years' work with a wide range of major corporations, including financial institutions and leading computer vendors. In his early career he was engaged in work on systems engineering and executive development with IBM in Europe and the USA. Since 1960 he has provided independent advice to senior management on corporate strategy, computer design, software policy, distributed data processing, database organization, information systems design, operations research, simulation and long-term planning. His client list ranges from AEG-Telefunken to Von Tobel Bank – including companies that are household names on both sides of the Atlantic. He has conducted seminars for more than thirty banking institutions world-wide and has presented public seminars in North America, South America, Europe and Asia. He has also published fifty-four books on management and information technology. His latest book, *Applying Expert Systems in Business*, was published in 1986 by McGraw-Hill, New York.

RICHARD FORSYTH

Richard Forsyth is a failed poet who now makes a living as a software specialist. He holds BA 1st class in psychology from Sheffield University (1970) and an MSc in computer science from the City University, London (1980); but so far no reputable institution has seen fit to grant him an honorary doctorate. From 1979 to 1984 he was lecturer, latterly senior lecturer, in computing at the Polytechnic of North London. Since 1984 he has been a self-employed author and researcher specializing in machine intelligence and its applications. He has written and edited several books, including *The Punter's Revenge: Computers in the World of Gambling* (co-authored with Tony Drapkin) published by Chapman and Hall Ltd.

KENNETH HAASE

Kenneth Haase is a graduate researcher at the Artificial Intelligence Laboratory of the Massachusetts Institute of Technology, specializing in the field of machine learning. His CYRANO discovery program (which began life as a rational reimplementation of Lenat's famous EURISKO system) has provided him with a test bed for investigating the conditions under which a computer may continually enhance its knowledge base without 'getting stuck' as its representation reaches the limits of its power, like previous systems. In 1987 he was a visiting lecturer at the AI Lab of the Free University, Brussels.

ANNA HART

Anna Hart is a principal lecturer in the Faculty of Science at Lancashire

Polytechnic, Preston. After reading mathematics she worked in industry as a software engineer before becoming a lecturer. She has been involved with expert systems for four years, and has written several papers and two books on the subject. Her interests focus on practical issues in developing useful computer systems. She is currently the leader of a cognitive science group of researchers, lecturers and students. One interest of this group is the nature of human knowledge and machine knowledge. Anna is happy to receive comments and problems from readers.

MOHAMAD MUSTAFA

Mohamad Mustafa is a PhD candidate in the Civil Engineering Department, Wayne State University. In 1985 he began research with Professor Arciszewski on the methodology of inductive learning. Work is being conducted in the Intelligent Computers Center. Mr Mustafa has co-authored two journal papers.

AJIT NARAYANAN

Ajit Narayanan has a BSc in communication science and linguistics from Aston University (1973) and was awarded a PhD in philosophy from Exeter University in 1975. He was a temporary lecturer in Philosophy at the University of Aston before taking up a lectureship in the recently formed Computer Science Department in 1980. He is co-editor of *Artificial Intelligence: Human Effects*, co-author of *An Introduction to LISP*, and author of *On Being a Machine (Vol. 1): Formal Aspects of AI*, all published by Ellis Horwood Ltd. He is on the editorial board of the recently launched journal *AI and Society* and is series editor of *AI Concepts and Foundations* for Ellis Horwood. Works currently under preparation are the second volume of *On Being a Machine* and a collection of articles dealing with law, computers and AI. Dr Narayanan is currently Head of the Department of Computer Science at the University of Exeter.

CHRIS NAYLOR

Chris Naylor holds degrees in psychology and philosophy from the University of Keele and in mathematics and statistics from the University of London. He is a member of the British Psychological Society, the Institute of Mathematics and its Applications, the Institute of Statisticians, the British Computer Society and several other learned bodies. Presently he is a full-time author, researcher and free-lance journalist. His recent books include *Build Your Own Expert System* published by Sigma Press. He is a regular contributor on AI and allied topics to a number of publications, including *PC Week* and *The Times*.

DEREK PARTRIDGE

Derek Partridge is Professor of Computer Science at the University of Exeter.

Prior to taking up that position in 1986, he was Professor in the Computing Research Laboratory at New Mexico State University, Las Cruces, USA (1975–85). His previous appointments include: instructor at Imperial College, London (1968–72); lecturer at the University of Nairobi in Kenya (1972–74); visiting lecturer at the University of Queensland, Australia (1981–82); and visiting fellow at the University of Essex (1982–83). Professor Partridge gained his PhD in computer science in 1972 from the Imperial College of Science and Technology, University of London, and a BS (Honours) in chemistry from University College, London in 1968. He has written over forty scientific papers and authored *AI: Applications in the Future of Software Engineering* (Ellis Horwood, 1986). He is also co-editor of a forthcoming book on the foundations of AI to be published by Cambridge University Press and has written an introductory AI textbook for Ablex Publishing of New Jersey.

ROY RADA

Roy Rada's educational credentials include: BA in psychology from Yale University, MD in medicine from Baylor College of Medicine, and PhD in computer science from the University of Illinois at Urbana. He has been Assistant Professor of Computer Science at Wayne State University and the head of a knowledge engineering section at the National (US) Library of Medicine, Bethesda, Maryland. His current position is Professor of Computer Science at the University of Liverpool. His research plan concerns studying the principles by which adaptive, multi-user, hyperdocument systems can be constructed.

INGO RECHENBERG

Professor Rechenberg is Head of the Bionik und Evolutionstechnik Unit at the Technical University of Berlin, Federal Republic of Germany. The research group under his direction investigates natural models for engineering systems. His speciality is the employment of Darwinian algorithms in the design of improved windmills, propeller blades, bridges and other man-made artefacts. He is also engaged in research into power sources of the future based on symbioses of micro-organisms (e.g. algae and bacteria producing hydrogen from cheap raw materials and sunlight).

MASOUD YAZDANI

Masoud Yazdani was born in Iran, but has lived in England since 1975. He obtained a BSc in computer science from Essex University before moving on to do research in AI at the University of Sussex. From 1981 to 1987 he was a lecturer in the Computer Science Department at Exeter University. Recently he has moved to Oxford to work as the training manager of Expert Systems International Ltd. His special interests include educational computing and computer creativity. He has authored numerous technical papers and edited a number of publications, most notably *Artificial Intelligence Review*, a quarterly survey and tutorial journal published by Blackwell Scientific Publications of Oxford.

Part one

Background

1

The logic of induction

RICHARD FORSYTH

> Our only hope therefore lies in a true induction.
> Francis Bacon, *First Book of Aphorisms*

> Induction simply does not exist, and the opposite view
> is a straightforward mistake.
> Karl Popper, *Conjectures and Refutations*

Most of today's so-called 'intelligent' computer systems would qualify as brain-damaged if they were people for the simple reason that they can be relied on to repeat the same behaviour in the same situation again and again and again. Predictability and reliability are desirable features of computer systems, but they are not the hallmarks of intelligence. Indeed a system that keeps repeating the same mistake over and over is, to the lay observer, demonstrably stupid. Yet this is exactly what today's most advanced software systems do (including master-level chess programs, commercially viable expert systems, etc.) – unless they are reprogrammed.

It is a theme of this book that artificial intelligence (AI) is and will remain a misnomer until systems that learn to adapt become commonplace. To put it another way: machine learning is the key to machine intelligence. This fact is still not widely recognized, even though the well-documented difficulties of know-ledge elicitation for expert systems have led to a revival of interest in automatic rule-induction techniques over the last few years (Michie, 1986).

It seems clear that this revival of interest in machine learning is overdue, is important, and will continue until systems capable of self-improvement become the norm rather than the exception. Indeed it is likely that many AI problems (e.g. speech understanding) are so difficult that they can only be solved by systems that go through a 'childlike' phase.

Putting it simply, learning is fundamental to intelligent behaviour – and that is a lesson that the AI community will have to learn if it is to achieve its objectives. Machine learning is far more than just a short cut in the 'knowledge acquisition' phase of constructing an expert system.

Furthermore, machine induction opens up the possibility of synthesizing totally new knowledge – of automating the process of scientific discovery and creating patterns and concepts that no one had ever thought of.

1.1   INDUCTIVE INFERENCE

Before discussing how, and in what sense, computers may be made to *learn*, we begin with a brief look at what philosophers and psychologists have said about the subject. We, too, may be able to learn from the past.

Induction – i.e. the derivation of general laws by examining particular instances – has long fascinated philosophers very much as a cobra fascinates its victims. It is both important and intractable, at least to a mind schooled in syllogistic reasoning: for no one has yet found a way to make induction truth-preserving, except in a closed system.

Clearly induction not only forms the basis for much of our day-to-day learning; it is at the foundation of the whole edifice of scientific discovery as well. Thus it is a cornerstone of human reasoning, but 'though science and indeed our daily life could not go forward without the inductive method, there has never been a proof of it' (Bronowski and Mazlish, 1960).

1.1.1   Inductive inference in philosophy

The problem is that inductively derived rules (whether created by persons or machines) cannot be proved correct. This age-old philosophical problem has broken the minds of the greatest thinkers since ancient times; and the doomed quest for a formal proof of the inductive method has hampered understanding of how it actually works. Only in the computer age have we come close to a systematic understanding of the act of induction. In short, the question of induction is a good example of how an intractable philosophical problem loses its sting (without actually being solved) when technological advance turns it into an engineering question.

A typical inductive inference goes something like this:

I have seen lots of black crows.
I have never seen a white crow.
Therefore, no crows are white.

Another old favourite is the sunrise 'problem':

Yesterday the sun rose in the East and set in the West.
Every day of my life it has risen in the East and set in the West.
Never in living memory has anyone seen it do anything else.
Therefore, it will rise in the East tomorrow too.

These innocuous acts of common-sense inference are in fact logically invalid, and philosophers have spent many sleepless nights attempting to find rational grounds for validating them – not so much because they expect the sun to rise in the West tomorrow, but because they would like to put such conclusions on firmer footing. After all, albino crows are in fact white.

Let us look at what philosophers (chiefly Francis Bacon and John Stuart Mill) have said about induction. They have devoted their attention primarily to its role in the scientific method.

Unfortunately, from a software designer's viewpoint, they have been less interested in how to do it than in how to justify it. Their objective was to frame rules governing inductive argument just as logicians, from Aristotle to Boole, have framed rules for deductive argument. As J. S. Mill put it (in his *System of Logic*): 'what induction is, and what conditions render it legitimate, cannot but be deemed the main question of the science of logic'.

In this endeavour they have been unsuccessful. Nevertheless, the AI practitioner who is chiefly interested in how to mechanize the process of induction can glean a number of hints from the work of the philosophers.

Francis Bacon had a very modern view of the deficiencies of any purely deductive science. He was not content with the scholastic approach to knowledge that had held sway in Europe since before the Christian era, and which had been renovated and refurbished in his own day by Descartes in particular. In his *First Book of Aphorisms*, he expressed his discontent as follows: 'The sciences we now possess are merely systems for the nice ordering of things already invented: not methods of invention or directions for new works.' Also in the *First Book of Aphorisms*, he stressed the importance of negative evidence, and the tendency of the human mind to overlook it (see Hampshire, 1956):

> It is the peculiar and perpetual error of human intellect to be more excited by affirmatives than by negatives; whereas it ought properly to hold itself indifferently disposed towards both alike. Indeed in the establishment of any true axiom, the negative instance is the more forcible of the two.

Bacon also pointed out that an inductive leap, to be of value, must go beyond the observations on which it is based. When it does, and is subsequently confirmed empirically, our confidence in it is strengthened:

> But in establishing axioms by this kind of induction, we must also examine and try whether the axiom so established be frame to the measure of those particulars only from which it is derived, or whether it be larger and wider. And if it be larger and wider, we must observe whether by indicating to us new particulars it confirm that wideness and largeness as by a collateral security; that we may not either stick fast in things already known, or loosely grasp at shadows and abstract forms; not at things solid and realized in matter.

Users of modern-day inductive systems, or indeed of statistical classification programs, will recognize this as a warning about the tendency of such systems to underestimate the error rate when the rules come out of the lab and go into service in the field.

Bacon had great faith in the method of induction, and was surprisingly modern (anticipating Babbage by two hundred years) in his belief that the work of the understanding could 'be done as if by machinery' (*Novum Organum*). Nevertheless he fully realized the danger of over-generalization. One of his cautionary remarks could serve as a slogan for the entire enterprise: 'the understanding must not therefore be supplied with wings, but rather hung with weights, to keep it from leaping and flying'.

Bacon was not in fact very influential in the progress of science, compared to Descartes or Newton for example, who popularized an axiomatic approach, and so there was little attempt to develop his systematization of induction for a long time after his death. It was not until John Stuart Mill laid down four primary 'experimental methods' for inducing general laws from particular cases that there was a significant advance on Baconian ideas about induction.

Mill considered that 'the business of inductive logic is to provide rules and models (such as the syllogism and its rules are for ratiocination) to which if inductive arguments conform those arguments are conclusive and not otherwise'; and he put forward four such rules and models himself. These were:

1. the method of agreement
2. the method of differences
3. the method of residues
4. the method of concomitant variation

These methods can be summarized as follows (see also Luce, 1958; Passmore, 1968):

1. *The method of agreement:* If two or more examples of a phenomenon under investigation have only one factor in common, the factor in which alone all the examples agree is the cause or effect of the given phenomenon.
2. *The method of differences:* If a positive instance of the phenomenon under investigation and a negative instance of the phenomenon have every circumstance in common except one, the single circumstance in which the two examples differ is the effect or the cause, or an indispensable part of the cause, of the phenomenon in question.
3. *The method of residues:* Remove from any phenomenon any part of it known to be the effect of certain antecedents and the remainder of the phenomenon is the effect of the remaining antecedents.
4. *The method of concomitant variation:* If one phenomenon varies regularly in some manner whenever another phenomenon varies in some particular way the first is connected with the second through some chain of causation.

Mill's four cardinal rules of induction suffer to some extent from antiquated terminology and from a preoccupation with causal determinism as the key to scientific investigation (which is no longer a fashionable view); nevertheless it is instructive when considering a computer-based learning program to ask oneself which of his four rules it uses. Normally one or more of his methods will be found at the heart of its induction strategy (see also Chapter 11).

Mill's first two methods (which are meant to be employed together) work best if there is no uncertainty in the causal chain which the scientist is attempting to explicate. The third method is best interpreted as heuristic advice to the scientific investigator. The fourth rule is the only one that makes much sense if one admits numerical data and uncertain information. It seeks correlation between two aspects or attributes of the phenomenon, and to that extent is the most general of the four rules, effectively subsuming the methods of agreement and differences. The method of concomitant variation involves looking for factors that vary together, or in inverse proportions; for example, the height and momentum of a weight when it is dropped to the ground, or the death-rate from cholera in a district and the distance from a particular well. Once a correlation between two quantities has been established, a law relating them can be proposed, and further tested (see also Chapter 7).

Mill's four methods, however, were specified before the computer age, and at first glance they appear to offer only very sketchy guidance for a program designer. When I first read them I thought they were merely interesting historical curiosities. However, when recast in a more modern format, they still serve as useful reference points for clarifying the whole business of induction by machine.

In Table 1.1 I have attempted to reformulate Mill's laws using more modern notations. One is a logical notation; the other is a probabilistic (Bayesian) notation. For example, the line

$$\text{not-}C \rightarrow \text{not-}A \Rightarrow A \rightarrow C$$

can be read as 'when the absence of C implies the absence of A there are grounds for believing that the presence of A implies the presence of C'. (Note that the inductive implication arrow $\Rightarrow$ is *not* a logically valid inference.) An alternative rendering of the same inductive implication is given on the line below in

---

Table 1.1   Mill's four laws (modernized)

---

1. *Method of agreement:*
$$C \rightarrow A \Rightarrow A \rightarrow C$$
$$P(A|C) = 1 \Rightarrow P(C|A) \geqslant 0$$

2. *Method of differences:*
$$\text{not-}C \rightarrow \text{not-}A \Rightarrow A \rightarrow C$$
$$P(\text{not-}A|\text{not-}C) = 1 \Rightarrow P(C|A) \geqslant 0$$

3. *Method of residues:*
$$\text{not}(C \rightarrow \text{not-}A) \text{ OR not}(\text{not-}C \rightarrow A) \Rightarrow A \rightarrow C$$
$$P(\text{not-}A|C) = 0 \text{ OR } P(A|\text{not-}C) = 0 \Rightarrow P(C|A) \geqslant 0$$

4. *Method of concomitant variation:*
$$A = f(C) \Rightarrow C = f(A)$$

---

probabilistic terms as

$$P(\text{not-}A|\text{not-}C) = 1 \Rightarrow P(C|A) \gg 0$$

which states that 'when the probability of not-A given not-C is 1 (certainty) there a grounds for believing that the probability of C given A is very much greater than zero'.

Actually a probability of 1 is unheard of outside textbook examples, so it would be safer to replace

$$= 1 \quad \text{and} \quad = 0$$

by

$$> 1 - e \quad \text{and} \quad < e$$

where e is some small error tolerance (whose exact value would be dependent on the domain) in all the above examples. The spirit of the rules, however, would not be affected.

This translation is not rigidly faithful to J. S. Mill's original meaning, but it is close to his intention, and I believe is more useful in the present context. To make the rules intelligible, it is instructive to replace the letters A and C by words. I offer three choices:

Antecedent	Consequent
Attribute	Category
Alcoholic	Cirrhosis

The first pair of terms is closest to Mill's original formulation. Thus

$$C \rightarrow A \Rightarrow A \rightarrow C$$

becomes

> If the Consequent always follows the Antecedent then there are grounds for believing that the Antecendent causes the Consequent.

but it is rather bare and abstract. (It also suffers from Mill's preoccupation with causal linkage, which is absent from the purely symbolic rendering.) The second pair of terms fits in best with current terminology in the field of computerized induction:

> If examples of Category C (almost) always have Attribute A then propose a rule that Attribute A implies Category C.

The third pair gives a more memorable mental image, and also highlights the practical dangers of leaping to conclusions via induction:

> If (almost) all Cirrhosis patients have a history of Alcohol abuse then hypothesize that Alcohol abuse is a cause of Cirrhosis of the liver.

This kind of reasoning step is in fact how medical (and other) researchers think;

but – unlike machines – they have a background of common sense and expert knowledge against which the limitations of such a potential over-generalization can be tested. After all, there are other causative factors besides excessive alcohol consumption in the development of this particular liver disease.

(The above example illustrates the fact that many very useful inductively derived rules are not certain: they usually work, and we hedge them with phrases like 'in most cases', 'highly likely' and so on. Ideally, we would like our inductive computer programs to be able to operate in the same way.)

One thing that becomes apparent from the above recoding exercise is that Mill's first three laws are only relevant for nominal or categorical data, while the fourth applies principally to data measured on a numeric scale. Thus the first three laws form a group (which we might term **non-parametric methods**) distinct from the fourth law.

Another point worth noting is that the fourth of Mill's four rules is the most general: in effect it subsumes the other three, since they are all special kinds of concomitant variation. For that reason the fourth rule is the most important. And once you accept that covariation need not be perfect to be informative, you can say that all today's induction programs are based on a procedure for detecting concomitant variation. But while noticing concomitant variation is essential to machine (and human) learning, it is not the whole story.

Bertrand Russell was another philosopher who wrestled with the problem of justifying inductive reasoning and eventually admitted defeat. As he says in *The Problems of Philosophy*, the inductive principle is 'incapable of being proved by an appeal to experience'. Its role in human thought, however, is so fundamental that 'we must either accept the inductive principle on the grounds of its intrinsic evidence, or forgo all justification of our expectations about the future' (Russell, 1912). In other words, if you do not believe in induction, you cannot believe anything (see also Russell, 1961).

He did, however, add a concern with statistical reasoning which was largely absent from Mill's treatment of the topic. The inductive principle, as he saw it, was essentially probabilistic. In brief, when two things, such as thunder and lightning, have been found to go together many times and never found apart, then 'a sufficient number of cases of association will make the probability of a fresh association nearly a certainty, and will make it approach certainty without limit'. The more common the joint occurrence (with no exceptions) the more secure the inductive generalization. In practice, we extend this principle – the weight of numbers – to cases of (imperfect) statistical association. For instance, as more and more studies piled up in which cigarette smoking was associated with a raised incidence of lung cancer, but not with the certainty of the disease, more and more people became convinced that smoking was a cause of lung cancer; but even today the evidence is not conclusive, and a few die-hards remain to be persuaded of the causative link.

Wittgenstein's contribution to the philosophy of induction was to emphasize, or re-emphasize, simplicity. He asserted in the *Tractatus Logico-Philosophicus*, paragraph 6.363, that 'the procedure of induction consists in accepting as true the simplest law that can be reconciled with our experiences' (Wittgenstein, 1961). Thus he recognized that many generalizations could be consistent with the evidence, and resurrected Occam's Razor as a means of choosing between them.

Over-elaborate explanations are difficult to disprove on the grounds of evidence alone, as the resilience of numerous superstitions testifies. Often such theories are only rejected because of internal contradictions. Indeed the history of science is littered with discredited hypotheses that were embellished with so many baroque flourishes that they collapsed under the weight of their own implausibility, even though they coincided with the known facts. A good case in point is Ptolemy's cosmology, which can be made to fit the facts of astronomical observation even today, by addition of a sufficient number of epicycles, but which was overturned by the Copernican theory because the latter had the virtue of simplicity.

Karl Popper (in Miller, 1987) is the living philosopher who has had most to say about the problem of induction, and his view, expressed trenchantly at the head of this chapter, is that the process does not exist:

> I hold with Hume that there simply is no such logical entity as an inductive inference; or, that all so-called inductive inferences are logically invalid – and even *inductively* invalid, to put it more sharply. We have many examples of deductively valid inferences, and even some partial criteria of deductive validity; but no example of an inductively valid inference exists (author's italics).

So what does go on in our heads when we encounter specific events and jump to general conclusions (such as reading the extracts cited in this chapter and deciding that philosophers live in a world of make-believe)? The answer, according to Popper (in Miller, 1987), is that all knowledge is, in the last analysis, guesswork:

> I hold that neither animals nor men use any procedure like induction, or any argument based on the repetition of instances. The belief that we use induction is simply a mistake. It is a kind of optical illusion. What we do use is a method of trial and elimination of error; however misleadingly this method may look like induction, its logical structure, it we examine it closely, totally differs from that of induction. Moreover, it . . . does not give rise to any of the difficulties connected with the problem of induction.

Although Popper's views appear nihilistic and downright perverse, he is actually closer to the spirit of the machine learning enterprise than any of the sages quoted earlier. His position is that knowledge is gained by making conjectures and refuting the ones that do not fit the facts, in science as in daily life. Therefore it is still rational to prefer, among competing hypotheses, those that have stood up to harsh criticism and multiple empirical trials. (This is how he smuggles an 'argument based on repetition of instances' back into his scientific methodology.) And it turns out that forming novel conjectures, most of which have to be weeded out after comparison with the data, is exactly what computers are good at – better, in certain circumstances, than people.

Where Popper can be criticized is: (1) in his blithe indifference to where hypotheses come from, i.e. the mechanics of conjecturing; and (2) in his one-sided view that all scientific hypotheses are universal laws.

The former criticism means that he has no practical help to offer in the actual building of an inductive engine; the latter means that he neglects statistical reasoning almost completely, due to an insistence that a single counter-example disproves a law (whereas no finite number of positive examples can prove a law). Not all scientific propositions, however, are universal. Some singular statements count as perfectly well-formed scientific hypotheses, for example: There are carbon-based life-forms on other planets; It is physiologically possible for a woman to run one mile in less than four minutes; Extra-terrestrial civilizations will arise before the end of the universe; Black holes exist; . . . and so on. Such assertions can be proved by a single instance; they cannot be disproved by accumulation of counter-examples. One could search all the planets circling all the stars in all the galaxies throughout the observable universe without fully disproving the conjecture that carbon-based life-forms exist elsewhere than earth. Yet one example would prove the conjecture correct. Indeed, the whole of AI is founded on a singular premiss: that it is possible to construct a thinking being without breeding it. So far all the evidence is contrary, but that has not disproved AI's fundamental principle, which could be vindicated (perhaps centuries in the future) by a single successful thinking machine. (This is not to deny that general laws are, broadly speaking, more useful than existential hypotheses.)

As a matter of fact the most useful kinds of hypotheses in real life are fuzzy rules of thumb, *already contradicted* by a small number of counter-examples, such as: falling out of aeroplanes at 8000 feet without a parachute is fatal. The statistical dimension is something that practical inductive programs cannot ignore even if the 'weight of numbers' has no grounding in pure logic.

Thus, although philosophy has not laid the blueprint for an inductive engine, it does provide some guidelines for people wishing to build one:

1. Use negative as well as positive evidence (Bacon);
2. Look for concomitant variation in the causal factors and the result (Mill);
3. The more frequently an association is observed, the more likely the association is to be generally true (Russell, *pace* Popper);
4. Prefer simple to complex generalizations (Wittgenstein).

This may seem no more than common sense, but that is a good sign; for induction is a common-sense process which philosophers seek to clarify and AI workers to mechanize.

1.1.2 Inductive learning in psychology

Induction in science is a public procedure. In daily life, however, induction goes on in private whenever we learn from experience. As such, it has been extensively studied by psychologists for over a century. So we might expect to find some useful hints on the mechanisms that underlie human learning in the psychological research literature. If we did, however, we would be in for a disappointment.

Broadly speaking, psychological theories of learning fall into two groups, stimulus–response (S–R) theories and cognitive theories. The S–R theorists regard the organism as a black box. They are interested in relating inputs (stimuli) with outputs (responses), but do not claim to model what is going on inside the animal's brain.

For example, mathematically inclined S–R theorists have proposed a number of mathematical formulae that might account for the notorious 'learning curve', depicted in hundreds of introductory psychology textbooks, which rises (or falls if a habit is being extinguished) smoothly and exponentially towards an asymptote. The shape and slope of this curve depend on parameters in the equations describing the animals' response patterns. But, until recently, the S–R psychologists who tested and refined such equations were interested purely in fitting the data. They would have been horrified if anyone tried to give the parameters they used the status of mental constructs. This attitude – despite vigorous attacks on it from inside psychology (e.g. Koestler, 1964) – was only broken down when psychologists from both camps became familar with computers and realized that algorithms (i.e. rules of behaviour) were quite as rigorous, and therefore quite as respectable scientifically, as mathematical equations.

Cognitive theorists, on the other hand, do attempt to describe the mental structures which are (presumably) created and destroyed within the nervous system as an organism (especially a human) learns from experience. Interestingly enough, they resort to extensive borrowing from the field of computer science to describe what they think is going on inside the skull. They have no prejudice against mentalistic models, they just have not found any that work very well.

Forsyth and Rada (1986) sum the situation up as follows:

> S–R theorists speak of "learning" and experiment mainly with rats and pigeons. Cognitive psychologists usually talk of "memory" and do most of their experiments on human beings. At present cognitive theorizing is in the ascendant (partly at least because cognitive theories lend themselves to computer simulation) but the debate continues between adherents of the two approaches. It will be a very long time before a unified psychological theory of learning emerges that fits the multiplicity of experimental data concerning human and animal learning.

In the meantime the AI worker looking to psychology for ideas on how to build learning systems will be disappointed. To be blunt, the psychologists do not know how it is done. For many years behaviourism was the prevailing orthodoxy in experimental psychology, and behaviourists eschewed mentalist concepts. The idea that a rat is forming and testing hypotheses when it runs a maze or that a pigeon is amending its own rule base as it pecks for food was a heresy for behavioural scientists from about 1920 till the late 1960s. It is scarcely surprising, therefore, that psychologists cannot explain something they have only recently admitted to exist.

Essentially the S–R theorists do not want to explain how learning actually works, and the cognitive theorists are unable to do so. As Holland *et al.* (1986) put it: 'Induction, which had been called the "scandal of philosophy", had become the scandal of psychology and artificial intelligence as well.' Part of the explanation for this dismal state of affairs lies in the disparity between neurons and notions. The modern psychologist who trains a rat to run a maze believes that it has developed some sort of **cognitive map** of the maze. The physiologist who cuts the creature up afterwards knows a good deal about how its nervous system works. But nobody yet knows how to reconcile these two levels of description. How is the software (the cognitive map) implemented in terms of the hardware (the neural interconnections)? The question has yet to be answered.

(There is an interesting parallel here, which there is insufficient space to explore as it deserves, between the SR vs cognitive opposition in psychology and the Connectionist vs symbolic approach to machine learning in AI. Very roughly, Connectionist systems (Hinton and Anderson, 1981) aim to model the brain, while symbolic systems – the mainstream of AI – aim to model the mind. As in psychology, so in AI: no one has yet unified the two approaches. It may be that the two types of description are incompatible. See also Chapters 11 and 12.)

Perhaps the only conclusion that would command a near-universal consensus among psychological researchers and at the same time make sense from the system-designer's point of view is that feedback, or knowledge of results, is absolutely crucial to the acquisition of novel skills, and must be provided as promptly as possible (see Hilgard and Bower, 1966; Bolles, 1979).

1.2   THE ACT OF INDUCTION

If learning is so poorly understood by philosophers and psychologists, how can upstart AI programmers hope to computerize the process? After all, they cannot even give a watertight definition of learning. The answer is that AI researchers are posing themselves a rather different problem. The philosphers wanted to know 'how can induction be rigorously validated?'. The psychologists want to know 'how does the brain store the results of experience?'. The AI programmer has a more modest goal, which involves answering the question 'in what ways can a machine develop general rules from specific examples, and how reliable are those rules in practice?' As the history of science makes abundantly clear, it is not answering but asking the right questions which is the key to progress.

Indeed it already appears that the results coming in from AI workers on induction by computer will throw new light on the unanswered questions of philosophy and psychology.

For the rest of this book we will say that learning is a phenomenon exhibited when a system improves its performance at a given task without being reprogrammed. Improvement can mean various things, including: a higher proportion of correct decisions, faster response, lower-cost solutions and wider range of applicability. We use the term **induction** (which means reasoning from specific cases to general principles) to describe the method by which learning is

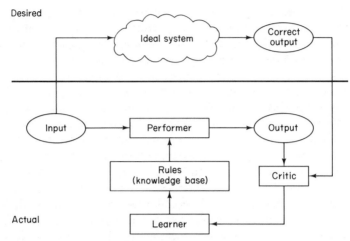

Fig. 1.1. A framework for learning. According to this diagram, learning is 99% pattern recognition and 1% reasoning.

effected. **Rule induction** covers a special, and prevalent, case of induction, in which the results of induction are expressible as condition–action rules.

It is important to note that, from this standpoint, a machine cannot learn anything unless its performance can be assessed objectively. For learning to take place, there must be a criterion according to which decisions or partial solutions can be scored. Otherwise no one can say whether the system has changed for the better or for the worse. Agreeing on a suitable measure, however, may not be a simple matter, as we shall see.

1.2.1   A framework for induction

Looked at from sufficiently far away, all systems designed to modify and improve their performance share certain important common features. Figure 1.1 is a diagram of the four major components of a typical learning system. Essentially this sketches a pattern recognizer which learns to associate input descriptions with output categories; but, as we shall see, many systems that are not overtly concerned with pattern recognition also fit into this general framework (Forsyth, 1984). Note that the system contains a **feedback** loop. We can briefly describe its main components in turn, by going round this feedback loop.

The **Critic** compares the actual with the desired output. In order to do so, there must be an 'ideal system', as we call it, against which the system's behaviour is measured. In practice this may be a human expert, or teacher. For instance, if the task is medical diagnosis, the ideal system may be the diagnosis given by a top consultant when faced with the patient whose history is being presented to the computer as input. The job of the critic is to apportion credit and/or blame for the system's responses. It must assess deviations from correct performance.

This can be simple or complex. In a simple case the Critic might compare (for example) rainfall as forecast with actual rainfall. If 0.6 mm of rain fell and the system predicted 1.7 mm then it is only a matter of subtracting one number from another and passing the difference on as feedback to the learning module. In other circumstances there may be more work for the critic to do to ascertain what went wrong. For example, after losing a game of chess, it may not be at all obvious where the computer made its mistakes. But however simple or complex the task of the critic, evaluative feedback is absolutely fundamental to the learning process. There are 'unsupervised learning' programs in existence, which do roughly the job that statisticians know as **cluster analysis**, i.e. tidying up a cluttered conceptual space, but this facility, though a component of learning, is not learning in the sense of improving performance at an assigned task. What such programs do is a precursor to the learning process proper, but it does not count as learning until the revised conceptual vocabulary is actually put to use.

To continue with the diagram of Fig. 1.1: the **Learner** is the heart of the system. This is the part of the system which has responsibility for amending the knowledge base to correct erroneous performance. A large number of learning strategies have been proposed since work on machine learning got under way in the 1950s, some of which will be examined in subsequent chapters.

The **Rules** are the data structures that encode the system's current level of expertise. They guide the activity of the performance module. The crucial point is that they can be amended. Instead of a read-only knowledge base (as in most current expert systems) the rules constitute a programmable–erasable knowledge base. Obviously they must only be modified under strictly defined conditions or chaos will result. Other forms of knowledge representation than condition–action rules have been used successfully, but we use the term 'rules' as a convenient shorthand.

Finally, the **Performer** is the part of the system that carries out the task. This uses the rules in some way to guide its actions. In other words, it is a kind of interpreter. Thus when the rules are updated, the behaviour of the system as a whole changes (for the better, if all goes according to plan). Naturally the Performer is the part of the system which varies most from one task to another, and is therefore the part of the system about which least can be said in general terms.

In discussions of machine learning systems, most attention is typically focused on the Learner and the Performer modules. But it is worth pointing out that the two commonest reasons for failure of machine learning systems stem from inadequacies in the other two functions, the Critic and the Rules:

1. Failure of the Critic: the chosen evaluation measure is misleading;
2. Deficiency in the Rules: the chosen representation is not capable of expressing the knowledge needed for satisfactory performance.

1.2.2   A taxonomy for learning

Two other terms need to be defined before our examination of practical learning methods – description language and training set.

The **description language** (or **rule language**) is the notation or formalism in which the knowledge of the system is expressed. There are two kinds of description language which are important. The first is the formalism used to represent the input examples. The second kind of description language is that chosen to represent the rules themselves. It should be noted that the expressiveness of the description language in which the rules are formulated is crucial to the success of any learning algorithm. It also has a bearing on how readily the knowledge can be understood, and hence on whether it can be transferred to people.

The notion of a **training set** is important in understanding how a machine learning system is tested. Typically there is a database of examples for which the solutions are known. The system works through these instances and develops a rule or set of rules for associating input descriptions with output decisions (e.g. disease symptoms with diagnoses). But, as Bacon pointed out, rules must be tested on cases other than those from which they were derived. Therefore there should be another database, the **test set**, of the same kind but containing unseen data. If the rules also apply successfully to these fresh cases, our confidence in them is increased (this issue is considered again in Chapter 2).

This preliminary definition of terms enables us to compare learning systems in a consistent manner.

Machine learning can be viewed from a bewildering number of perspectives – as optimization, concept formation, pattern recognition, automatic classification, scientific discovery, programming by example and many more. But the simple common theme of generate + test (which is the dynamic underlying the static block diagram of Fig. 1.1) provides a unifying principle. All learning systems, however clever they are about avoiding brute-force exhaustive search, propose new potential solutions and test those potential solutions (see Section 1.1.1 on Karl Popper). This means that there are two fundamental questions we can ask about an automatic induction system:

1. How are new knowledge structures generated from old ones?
2. How are candidate knowledge structures evaluated?

There are many possible taxonomies of the field of rule induction; but the answers to these two simple questions help to organize an area that up till now has been characterized by somewhat anarchic eclecticism. If we know the answers to those two questions for a particular system, we have grasped the essence of its operation.

A more detailed classification scheme divides up learning systems into 256 types based on the answers to eight two-way questions. Strictly speaking, these dichotomies are mostly polarities, i.e. a real system will often fall between the two extremes, but lumping all systems to one side or the other of an imaginary midpoint simplifies the scheme and is useful for two reasons: (1) it provides the reader with a standard checklist of questions to ask (attributes to look for) in attempting to understand a novel learning system; (2) it relates learning systems together, and may even suggest new meta-rules or PhD projects (e.g. Why are there no existing systems with such and such a combination of attributes?)

Domain:
1. General purpose vs specific
   Does the system apply to a variety of application areas or is it specialized to one field?
   General-purpose example: ID3
   Specific example: Meta-dendral

Induction method:
2. Incremental vs one-shot learning
   Does the system maintain a best-so-far rule or description which is amended as new examples arrive one by one or does it look at the entire training set before forming its rule(s)?
   Incremental example: UNIMEM
   Single-shot example: CN2
3. Subsumption-based vs non-hierarchic
   Does the induction process rely on an inheritance lattice that orders concepts from general to specific, or does it work without reference to the generality of the descriptions it generates?
   Subsumption-based example: LEX
   Non-hierarchic example: Holland's genetic algorithm
4. Deterministic vs non-deterministic
   Does the system always give the same results from the same data or is there a random element in its rule generation?
   Deterministic example: BACON.4
   Randomized example: BEAGLE

Critic:
5. Logical evaluation vs quantitative evaluation
   Does the system classify trials only as successes or failures, or does it measure the distance from the correct answer according to a metric?
   Logical example: Perceptron
   Quantitative example: EURISKO

Representation:
6. Unary features vs structural predicates
   Are examples presented to the system as feature vectors, or can the system accept examples which have internal structure described by multi-term predicates?
   Unary example: Assistant
   Structural example: Winston's program

7. Humanly intelligible vs black box
   Is the rule language readable by people or is it in an opaque internal code?
   Intelligible example: Induce 1.2
   Black box example: Boltzmann machine
8. Fixed language vs extensible language
   Is the system restricted to a description language given by its designer or can it extend its own vocabulary by defining new concepts and functions? (This is very much a matter of degree.)
   Fixed language example: AQ11
   Extensible language example: CYRANO

Do not worry if you have not (yet) come across most of the systems cited above as examples. They merely serve as a preliminary demonstration of the feasibility of the eight attributes, by showing at least one example from both ends of the spectrum in each case. Many of them will be discussed in subsequent chapters.

This list of attributes is not presented as the ultimate classification scheme for machine learning, but is offered as an aid for the reader who is new to the subject. It should help to impose order on the variety of systems described in the remainder of this book. We can put it to the test, and at the same time introduce one final important concept (the **search space**) by applying it to a well-known induction system.

1.3   IN SEARCH OF KNOWLEDGE

It is a fundamental notion of machine learning research that the process of induction can be viewed as a search through an abstract space of potential rules or descriptions. Tom Mitchell (1982) was the first to make this important point in print.

A rule language defines a vast (possibly infinite) set of potential rules or concepts. The job of a learning algorithm is to hunt through that enormous space for useful descriptions in an efficient manner. In nearly all realistic situations, the proportion of valuable descriptions to syntactically valid descriptions is extremely low: at needle-in-haystack level or worse. The main problem (assuming that the rule language is capable of describing any correct rules at all) is how to ignore the great majority of useless descriptions without missing the useful one(s).

Mitchell's insight was that the voluminous AI literature on search as a problem-solving technique could be harnessed in the quest for efficient learning algorithms. Before then, the two topics of learning and search had been treated as separate. So it is appropriate to round off this introductory chapter by describing, as our first concrete example, the algorithm that Mitchell devised for searching a space of possible concepts (which he called the **version space**). The method is known as the **candidate-elimination** algorithm.

For computer programmers it can be described as a cross between the Sieve of Eratosthenes and the Binary chop. The sieve of Eratosthenes is a way of finding prime numbers by setting up an array of odd integers and eliminating those which are divisible by numbers lower down in the array. The binary chop, or binary search, is a technique for converging on a solution, or an approximation to a solution, by repeatedly readjusting inwards the two extreme points between which the solution is known to lie. Both are well-known programming techniques.

The basic idea behind the candidate-elimination algorithm appears absurd at first sight: list all possible descriptions, then cross off the ones that do not apply to the training data. Any that are left after the crossing-out process must be correct descriptions. This procedure constitutes an elegant method (at least with noise-free training instances) of converging on the description or descriptions of a concept (Mitchell, 1977, 1982).

What could be simpler than taking all possible descriptions and eliminating the ones that conflict with the training set? The catch is, of course, that the set of all possible descriptions is (except in trivial cases) far too large to enumerate individually. But despite the enormity of the search space, the method becomes practical by taking account of the fact that a partial ordering exists among the concept descriptions, from general to specific. Thus any two descriptions can be compared and ranked according to which is the more general. For instance, 'deaf white cat' is more specific than 'white cat'. (This remains true in principle even if, empirically, all white cats happen to be deaf.)

This realization allows the system to maintain two boundary sets – S, the set of the most specific possible descriptions compatible with the training data, and G, the set of the most general possible descriptions still compatible with the training data. Between them, these two finite sets define the edges of a far larger set in a compact form.

The S and G sets are gradually made to converge as more and more training instances are processed. The convergence is achieved as follows:

1. When a positive instance is encountered, any description in G that does not cover it is eliminated, and all elements of S are generalized as little as possible so that they do cover it;
2. When a negative instance is encountered, any description in S that covers it is deleted, and all elements of G are specialized as little as possible so that they no longer cover it.

The S set can be initialized with the description of a 'seed' training example (which is a positive instance of the concept to be discovered) or alternatively with all possible maximally specific descriptions, and the G set is initialized with the null description. (Thus the G set starts by stating that all examples are positive examples.) In effect the S set describes sufficient conditions for belonging to the concept being learned and the G set describes necessary conditions. When the two sets converge, the concept is fully defined. An illustration of this procedure appears as Fig. 1.2.

Mitchell's masterly exposition convinced some members of the AI community

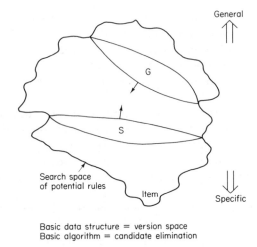

Basic data structure = version space
Basic algorithm = candidate elimination

Fig. 1.2. Version space. Mitchell's algorithm is a kind of cross between the sieve of Eratosthenes and the binary chop.

that the induction problem had, in all essentials, been solved. However, like many theoretically optimal procedures, the candidate-elimination algorithm is very brittle in practice. It goes wrong with quite modest amounts of noise in the training data. Thus it is chiefly suited to domains, such as symbolic integration or chess problems, where the examples are themselves generated by formal rules; it is not suited to domains, such as weather forecasting or disease diagnosis, where the data is subject to random perturbations or observational errors. (Mitchell has extended the algorithm to cope with very small amounts of noise; but these remarks still apply.)

Thus Mitchell's general idea of learning as a search has survived and proved fruitful, though his particular search algorithm is merely one in a growing catalogue of induction techniques. We can describe it in terms of the attribute list of the previous section as follows:

1. Is it general purpose or specific? General purpose in so far as it is not tied to one subject-matter (though in practical terms it is limited to well-defined problem areas);
2. Is it incremental or single-shot? Incremental because the training examples are examined one at a time;
3. Is it subsumption-based or not? It is the archetypal subsumption-based system, since it relies entirely on the general-to-specific ordering of concepts;
4. Is it deterministic or non-deterministic? It is deterministic: given the same examples in the same order it will always produce the same results;
5. Does it use logical or quantitative evaluation? It uses logical evaluation: descriptions are either correct or not; there is no measure of near misses;

6. Does it use unary or multiple predicates? It uses unary predicates, although later work has extended it to deal with structural predicates;
7. Are its descriptions humanly intelligible or opaque? They are intended to be legible by people (although the basic method could work with other representations);
8. Does it use a fixed or extensible rule language? The language is fixed. (If it created new descriptors it would have to insert them in the generality lattice and start the G/S convergence process all over again.)

Thus the answers to all eight questions are Yes for the candidate-elimination algorithm. It defines an end-point of (11111111) in the induction-system typology outlined in the previous section. (Since you ask, I cannot think of a 00000000 system to contrast it with, though I have been involved personally with the creation of a financial rule generator that has not been reported but which would qualify as a 00000001 type.)

This chapter has now sketched a background against which to view the field of machine learning, from philosophical discussions to psychological theories of learning. It has outlined a conceptual framework within which modern efforts to computerize the act of induction can be understood, and it has introduced some important terminology. We can now proceed to explore some of the many aspects of machine learning more fully in the remaining chapters of the book.

1.4 REFERENCES

Bolles, R. (1979) *Learning Theory*, Holt, Rinehart and Winston, New York.
Bronowski, J. and Mazlish, B. (1960) *The Western Intellectual Tradition*, Hutchinson, London.
Forsyth, R. (ed.) (1984) *Expert Systems: Principles and Case Studies*, Chapman and Hall, London.
Forsyth, R. and Rada, R. (1986) *Machine Learning: Applications in Expert Systems and Information Retrieval*, Ellis Horwood, Chichester.
Hampshire, S. (ed.) (1956) *The Age of Reason*, Mentor Books, New York.
Hilgard, E. R. and Bower, G. H. (1966) *Theories of Learning*, Appleton-Century-Crofts, New York.
Hinton, G. E. and Anderson, J. (eds) (1981) *Parallel Models of Associative Memory*, Lawrence Erlbaum, Hillsdale, N.J.
Holland, J. H., Holyoak, K. J., Nisbett, R. E. and Thagard, P. R. (1986) *Induction: Processes of Inference, Learning and Discovery*, MIT Press, Cambridge, Mass.
Koestler, A. (1964) *The Act of Creation*, Hutchinson, London.
Luce, A. A. (1958) *Teach Yourself Logic*, English Universities Press, London.
Michie, D. (1986) *On Machine Intelligence*, Ellis Horwood, Chichester.
Miller, D. (ed.) (1987) *A Pocket Popper*, Fontana Press, Glasgow.
Mitchell, T. (1977) Version spaces: a candidate elimination approach to rule induction. *Internat. Joint Conf. on AI*, **5**, 305–10.
Mitchell, T. (1982) Generalization as search. *Artificial Intelligence*, **18**, 203–26.

Passmore, J. (1968) *A Hundred Years of Philosophy*, Penguin Books, Harmondsworth, Middx.

Popper, K. (1972) *Conjectures and Refutations* (4th edn), Routledge and Kegan Paul, London.

Russell, B. (1912) *The Problems of Philosophy*, Oxford University Press, Oxford.

Russell, B. (1961) *History of Western Philosophy*, Allen and Unwin, London.

Wittgenstein, L. (1961) *Tractatus Logico-Philosophicus*, tr. by Pears and McGuinness, Routledge and Kegan Paul, London.

2

Machine induction as a form of knowledge acquisition in knowledge engineering

ANNA HART

2.1 INTRODUCTION

Machine learning is one area of artificial intelligence (AI) research. In many ways it epitomizes the strengths and weaknesses of AI work, and this is hardly surprising as learning is an intrinsic, but complex, part of intelligent behaviour. Expert systems are commonly referred to as an early phase in the commercialization of AI, and they have had an interesting and difficult gestation period in industry and commerce. This chapter is based on experience of expert system projects outside research laboratories in commercial environments, and describes some very important principles which must be considered in the development of usable and useful systems. It outlines the complexities of human expertise, suggests a role for expert systems against this background, and then discusses the usefulness of machine induction in expert system development. In this way important issues are highlighted, setting a context for further chapters on various aspects of learning.

2.2 HUMAN EXPERTISE

Intelligence is far easier to recognize than to define, and so AI researchers often concentrate on trying to produce what they consider to be 'intelligent' behaviour in machines, rather than defining intelligence or knowledge. Indeed the Turing test devised by Alan Turing (Turing, 1950) as a means of deciding whether or not a computer could be said to be 'intelligent' is based on a dialogue between a person and 'second party' via a terminal. The computer is deemed to be behaving in an intelligent manner if the person cannot determine, on the basis of the dialogue, whether the other party is a person or a machine. Some authorities openly acknowledge that they side-step the issue of 'what is knowledge'

(Feigenbaum and Barr, 1981) or even warn against asking too many penetrating questions which might lead to this basic philosophical issue. While this is to a certain extent understandable, it has led to an AI view of knowledge, and much of the work has underlying assumptions about the nature of expertise, knowledge and intelligence. When these basic tenets are taken to extremes then they can lead to the failure of projects, owing to fundamental misconceptions about the feasibility and power of computer models of cognition and thought. It is therefore useful at least to reflect on the question of what is knowledge, and how computer systems can play a part in human problem-solving.

Here we shall present a more extreme picture of some of these basic assumptions in order to set the scene for further discussion. Some early work by Newell and Simon (1963) was an attempt to study human problem-solving techniques, and then to construct a General Problem Solver program with powerful general techniques. The work did not meet its overly optimistic objectives, and it was soon realized that general strategies are insufficient on their own. Most tasks are knowledge intensive, requiring varying amounts of both general knowledge and problem (or domain) specific knowledge. Later work then produced the first 'expert systems' where developers tried to model the knowledge and reasoning strategies used by human experts in their domain. They tried to produce computer programs which could perform at a high level of expertise and competence on specific tasks, e.g. diagnosis of blood infections (MYCIN), configuring VAX computer systems (R1, or XCON), and interpreting mass spectrographs (DENDRAL). (See References for further details.) Key problems in this area are knowledge elicitation, where the developers try to extract from human experts the details of their knowledge, and knowledge representation, when they try to represent the knowledge on a computer system. Tacit assumptions which are often made are:

1. Knowledge is modular, i.e. it can be broken down into sub-parts and subsystems;
2. All the important knowledge can be made explicit, verbalized, and then adequately represented as data structures and procedures;
3. All the knowledge exists in an expert's head, and the problem is to 'mine' it out piece by piece, refining a computer system by successively adding rules to it;
4. The problem space is 'closed', i.e. all the relevant knowledge for a set of tasks in a domain can be isolated and contained within a computer knowledge base.

Since the early systems there have been relatively few true 'success' stories, and this has caused some people to reassess the nature of expertise, and to voice reservations about the power of AI techniques and the wisdom of certain philosophies.

In particular the Dreyfus brothers (1986) have done extensive studies of human expertise and concluded that current computer technology is necessarily restricted in its power. They describe the progression from novice to expert in five stages. Their theory is that a novice works with context-free rules and features, but that as he or she becomes more proficient the context and situational elements become more important leading to holistic problem-solving. In other words, people learn to have the confidence to break rules, and to act intuitively based on experience and without conscious recourse to rules. True experts are able to 'do what normally works', without being aware of how they are doing what they are doing. Their behaviour is ongoing and reflective, and they are immersed in their tasks. A consequence of this view is that knowledge is stored implicitly in the form of experiences, values and beliefs, and that the view of 'facts and rules' is inadequate for all except the early stages of knowledge and skill acquisition. Winograd and Flores (1986) who used to be strong defendants of AI have now concluded that there is more to human expertise and professional competence than the explicit representation of objective knowledge, and that experience and context are very important. They argue that our implicit beliefs and assumptions cannot all be made explicit, and that practical understanding based on situations is more important than detached theoretical understanding. They also suggest that humans may not always need formalized representations in order to act, and that computers as symbol manipulators have inherent limitations. In short these researchers are stressing the potential power and versatility of human cognition. That is not to say that people are infallible or that they always make good decisions. The point is that computers are necessarily different, and it cannot be assumed that all facets of intelligence or knowledge can be adequately or even usefully represented on computers.

Cognition is certainly a complex process. Experiments in perception (Gregory, 1986) seem to indicate a sophisticated mechanism of interpretation of images in the context of previous experience, and also holistic pattern recognition. There is evidence that memory is complex and associative (Thomson and Tulving, 1970) and people are able to reason in sophisticated ways, e.g. by analogy, by simulation, and by reconstruction of situations and scenarios. People are also driven by emotion and human values, not merely by facts and figures. This can produce bias, prejudice or stereotyping, but also allows a versatile framework for behaviour and adaptation. Paradoxically our strength is our very weakness. By being able to act instinctively and view problems or situations holistically we can sometimes 'miss the obvious'; on the other hand we are not bound by predefined rules and constraints. Even those who stress the limitations of human reasoning power and advocate that it should be augmented by a logical (in this case mathematical) framework, allow that in unusual or difficult cases a human being can outperform a set of mathematical tables (Faust, 1984). The scientist Peter Medawar (1969) argues convincingly that discovery is brought about by chance, leaps of intuition, unusual ideas, etc. and is not constrained by formal logic or inductive reasoning.

Lyotard (1984) goes further and warns against the dream of machine thought. Admitting that the positivist type of knowledge is present and important, he emphasizes the importance of critical reflexive knowledge associated with aims and values. He argues that knowledge goes beyond that which is 'true', taking into account efficacy, justice, values and happiness. His message is that we should not reduce knowledge to that which can be represented on computers, and that we should continue to value human judgement.

There is certainly empirical evidence for implicit knowledge, and a mismatch between people's reported strategies and knowledge, and their actual performance (Berry, 1987). Computer models of neural nets, which mimic the interconnections in the brain, have demonstrated that memory and learning can be modelled effectively via implicit storage in connection strengths rather than explicit representations (McClelland and Rumelhart, 1986). This adds weight to the view that explicit knowledge representation is only part of the picture.

Discussions like these have existed in philosophy for some time, and are well documented (Haugeland, 1986; Pratt, 1987). The move towards logic and mathematics as the ultimate form of reasoning is not new. What we should ask is not whether or not computers are intelligent, but what we can make them do to help people in their problem-solving environments.

Computers cannot experience in the same way that we do; they lack motives and values; they have no semantic understanding of the symbols which they process. On the other hand they do have very powerful features which we can exploit. Once programmed they are accurate and indefatigable; they are good at computation and logic; they can be fast and efficient, and are not prone to tiredness, mood, stress or emotion. They cannot become experts in the ways described by the Dreyfus brothers and Winograd and Flores. However they can be very powerful tools to assist people. They can prompt, remind, critique; they can search through large spaces of possibilities; they can be programmed to remember very many cases; and they can store and manipulate large banks of data. They can therefore be assistants, but are unlikely to be true authorities.

It is therefore not a trivial task to give a definition of an expert system. What is more important is to analyse the environment of a potential user of a computer system, and to design a system which will be of use. Rather than capturing the expertise of a human expert this is a case of designing a 'joint cognitive system', namely the computer and the user. The aim is to exploit the best features of each of them, creating a state of symbiosis, where the user is better with the system than without it, but has the freedom and confidence to develop the intuitive knowledge which is seen to be so important.

This may of course involve modelling certain reasoning strategies and building a knowledge base which contains representations of the information which is seen to be important for that tool. It requires the production of a suitable man–machine interface so that the user can retrieve useful information (or knowledge) and understand its relevance. But it also requires an understanding of the tasks performed by the user, and his strengths, interests, values and problems. It demands an appreciation of the role of the system and its effect on the user; it requires a 'user-centred' approach to system design, not an 'expert-centred' approach. The system to be studied is that of the computer and user, in an attempt to make the user more proficient, i.e. more expert. In certain cases the user may well be the expert, but the principle is the same.

2.3 KNOWLEDGE ELICITATION

In order to be effective the knowledge elicitation process must be seen against this background. It is quite possible to elicit knowledge from a human expert – he or she will have much knowledge. This knowledge is of different types and used for different tasks. Much of it will be context-dependent, and it is extremely important to have a framework of system design in mind when eliciting the knowledge; this sets a context and purpose to the whole process.

It is commonly reported that the knowledge acquisition process is difficult. Experts can experience difficulty in verbalizing their knowledge in a form which can then be represented on a computer system. Introspection is necessarily restricted in its power, and explanation can be a *post hoc* rationalization of a process which may even be fictitious. While some people have assumed that the knowledge is actually there in the form of rules of thumb which have not previously needed to be stated explicitly, our discussions on knowledge suggest that the problem may be more fundamental, and that the very nature of the knowledge may be implicit. It is almost certainly the case, therefore, that there are two types of implicit knowledge; that which is in the form of rules, but which has become second nature, and that which is necessarily implicit and cannot be described.

Also, much of the useful knowledge is uncertain, and would better be described as belief. Problems are often ill-specified, data may be imprecise or incomplete, and experts respond to situations intuitively rather than by a set of logical deductions. Attempts to model uncertainty in expert systems often require people to estimate probabilities and factors whose meaning is not understood. Probability theory is alien to many people, and so attempts to estimate probabilities can present very real problems in knowledge elicitation (Hart, 1986a). Furthermore, the knowledge is not static. People continue to learn from experience, and to refine and change their views and beliefs. The extent to which this happens obviously depends on the domain, but the consequences are that knowledge bases will need updating after they have gone into use. John McDermott made this comment years ago in the context of XCON (McDermott, 1980, 1981). In fact he calls the knowledge acquisition problem the knowledge maintenance problem. It is therefore not simply a matter of extracting knowledge and building a static model of it; the model needs to be able to support changes. These are all good principles from software engineering, but the nature of the information which is being handled makes the problem more difficult for expert systems.

In traditional system development a systems analyst is often used to form a bridge between users and technical personnel. They also serve as a catalyst for projects, co-ordinating and sometimes generating ideas. In expert system development the analogous person is called a knowledge engineer. A knowledge engineer needs interpersonal skills, technical knowledge, communication skills, and a knowledge of subjects like psychology, social sciences, etc. The knowledge engineer observes, suggests, prompts, looks for patterns and contradictions, and tries to ensure that the emerging model and system serve their purpose (Hart, 1986b; Kidd, 1987). It is often a time-consuming process, involving hours of interviews with expert(s), and there is no consensus as to how the process should take place. Common methods are listed as follows:

1. interviews; structured or unstructured
2. talking through case studies
3. observing interactions
4. protocol analysis
5. card-sorting and other techniques from psychology
6. task analysis
7. examining records
8. automated tools, or expert system shells
9. machine induction

For further details see Kidd (1987).

2.4   INDUCTIVE KNOWLEDGE GENERATION

Chapter 1 has already discussed inductive reasoning as a method of learning. It is accepted that we use induction to draw generalizations from specific cases and thereby learn. Unlike deduction, which is a logical process, induction is necessarily uncertain and 'unproven'. Computers can be used to suggest generalizations from data. The process is essentially data analysis. However, it is very important to appreciate an important difference between machine induction and human induction. Human reasoning is all carried out in the context of general and domain knowledge (as discussed earlier in this chapter), whereas most inductive knowledge generators have no such base of knowledge, and use general techniques to detect patterns. This can have the advantage of a form of objectivity in the sense that there is no prejudice or preconception, and that computer systems can detect correlations which human beings would not always see. On the other hand it means that the discovery is done away from the richness of general knowledge, and a computer might suggest some pattern which as 'obviously' inappropriate. The lack of semantic understanding can be a big handicap.

Another feature of inductive systems is that they tend to search for a minimal set of rules or the 'simplest' pattern which describes the input. In this way the output can be efficient but clinical in the sense that it lacks the richness of knowledge usually associated with the domain by a human expert.

There has been some excitement that eventually computers would be able to synthesize or discover knowledge using machine induction (Michie and Johnston, 1985). Claims were made that computers would be able to solve world problems by generating knowledge unknown to men. It is quite true that there are a few cases of economic success resulting from the use of an inductive generator as a data analysis tool, but the claim is fundamentally misguided owing to a misunderstanding of knowledge and induction. It is very important to place these claims in context, and to give guidelines for the use of induction.

In the context of expert system development the induction enthusiasts see induction as a method of bypassing the 'knowledge acquisition bottleneck'. Instead of spending hours and hours trying to elicit knowledge from an inarticulate expert the idea is to collect large sets of example problems, together with their answers, and to let the computer discover the rules and so generate knowledge. Typically the cases might be patient details, namely their symptoms and the 'correct' diagnosis. The expert doctor may be able to describe the symptoms (either from case notes or by constructing examples) and the diagnosis, without explicitly telling the knowledge engineer how the decision process took place, which symptoms were considered, when and how. The computer could then analyse the cases and discover rules indicating which symptoms to examine and how to come to a diagnosis. The examples, often called the training set, would have to contain examples of patients with the disease under consideration, and examples of those without (i.e. positive and negative cases). These generated rules would then form the basis for a medical diagnosis system to assist in this domain.

In the context of machine learning the term 'concept' is used to mean a class value, and does not carry the same meaning as in common language. For the case of medical diagnosis the concept to be learnt would be DISEASE which would be either present or absent. The system would produce rules to determine whether or not the disease was present, and would then be described as having learnt the single concept. In many instances, and typically medicine, it is desirable to diagnose more than one class (or disease) and this would be called multiple concept learning. For general problems the 'symptoms' are often referred to as attributes (which can take categorical values, e.g. RED/BLUE/GREEN, or integer values, e.g. AGE), and the diagnosis is referred to as the class which must be categorical.

Now let us consider an overly simple case. Suppose that the training set of examples contained an example covering every 'type' of problem which could occur for the intended system. 'Type' is deliberately vague because it is complex. It does not merely mean one of each type of class or answer; rather the line of reasoning behind the decision, i.e. the route down a decision tree. For example, if we were considering the selection of personnel for a job, then two candidates could be considered suitable but for quite different reasons. The criteria for selection could be different in each case, although the decision was exactly the same. As you do not know in advance what the reasoning is, then it is difficult to assess what different 'types' are needed. However, for such a complete training set it is clear that if the system induced rules which worked for the training set then they would obviously work in general. Machine learning could then be said to have discovered knowledge, as the rules would be adequate for any new example presented to them. Even if human experts did not recognize the rules or even believe them, the rules would work. They may not even have any physical or causal reason for working, but that would not matter. In practice it is utterly impossible to have a complete and correct training set and to know that you have such. The output may or may not have some general validity, but the fact that it was produced by an inductive system is insufficient reason for accepting it. It is therefore vitally important that care is taken in drawing up the training set and in interpretating the output.

2.5   INDUCTIVE METHODS

There are various ways of inducing patterns from input examples. Typical strategies are outlined below, although this chapter is more concerned with general principles than with specific algorithms.

1. Engineering and systems theory present numerical methods of pattern recognition using statistical techniques;
2. Starting with specific examples you can eliminate attributes which appear to be irrelevant, until you have a minimal effective set;
3. You can perform logical operations on descriptions of the examples and reduce them to minimal descriptions;
4. You can generate and test hypotheses about the data;
5. You can build a decision tree by successively selecting attributes which discriminate well on the examples.

Readers who are familiar with statistics as a discipline will have noticed the similarity between these techniques and hypothesis testing. In fact statistical inference is a classic example of inductive reasoning. There the method is as follows:

1. State assumptions about the population and test them if possible;
2. Take a random sample from the population;
3. Perform a test on the sample;
4. Draw conclusions about the population as a whole.

The population is analogous to the complete set of problems; the random sample to the training set; and the test results to the induced rules. In addition, in statistics it is usual to attribute some degree of confidence to the conclusions (e.g. Ehrenberg, 1982). Many of the principles which follow come from the good practice associated with statistical methods.

2.6   USING INDUCTION WISELY

We shall now illustrate some of the issues associated with the use of induction in practice.

Consider the very simple training set in Table 2.1 which shows examples of patients and diagnoses of measles/not measles. One reasonable rule for learning the concept is

Table 2.1   Characteristics of patients and the diagnosis

Attributes			Class
TEMPERATURE	SPOTS	AGE	DIAGNOSIS
YES	YES	7	MEASLES
NO	YES	1	NOT MEASLES
YES	YES	8	MEASLES
YES	NO	2	NOT MEASLES
NO	NO	21	NOT MEASLES
NO	YES	38	NOT MEASLES
YES	NO	24	NOT MEASLES
YES	YES	7	MEASLES
YES	YES	8	MEASLES
YES	YES	4	MEASLES

**IF SPOTS AND TEMPERATURE THEN MEASLES
ELSE NOT MEASLES**

If you looked at the data then this is probably the rule which you spotted. However, from the data alone an equally valid rule would be

**IF $3 < AGE \leqslant 9$ THEN MEASLES
ELSE NOT MEASLES**

The second rule seems less natural, and it is valuable to reflect on this example. Our common knowledge about diseases tells us that SPOTS and TEMPERATURE are far more likely to be symptoms of measles than AGE. However, this depends on a semantic understanding of the terms, and general knowledge about medicine. By chance, for this particular training set, the attribute AGE provides a good rule. This is because age is correlated with the disease – children are far more likely to have measles than adults, although clearly a diagnosis could not be made on the basis of that single attribute.

One could argue that the attribute AGE should not be present in the training set, and that that would remove the problem. There is an element of truth in this, and it is certainly extremely important that the training set is drawn up by someone with a knowledge of the domain, and the most 'natural' attributes selected. After all the rules or generalizations are expressed in terms of the attributes so a good or natural set of attributes is more likely to lead to a natural set of rules. Often in practice you would not know that an attribute was not important, and so include it in the hope that it gave better results. As this case shows, this might not be the actual outcome. On the other hand a physician might have good reason for including AGE if he or she considers it a factor which is taken into consideration while not being the deciding factor. As an overriding principle, the quality of inductive output depends very heavily on the quality of the input.

As a further case study, consider the training set of Table 2.2 which shows examination results for a set of students, together with decisions about progression. Depending on their performance, the students can be awarded a pass, they can be referred so that they have to resit at least one examination before a final decision can be made, or they can fail. If they perform exceptionally well then they can be awarded a distinction.

Table 2.2

	Marks in subject			
A	B	C	D	Result
30	65	79	50	Refer
40	32	62	50	Refer
65	70	66	86	Distinction
30	32	30	50	Fail
40	42	56	60	Pass
50	60	77	74	Pass
25	32	30	50	Fail
72	64	75	75	Distinction
38	40	45	42	Pass

An inductive system generated the following set of rules:

IF SUBJECT A > 58 THEN DISTINCTION
IF SUBJECT A ⩽ 58 AND SUBJECT C ⩽ 37 THEN FAIL
IF SUBJECT A ⩽ 58 AND SUBJECT C > 37 AND SUBJECT D ⩽ 55 AND SUBJECT D > 46 THEN REFER
ELSE PASS

Compare these rules with the actual examination regulations:

1. The pass mark is 40;
2. A marginal fail is a mark greater than 34 but less than 40;
3. A distinction is awarded if the student has passed all subjects with an average of at least 70;
4. A pass is awarded if all subjects are passed;
5. A pass is awarded if there are at most two marginal fails;
6. A referral is allowed if there are at most two fails;
7. The student fails if there are more than two failures.

Table 2.3 shows the data recoded more in the style of the regulations. This time the induced rules are:

IF AVERAGE > 68 THEN DISTINCTION

Table 2.3 The examination data recoded so that they more closely match the criteria for decisions about the results. The induced results are better from these data than from Table 2.2

NUMBER OF PASSES	NUMBER OF MARGINAL FAILS	AVERAGE MARK	RESULT
3	0	56	REFER
3	0	46	REFER
4	0	72	DISTINCTION
1	0	36	FAIL
4	0	49	PASS
4	0	65	PASS
1	0	34	FAIL
4	0	71	DISTINCTION
3	1	41	PASS

IF AVERAGE > 53 AND AVERAGE ⩽ 68 AND NUMBER OF PASSES ⩽ 3
THEN REFER
IF AVERAGE > 53 AND AVERAGE ⩽ 68 AND NUMBER OF PASSES = 4 THEN
PASS
IF AVERAGE ⩽ 53 AND NUMBER OF PASSES = 4 THEN PASS
IF AVERAGE ⩽ 53 AND NUMBER OF PASSES = 1 THEN FAIL
IF AVERAGE ⩽ 53 AND NUMBER OF PASSES = 3 AND MARGINAL FAILS = 1
THEN PASS
IF AVERAGE ⩽ 53 AND NUMBER OF PASSES = 3 AND MARGINAL FAILS = 0
THEN REFER

Notice how the new training set gets closer to the actual rules, but is still inaccurate owing to the incompleteness of the examples. While in this case it was relatively easy to describe the examples in a 'good' style, in practical examples it is not at all clear what constitutes good style. The moral from this case study is that changing the attributes can make a profound difference on the quality of the induced rules. This study also demonstrates a problem with integer attributes. Most inductive techniques work much better on categorical data than on integers. Notice here that the mark for a distinction is chosen as 68. As can be seen from the data any value between 66 and 71 could have been selected. These cut-off points which emerge when integer attributes have been used need careful investigation. They should have some significance to the domain expert, and it is a good idea to perform some kind of sensitivity analysis on them. The point that is chosen is clearly very dependent on the input data.

A training set can be drawn from existing case histories or notes, or compiled by an expert. Whichever is the case it needs careful compilation and filtering. It needs to be expressed in an effective way using attributes and descriptions which are natural in the language of the domain, and the output should be investigated with care.

Induction can sometimes raise as many questions as it answers. For example, in the examination problem what is the decision if the average is less than 53, and the number of passes is 2? No example in the training set covers this event. Either it is an impossible combination, or the training set needs refining. Questions like these can form the basis of a useful discussion with the expert. So can questions about which attributes were chosen, why some attributes were omitted, and the order in which attributes are selected in the output. The basis of this discussion is not that the induced results are right and that the expert has to justify them, but that induction has highlighted interesting questions about the domain. The actual induced results may, in the end, form no part of the knowledge base, but they may act as a catalyst for discussion and evaluation of a model of the knowledge.

In a different study the following anomalies arose (for more details of this work see Hart, 1987):

> IF STUDENT HAS ENTRY REQUIREMENTS AND AGE < 19 AND EXAM GRADE IS D THEN ACCEPT
> IF STUDENT HAS ENTRY REQUIREMENTS AND AGE < 19 AND EXAM GRADE IS C THEN REJECT

Here a better-qualified student is being rejected while another is accepted. The data does not show any other criteria for the decision. This is another case of an inadequate training set.

In the same study these rules were also obtained:

> IF STUDENT DOES NOT HAVE ENTRY REQUIREMENTS AND NO EXAMS ARE OUTSTANDING AND AGE ≤ 26 THEN REJECT
> IF STUDENT DOES NOT HAVE ENTRY REQUIREMENTS AND NO EXAMS ARE OUTSTANDING AND AGE > 26 AND AGE ≤ 45 THEN ACCEPT
> IF STUDENT DOES NOT HAVE ENTRY REQUIREMENTS AND NO EXAMS ARE OUTSTANDING AND AGE > 45 THEN REJECT

Here the program has 'discovered' mature students. These are students with no formal qualifications but experience, and they can have exceptional entry to courses. However, the judgement involved in such a decision is far more involved than a mere consideration of age. As this wealth of information was not available in the training set, and more crucially because it was not necessary in order to discriminate between cases, the induced rules reflect nothing of the complexity of this decision process.

Some attributes can behave like labels, by acting as unique identifiers for the examples; for example, the application number in this study. Attributes which thus identify individual cases are excellent discriminators within the training set, and are likely to be chosen by the system. However, they clearly have no predictive power. Names, ages, etc. can have similar effects. In statistical terms there are too many degrees of freedom associated with the attribute in comparison with the number of different examples.

A minimal set of discriminating rules will provide a very 'shallow' set of knowledge. There is no context, no explanation, and no justification except that the rules work for the input data. In the context of our discussion of useful expert systems the results need a great deal of work before they can become part of a knowledge base. A decision tree can hardly be called a knowledge base at all; it certainly meets very few of our earlier criteria for joint cognitive systems.

2.7 VALIDATING THE OUTPUT

The output must be discussed and evaluated with a human expert. Only a human expert can produce the dialogue which augments the crude rules in order to construct a meaningful system. The results should also be tested on further examples to evaluate performance. Induced rules which are based on an untypical set of data will perform badly on other examples. If the number of examples is restricted then the set should be divided into subsets, one of which is used to induce rules and the other to validate them. This can be done several times, and the various outputs checked for consistency.

In the context of testing it is important to consider the importance of the decision and risk involved, not merely 'percentage correct'. It is far too easy to neglect the base rate in the calculation of a success rate. For example, if a particular instance occurs 10% of the time you can get a 90% success rate by always predicting that it is not there. This is hardly impressive, or knowledgeable.

If the output is a decision tree then it is likely that the lower parts of the tree are less accurate than the higher ones, because they are based on fewer examples. This obviously makes them very sensitive to the input data. There are various ways of dealing with this problem. One is to have some criteria for stopping growth of the tree; e.g. a measure of the information content in the remaining examples, and a criterion which stops growth when this gets low. An alternative strategy is to grow the tree to its full length and then to prune back parts which are not effective. Typically this involves comparing the extra information gained by growing the tree against the cost of so doing. This is adequately described elsewhere (Breiman *et al*, 1984).

There is one other problem. In statistics the study of outliers is difficult and interesting. Outliers are data points which appear different from the main data set. They are like stray points. Outliers can be caused by errors in measurement or they may be genuinely interesting cases, and it is not always easy to know which they are or how to deal with them. In induction this is an important problem too. Expert systems should be able to help with interesting and unusual cases as well as the common ones. In fact it may well be these exceptional cases which are of most interest to the user. On the other hand, you do not want to include a set of rules which describe a noisy or erroneous example. Inductive techniques are unlikely to be able to handle these outlier points and although they may be obvious from a full tree, pruning a tree may remove them. Once again this forms the basis for a discussion with the expert.

2.8   GENERAL GUIDELINES

When selecting examples for a training set it is important to ensure that you have a good set for each of the classes of problem. This can mean that a standard random sample is inadequate, because it describes the distribution of events, not the set of problem types. Some problem types are more common than others, but the set should adequately describe them all. Data may need filtering.

Errors or imprecision in the input can cause spurious output; an error in a class is usually more serious than in an attribute value.

Skill is needed in the selection of attributes. If a joint pair of attributes is seen to be important then they should be coded as such (i.e. **A AND B**; true or false) rather than individually as a pair of attributes (A true or false; B true or false). This needs the skill of the expert.

Beware of attributes which are like labels, such as identifying numbers. These are excellent for describing the training set examples, but useless for prediction.

The output must be tested on further examples.

Watch out for results which are dependent on a few examples; they may be spurious or interesting. Induced results may be very shallow and inadequate.

Look for contradictions and gaps in the data. They can lead to interesting discussions.

Integer attributes lead to rules with cut-off points which need analysis and justification. In general integer attributes need careful treatment.

The results are a minimal set of rules or patterns. It is useful to discuss attributes which do not appear in the output. They may be correlated with others, or redundant. Such comments are essential if a rich and informative knowledge base is to be created.

Be prepared to modify and refine the training set, but do not impose some preconceived solution on the system.

2.9   KNOWLEDGE MAINTENANCE

We have commented that the knowledge acquisition problem is really a knowledge maintenance problem, and that knowledge bases will need continual refinement. Some users ask why the system cannot update its own knowledge base when it is found to be inadequate. Induction has been suggested as a method here.

Once a knowledge base has been created then inductive techniques could be used to update it. This has the advantage that the inductive method need not be a very general one, but based on knowledge about the domain. Indeed some expert systems have their own knowledge acquisition programs which in some way attempt to do this. Architectures of systems have been proposed where there is deep knowledge (considered to be factual, causal or generally accepted) supporting heuristic knowledge, and that the heuristics could change in the light of experience. The causal knowledge would be used to induce new heuristics or to amend the existing ones. The main problem with this is one of validation. Who takes responsibility for the knowledge base, as it may after a time have heuristics and 'knowledge' which are alien to the human experts. Partridge discusses the problem of learning in this way, but still believes that it is an essential feature of intelligent systems (Partridge, 1986). Of course, such learning still suffers from being in the context of limited knowledge, and certainly a lack of general knowledge and common sense. For an example of this learning approach see Van de Velde (1986).

It is also fair to comment that research is under way to cope with noisy training sets (e.g. Quinlan, 1985). Many of the principles outlined here will still be valid.

2.10 CONCLUSIONS

Human knowledge and intelligence are difficult to describe and define. However, computer intelligence is essentially different, and the development of 'intelligent' machines raises the question of how they can best be designed to meet users' needs. Such systems contain representations of knowledge and reasoning extracted from human experts. Owing to the complex nature of knowledge it is impossible to elicit some kinds of human knowledge, and difficult to elicit others. Machine induction, while far less sophisticated than human learning, can sometimes be a useful tool to assist in suggesting a model of knowledge. However, it must be used with care, and the results evaluated and very much refined before they can be built into a useful knowledge base.

2.11 REFERENCES

Berry, D. (1987) The problem of implicit knowledge. *Expert Systems Journal of Knowledge Engineering,* **4** (3).

Breiman, L., Friedman, J. H., Olshen, R. A. and Stone, C. J. (1984) *Classification and Regression Trees,* Wadsworth International, Belmont, California.

Dreyfus, H. and Dreyfus, S. (1986) *Mind over Machine,* Free Press, New York.

Ehrenberg, A. S. C. (1982) *A Primer in Data Reduction,* John Wiley, London.

Faust, D. (1984) *The Limits of Scientific Reasoning,* University of Minnesota Press, Minneapolis.

Feigenbaum, E. A. and Barr, A. (1981) *The Handbook of Artificial Intelligence,* Vol. 1, Pitman Books, London, (see especially p. 144).

Gregory, R. L. (1986) *Eye and Brain: The Psychology of Seeing,* Weidenfeld and Nicolson, London.

Hart, A. (1986a) Problems of handling uncertainty in knowledge engineering, in *Proc. 2nd International Conference on Expert Systems, London,* Learned Information, Oxford, pp. 253–63.

Hart, A. (1986b) *Knowledge Acquisition for Expert Systems,* Kogan Page, London.

Hart, A. (1987) The role of induction in knowledge elicitation, in A. Kidd (ed.), *Knowledge Acquisition for Expert Systems: A Practical Handbook*, Plenum Press, New York.

Haugeland, J. (1986) *Artificial Intelligence; The Very Idea*, MIT, London.

Kidd, A. (ed.) (1987) *Knowledge Acquisition for Expert Systems: A Practical Handbook*, Plenum Press, New York.

Lyotard, J. F. (1984) *The Postmodern Condition: A Report on Knowledge*, Manchester University Press.

McClelland, J. L. and Rumelhart, D. E. (1986) *Parallel Distributed Processing: Explorations in the Microstructure of Cognition*, Vols 1 and 2, MIT Press, Cambridge, Mass.

McDermott, J. (1980) R1: an expert in the computer systems domain. *AAAI*, **1**, 269–71.

McDermott, J. (1981) R1: the formative years. *AI Magazine*, **2** (2), 21–9.

Medawar, P. (1969) *Induction and Intuition in Scientific Thought*, Methuen and Co., London.

Michie, D. and Johnston, R. (1985) *The Creative Computer*, Pelican, London.

Newell, A. and Simon, H. A. (1963) GPS: a program that simulates human thought, in E. Feigenbaum and J. Feldman (eds), *Computers and Thought*, McGraw-Hill, New York, pp. 279–93.

Partridge, D. (1986) *Artificial Intelligence: applications in the future of software engineering*, Ellis Horwood, Chichester, UK.

Pratt, V. (1987) *Thinking Machines: The Evolution of Artificial Intelligence*, Blackwell, Oxford.

Quinlan, R. (1985) *Induction of Decision Trees*, Technical Report 85.6, New South Wales Institute of Technology, Australia.

Thomson, D. M. and Tulving, E. (1970) Associative encoding and retrieval: weak and strong cues. *Journal of Experimental Psychology*, **86**, 255–62.

Turing, A. (1950) Computing Machinery and Intelligence. *Mind*, London.

Van de Velde, W. (1986) Explainable knowledge production. *Proc. Seventh European Conference on Artificial Intelligence*, Brighton, pp. 8–22.

Winograd, T. and Flores, F. (1986) *Understanding Computers and Cognition: A New Foundation for Design*, Ablex Publishing Co., Norwood, N.J.

FURTHER READING

Alty, J. L. and Coombs, N. J. (1984) *Expert systems: Concepts and Examples*, Manchester NCC.

Waterman, D. A., Hayes-Roth, F. and Lenat, D. B. (1983) *Building Expert Systems*, Addison-Wesley, London.

3

Inductive learning: the user's perspective

TOMASZ ARCISZEWSKI AND MOHAMAD MUSTAFA

3.1 INTRODUCTION

'Tool builders have focused, not improperly, on tool building, how to build better-performing machines. But tool use involves more. The key to effective application of computational technology is to conceive, model, design and evaluate the joint human–machine cognitive system . . .'

D. Woods, 1986

Computer learning from examples has been a subject of interest to scientists since the early 1950s, when Turing (1950) proposed this application for computers. For a long time inductive learning was a rather theoretical subject without practical implications. Only recently has the development of a number of inductive systems applicable to practical problems changed this situation and stimulated interest in the methodology of use of such systems in different areas of science and technology.

The new class of inductive systems available contains several groups of computer tools based on different learning algorithms. However, all these different inductive systems can be used for the same purpose of computer extraction of decision rules from examples, and therefore they should be considered jointly from the user's point of view, particularly in that their applications can be covered by the same methodology of inductive learning.

The first group of inductive systems is based on the inductive algorithm ID3 proposed by Quinlan (1983), which uses the statistical theory of information originally proposed by Shannon (1948). The best-known commercially available inductive systems in this group are EXPERT-EASE (Software Review, 1985), EX-TRAN7 (Michie, 1984) and Super Expert, developed by Intelligent Computer Terminals. The second group of inductive systems has been developed by Forsyth (1986, 1987) and is based on the evolutionary approach to decision rules generation (Forsyth, 1981) using Darwinian principles. Commercially available inductive systems from this group are called subsequent BEAGLEs and were produced by Warm Boot Ltd. The concept of the evolutionary development of decision rules has also been used by Michalski in two learning algorithms. AQ11 (Michalski and Larson, 1978) produces decision rules by employing a 'top-down' approach in which initial general rules are narrowed down to reflect new evidence in the process of generation. His second learning algorithm, INDUCE (Dietterich and Michalski, 1981), works in the opposite way, starting with narrow rules which are gradually generalized. These algorithms have been used in experimental inductive systems which are not commercially available. The next group of experimental inductive systems is based on two different learning algorithms, PLA (probabilistic learning algorithm) and Reduct-PLA, proposed by Ziarko and Wong (Wong and Ziarko, 1986; Ziarko, 1987). These algorithms were derived from the underlying probabilistic model of rough sets proposed by Pawlak (1982). PLA is an inductive learning algorithm capable of generating generalized decision rules from non-deterministic information: these decision rules form a decision tree with certainty factors automatically assigned to individual rules. Reduct-PLA (Ziarko, 1987) produces a collection of decision trees, or forest, where each decision tree contains rules related only to a given conclusion. Several experimental computer programs based on these two algorithms, including ANLYST1, ANLYST2 and ANLYST3, developed by Voytech Systems, Inc. are being tested in the Intelligent Computers Center at Wayne State University.

There have been several successful experimental applications of inductive systems in science. The best known are the use of an inductive system based on INDUCE for the problem of classification of cells into cancerous and normal (Dietterich and Michalski, 1981), and the applications of BEAGLE to the classification of glass fragment evidence in forensic science (Spiehler, 1987). However, there are very few engineering applications of inductive systems. EX-TRAN7 was used by Modesitt for generating decision rules for analysis of test data for the space shuttle main engine (Modesitt, 1987) and by Sillen (1987) in engineering problem-solving. ANLYST was used by the authors for the experimental generation of decision rules governing the conceptual design of steel members under bending (Arciszewski *et al.*, 1987). The present situation can be explained by the novelty of such systems and by the lack of methodology for their use. It is no coincidence that at present only very large companies with expert systems divisions, such as Rockwell International, or very small, highly specialized expert systems companies such as Novacast AB of Sweden, are actively involved in inductive systems engineering applications. The mainstream applications are still to come. It should be noted that these mainstream applications are being delayed not by the lack of necessary software or hardware but by the lack of methodology. Michalski in Michalski *et al.* (1983) presented the first outline of this methodology, but he was mostly concerned with the internal workings of an inductive system during the learning process. This is the point of view of a developer, not user, of inductive systems, and therefore the results of Michalski's work have had only limited practical impact. Also, the available publications on the applications of inductive systems provide very limited methodological information. In all known cases this information was obtained as a by-product of projects oriented towards specific results, specifically only towards the generation of decision rules controlling the specific problems under investigation. There have been at least two such projects, which have also produced some methodological results; these were mentioned above (Modesitt, 1987; Sillen, 1987). The methodological information resulting from these projects is very important and useful, but its fragmented character makes it insufficient for building a consistent methodology. The present state of the art and growing practical importance of inductive systems create the need, however, to develop such methodology, which would be oriented towards the inductive system user.

In this chapter, the methodology of inductive learning is understood as a subarea of inductive learning. Its subject is the process of generating decision rules from examples, and methods of control and optimization of this process in order to minimize the time required to extract a set of decision rules from a given body of examples. The methodology of inductive learning considers the process of learning from the inductive system user's point of view. The user applies an inductive system as a kind of black box, and his understanding of the mathematical or computer aspects of learning is usually very shallow. So defined, the methodology of inductive learning will provide detailed methodological knowledge for a large class of potential inductive system users in science and technology. Its development should also stimulate further applications of inductive systems, particularly in engineering.

The authors have systematically studied the methodology of inductive learning since 1985. In that year the first experimental inductive systems, developed by Dr Ziarko of the Computer Science Department, University of Regina, were installed in Wayne State University's Civil Engineering Department. A close working relationship was established between these two departments. Its results are a string of inductive systems, specially tailored and developed for engineering applications, and initial methodological experience gained during the years spent testing these inductive systems. The results of this research have been presented (Arciszewski *et al.*, 1987; Arciszewski and Ziarko, 1988, to appear; Hajdo *et al.*, 1988). The initial methodological results were described in Arciszewski *et al.* (1987). Dr Ziarko of the Computer Science Department, University of Regina, Canada, Dr Reynolds of Wayne's Computer Science Department and Mr Forsyth of Warm Boot Ltd, are in contact with the authors and their experience is being used in the current research.

In 1987 the Intelligent Computers Center was established in Wayne's Civil Engineering Department. A number of computer hardware and software grants were received and used to install a network of computers, including a Texas Instruments Explorer LX computer and several Texas Instrument Business Professional computers, with all necessary software. A group of interested PhD students has been selected and have begun systematic research on different engineering applications of inductive systems, with special interest in the methodological aspect of inductive learning in engineering.

3.2 RESEARCH OBJECTIVES

The objective of this chapter is to present the results of experimental work on the methodology of inductive learning conducted in the Intelligent Computers Center at Wayne State University. Several different models of the inductive learning process are proposed, discussed and compared. The problem of selecting examples for inductive learning is analysed and recommendations made. A system of inductive learning process control criteria is also proposed. Individual developed criteria were used to monitor and control a number of inductive learning processes; these results are described and initial conclusions presented.

3.3 BASIC ASSUMPTIONS AND CONCEPTS OF THE RESEARCH

In this research, inductive systems were considered as new engineering tools. These tools were assumed to be black boxes which can be used for the extraction of decision rules from examples by inductive learning experts. Such experts may not necessarily be computer scientists, but they should have a background in design methodology and should know how to deal with complex processes involving decision rules. The basic research question was then how to use these tools, and global, or shallow, understanding of the inductive learning process was the ultimate objective. So formulated, our research assumes here the integration of inductive learning and the methodology of engineering design, and reflects the general philosophy of research being conducted in the Intelligent Computers Center.

The next assumption was that the inductive learning process should be considered as a monitored multi-stage process. It was also assumed that not only the final result, or the final set of decision rules, is important. From the engineering point of view the understanding of the learning process is equally important, and in the cases of research applications it is even more important. This understanding should include:

1. The ability to relate individual decision rules to their 'parent example';
2. The ability to trace the 'history' of the generation of individual decision rules, including all their changes and the character of these changes;
3. The ability to control the learning process using corrective examples;
4. The ability to know when this process is completed.

It was also assumed that a class of different inductive learning process models should be identified and individual models used for different inductive learning purposes.

The important assumption was that the inductive learning process can be controlled and that criteria can be identified and used for this control.

All the above assumptions should be valid for qualitative and quantitative knowledge acquisition, and the same methodology can be developed for dealing with these two types of knowledge. Qualitative knowledge is understood here as general knowledge useful for the purposes of conceptual design, while quantitative or detailed knowledge represents decision rules extracted from numerical examples of solutions to a given problem, which were produced under different assumptions. In this chapter only the results of inductive experiments conducted using quantitative examples are described, but our experiments with qualitative examples justify our assumption (Arciszewski *et al.*, 1987).

The quantitative examples used were computer-generated. They were produced using a specially developed LISP program for the Texas Instruments Explorer LX, which was prepared in the Intelligent Computers Center for the design of steel beams under bending. Forty-five examples were used, related to two conclusions, in this case cross-sections of steel beams. The computer generation of examples used can be compared with the computer experimentation being conducted by Adeli (1987) for expert systems applications.

All inductive learning experiments described in this chapter were conducted using an experimental inductive system, ANLYST, developed by Ziarko and described in Wong and Ziarko (1986) and Ziarko (1987).

3.4 MODELS OF THE INDUCTIVE LEARNING PROCESS

In 'traditional' inductive learning a body of all available N examples is usually entered and analysed in a single learning stage. From the global point of view the model of such a process can be called a 'point model' (Fig. 3.1). The application of the point model usually produces the desired results, and it also requires a relatively short time. This model is most effective in product-oriented applications, when the inductive system user is interested only in the final results, i.e. the final set of decision rules. In addition to this the domain should be well known and understood, and the expected rules should be relatively simple and easy to verify. In many cases, however, this model is insufficient. The best example of such a situation is the use of a personal computer with limited working memory, which can handle only a relatively small but unknown number of examples. In this case the point model may produce no results and time is wasted. There is also a large class of engineering and research problems where the point model is useless. In all these problems the ultimate objective is to develop a better understanding of the domain of the examples, and the final decision rules are

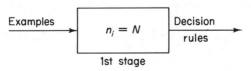

Fig. 3.1. Point model.

insufficient and often cannot be verified and properly interpreted. To deal with all such problems, a new class of multi-stage models of the learning process is proposed here. The class of multi-stage models has two subclasses: linear and mixed models.

Linear models of the learning process are defined here as models with at least two learning stages. In this case the set of N available examples is divided into at least two subsets. The first subset is analysed in the first stage of the learning process while the second one is added in the next stage. Linear models can be additionally classified as uniform, when all sets of examples have the same power, and semi-uniform, when the power of individual example sets n_i is differentiated, but these differences are insignificant, i.e. less than 10% (Fig. 3.2).

Mixed models are defined as multi-stage models with individual stages having sets of examples of significantly differentiated powers, i.e. more than 10%. These models can be additionally classified into front point, central point and back point models, considering the location of the largest set of examples having a power at least 25% larger than other sets of examples used in the given learning process (Fig. 3.3).

The authors' experience with inductive learning strongly indicates that it is important for an inductive learning expert to be able to identify the relationship between rules generated during individual stages of the learning process and to present these relationships in simple graphical form. For this reason two different forms of recording of a learning process were proposed. The first one can be called an 'inductive learning process spreadsheet' and the second one a 'decision rules network'.

In an inductive learning spreadsheet all decision rules are recorded in a table with rows representing individual stages of the learning process. Related

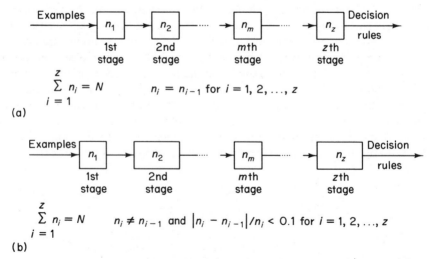

Fig. 3.2. Linear models: (a) uniform linear model; (b) semi-uniform linear model.

$$\sum_{i=1}^{z} n_i = N$$

$$n_i \neq n_{i-1} \text{ and } 0.1 < |n_i - n_{i-1}|/n_i < 0.25 \text{ for } i = 1, 2, \ldots, z$$

(a)

$$\sum_{i=1}^{z} n_i = N$$

$$n_1 \neq n_{i+1} \text{ and } |n_1 - n_{i+1}|/n_1 \geqslant 0.25 \text{ for } i = 1, 2, \ldots, z-1$$

and

$$n_j = n_{j+1} \text{ for } j = 2, \ldots, z-1$$

or $\quad n_j \neq n_{j+1} \text{ and } |n_j - n_{j+1}|/n_j < 0.1 \text{ for } j = 2, 3, \ldots, z-1$

or $\quad n_j \neq n_{j+1} \text{ and } 0.1 < |n_j - n_{j+1}|/n_j < 0.25 \text{ for } j = 2, 3, \ldots, z-1$

(b)

$$\sum_{i=1}^{z} n_i \neq N$$

$$n_c \neq n_{c-1} \text{ and } n_c \neq n_{c+1} \text{ and } |n_c - n_{c \pm 1}|/n_c \geqslant 0.25$$

and

$$n_i = n_{i-1} \text{ for } i = 1, 2, \ldots, z \text{ and } i \neq c$$

or $\quad n_i \neq n_{i-1} \text{ and } |n_i - n_{i-1}|/n_i < 0.1 \text{ for } i = 1, 2, \ldots, z \text{ and } i \neq c$

or $\quad n_i \neq n_{i-1} \text{ and } 0.1 < |n_i - n_{i-1}|/n_i < 0.25 \text{ for } i = 1, 2, \ldots, z \text{ and } i \neq c$

(c)

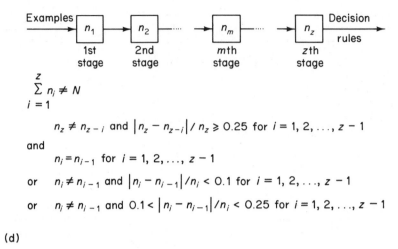

$$\sum_{i=1}^{z} n_i \neq N$$

$$n_z \neq n_{z-i} \text{ and } |n_z - n_{z-i}|/n_z \geqslant 0.25 \text{ for } i = 1, 2, \ldots, z-1$$

and

$$n_i = n_{i-1} \text{ for } i = 1, 2, \ldots, z-1$$

or $n_i \neq n_{i-1}$ and $|n_i - n_{i-1}|/n_i < 0.1$ for $i = 1, 2, \ldots, z-1$

or $n_i \neq n_{i-1}$ and $0.1 < |n_i - n_{i-1}|/n_i < 0.25$ for $i = 1, 2, \ldots, z-1$

(d)

Fig. 3.3. Mixed models: (a) mixed model; (b) front-point mixed model; (c) central-point mixed model; (d) back-point mixed model.

decisions are shown in individual columns or parts of the table. A code denotation can be used: the first symbol represents the number of the test, the second one the number of the stage, while other symbols are values of individual attributes, with zeros representing inactive attributes. All results can be easily recorded using any available spreadsheet. An example of such a form is shown in Fig. 3.4. This figure shows the results of two tests, each conducted in seven stages for nine-attribute examples. These examples were generated for steel beams under bending using quantitative data. In this case individual examples represent a combination of numerical assumptions, and the resulting conclusion (attribute no. 9) is a cross-section appropriate for these assumptions. It can be observed, following the sequence of examples, how individual decision rules change and grow more complex.

The decision rules network also contains individual decision rules identified by the code proposed above. In addition to this, however, the network also presents relationships between individual rules, shown as arrows in Fig. 3.5. A sequence of decisions connected by arrows gives a decision rule path. This path can be identified using three different path selection criteria. It was assumed that for a given rule generated in the ith stage the related rule generated in the $(i+1)$th stage can be selected using the following criteria based on attribute changes occurring at the $(i+1)$th stage with respect to the ith stage:

1. maximum number of attributes
2. minimum number of attributes
3. average number of attributes

The application of the first criterion produces the so-called 'maximum path',

Test number	Stage number	Rule number	Attribute values								Conclusion
			1	2	3	4	5	6	7	8	
1	1	1	1	1	1	0	0	0	0	0	2
	2	1	0	1	1	0	0	0	0	0	2
	3	1	0	1	1	2	0	0	0	1	2
	3	2	0	1	2	1	0	0	0	0	2
	3	3	0	1	1	3	0	0	0	0	2
	4	1	0	1	2	2	0	0	0	1	2
	4	2	0	1	2	1	0	0	0	1	2
	4	3	0	1	1	0	0	0	0	1	2
	5	1	0	1	2	2	0	0	0	1	2
	5	2	0	1	1	3	0	0	0	1	2
	5	3	0	1	2	0	0	0	0	1	2
	5	4	0	1	0	1	0	0	0	0	2
	6	1	0	1	2	2	0	0	0	1	2
	6	2	0	1	1	3	0	0	0	1	2
	6	3	0	1	1	2	0	0	0	1	2
	6	4	0	1	0	1	0	0	0	0	2
	7	1	0	1	0	1	0	0	0	0	2
	7	2	0	1	1	3	0	0	0	1	2
	7	3	0	1	1	2	0	0	0	1	2
	7	4	0	1	0	1	0	0	0	0	2
2	1	1	0	0	0	1	0	0	0	0	2
	2	1	0	1	0	1	0	0	0	0	2
	3	1	0	1	0	1	0	0	0	0	2
	4	1	0	1	0	2	0	0	0	1	2
	4	2	0	1	0	1	0	0	0	0	2
	5	1	0	1	0	2	0	0	0	1	2
	5	2	0	1	0	1	0	0	0	0	2
	6	1	0	1	2	2	0	0	0	1	2
	6	2	0	1	0	3	0	0	0	1	2
	6	3	0	1	0	1	0	0	0	0	2
	7	1	0	1	1	2	0	0	0	1	2
	7	2	0	1	1	3	0	0	0	1	2
	7	3	0	1	2	2	0	0	0	1	2
	7	4	0	1	0	1	0	0	0	0	2

Fig. 3.4. Inductive learning process spreadsheet.

denoted by MXP. The second criterion gives a minimum path, denoted by MINP. The last criterion leads to the average path, denoted by AVP.

It would be expected that MINP would be useful. Our initial results indicate, however, that MINP can be ignored since the decision rules obtained following this particular path have no significant meaning for the specific engineering problem under consideration.

Two examples of decision rules networks are shown in Fig. 3.5. These networks contain sets of decision rules for the first and second test shown in Fig. 3.4 and discussed earlier in this section. It clearly demonstrates why a network gives such good insight into a learning process. Three types of paths are also shown in these examples. It can be observed that in the first test the learning

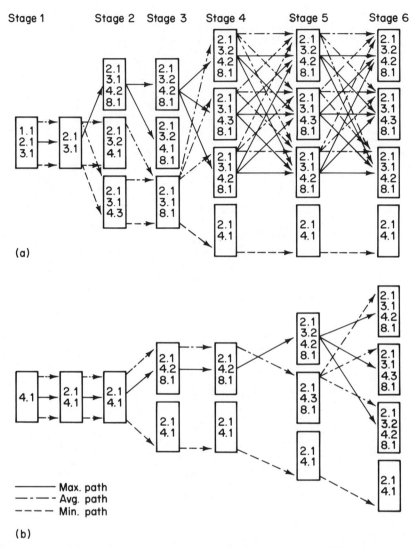

Fig. 3.5. Decision rules network: (a) 1st test: coincidental selection; (b) 2nd test: random selection.

process has been completed and individual rules do not undergo modifications and changes starting with stage 5 of the process, while in the case of the second test (employing a different sequence of the examples used in the first test) the learning process is not over even at stage 7 and individual rules are still under development.

3.5 SELECTION OF EXAMPLES

When a point model of the learning process is used the sequence of examples entered is immaterial. Simply all available examples are used and there is no need to analyse the character of individual examples and to 'design' their sequence. There is a much different situation when multi-stage models of the learning process are used. In this case the selection of examples for individual stages is important and should be made using four different approaches: purely random, coincidental, balanced and corrective.

In all cases of inductive learning the first group of examples should include examples supporting all considered conclusions. The character of examples in a given group should be strongly differentiated and each group should contain examples representing the entire spectrum.

The purely random selection of examples occurs when a special selection procedure is used. In this case all examples are numbered and their sequence determined through random generation. In our experiments a special computer program was developed for the purposes of random generation of sequences of numbers, representing individual examples to be used in a given learning process. This program was based on the stochastic simulation of morphological analysis; its basic concepts are described in Arciszewski (1987).

The coincidental selection of examples occurs when the computer learning expert selects examples for individual stages without analysing them. This selection is called coincidental to stress the fact that it is not purely random and may be affected by the expert's preferences, a subconsciously used domain understanding, or other factors.

The balanced selection of examples is usually required when using a personal computer with very limited working memory. In this case the body of all examples is carefully analysed by domain experts and divided into several groups. The character of these examples in a given group strongly reflects expert knowledge about the given task. This preparation of examples is very time-consuming and often difficult, but cannot be avoided when using a personal computer. Otherwise the learning process may be disrupted before the learning is over and the rules generated will be useless.

The selection of examples also includes the selection of corrective examples. Corrective examples are a class of special examples which have to be developed and used to eliminate incorrect decision rules, which sometimes occur. These incorrect rules are usually eliminated by the inductive system itself, when more examples are added, but sometimes they persist and must be dealt with accordingly. In this situation the addition of corrective examples, prepared specifically to eliminate a given incorrect decision rule, seems to be the best approach; more details are found in Arciszewski *et al.* (1987).

3.6 CONTROL CRITERIA

The inductive learning process can be considered from the control point of view, and two levels of control should be distinguished: global and local. The global control level can be used to monitor the entire learning process, while the local level enables the monitoring of the development of individual decision rules, or backtracking of individual paths in the rules 'network', as proposed in Section 3.4. The subject of this control process is the decision rules and attributes used to formulate these rules. Thus all proposed control criteria can be classified as global or local, and rules and attributes oriented. Individual classes of control criteria can be used for different purposes and are complementary. All proposed control criteria are to be used at individual learning stages, as the learning process progresses. Their general concept is shown in Fig. 3.6.

The class of global control criteria has two criteria. The first one, the general control rule criterion (GCRC), is defined as the total number of rules developed up to the jth stage of the learning process. Several results of the application of this criterion in a seven-stage learning process are shown in Fig. 3.7. These results were obtained for the same body of examples (steel beams under bending) described in Section 3.4. Results were produced using coincidental and random selection of examples. The two selection approaches produced identical final

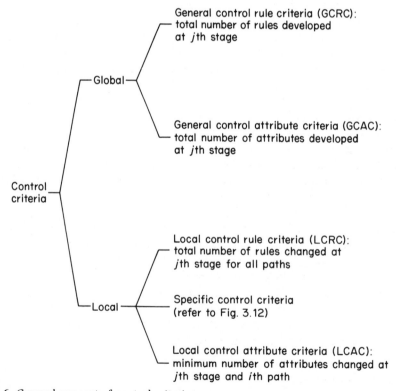

Fig. 3.6. General concept of control criteria.

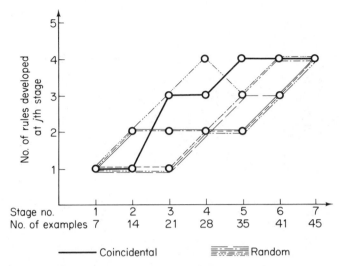

No. of rules developed at jth stage

Stage no.   1   2   3   4   5   6   7
No. of examples   7   14   21   28   35   41   45

———— Coincidental   ≡≡≡≡ Random

Fig. 3.7. Global control rule criteria (GCRC): number of rules developed at jth stage versus number of samples.

results, but there is a significant difference between the two relationships GCRC–number of examples used, obtained for these two approaches. It seems that the coincidental approach produces the expected results earlier, and relationships generated using random selection finally converge to this relationship. Thus the coincidental selection of examples can be recommended, particularly when the user wishes to minimize the time and cost of learning.

The second global criterion, the general control attribute criterion (GCAC), is defined as the total number of attributes developed at the jth stage of the learning process. The results of the application of this criterion in the learning process described above are shown in Fig. 3.8. The conclusions given above and regarding coincidental and random selection of examples are valid in this case also.

The class of local control criteria has two local criteria and a complex subclass of specific criteria, which will be discussed later. The first criterion, the local control rule criterion (LCRC), is defined as the number of rules changed at the jth stage for all paths in the rules network. Fig. 3.9 demonstrates several examples of relationships LCRC–number of examples used, obtained for our body of examples using the linear model of the learning process and coincidental and random seletion of examples.

The second criterion, the local control attribute criterion (LCAC), is defined as the minimum number of attributes changed at the jth stage in the ith path of the rules network. This criterion can be used to monitor maximum, minimum or average paths related to individual decision rules. This criterion was used to monitor changes occurring in maximum and average paths related to three

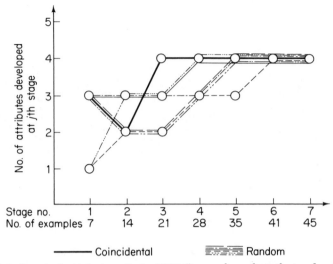

Fig. 3.8. Global control attribute criteria (GCAC): number of attributes developed at *j*th stage versus number of examples.

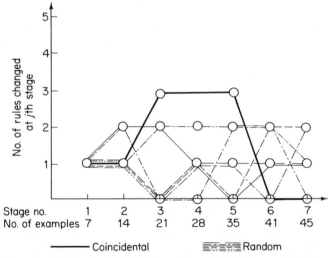

Fig. 3.9. Local control rule criteria (LCRC): number of rules changed at *j*th stage versus number of examples.

different rules generated for our body of examples. In all cases both coincidental and random selections of examples were used. Figure 3.10 presents relationships LCAC versus number of examples for the coincidental selection of examples for the maximum and average paths. These relationships should be compared with those obtained for identical rules but using random selection of examples, shown in Fig. 3.11. As before, coincidental selection of examples led to a learning process with smaller changes and 'faster' learning, measured by the number of examples necessary to complete the learning.

The proposed local criteria are useful, but unfortunately insufficient for the understanding of an ongoing learning process. For this reason a subclass of local, specific criteria is proposed. The subclass of local, specific criteria has a hierarchical character and contains a group of twelve control criteria. All these criteria cover different aspects of changes occurring with attributes during the

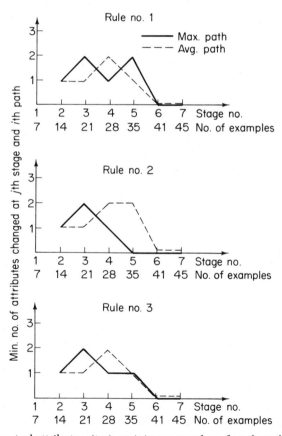

Fig. 3.10. Local control attribute criteria: minimum number of total attributes changed at *j*th stage and *i*th path versus number of examples. Coincidental selection.

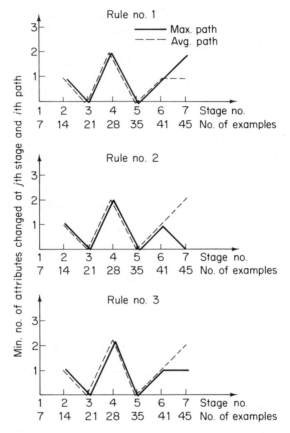

Fig. 3.11. Local control attribute criteria: minimum number of total attributes changed at *j*th stage and *i*th path versus number of examples. Random selection.

learning process and can be used to monitor this process. All specific criteria can be divided into two groups: total and single-attribute criteria.

Total specific criteria can be used to monitor changes occurring within the entire body of attributes. These criteria apply to individual characteristic paths, including maximum, average and minimum paths, as defined in Section 3.4. Two different changes are considered for a given *i*th path and the *j*th stage of the learning process. The first monitored change represents the number of attributes added or deleted, and the second one is the number of attributes which change their values. The entire system of all proposed specific control criteria is shown in Fig. 3.12. Figures 3.13 and 3.14 show examples of the relationships of these total specific criteria versus the number of examples for the maximum and average path in the developed network of decision rules.

In the case of single-attribute criteria, similar changes are considered, but only

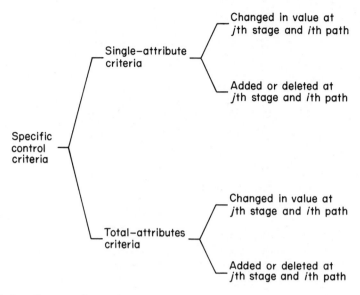

Fig. 3.12. Specific control criteria.

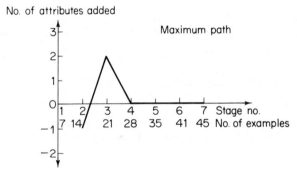

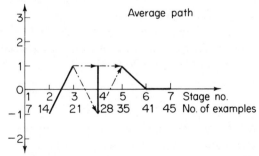

(a)

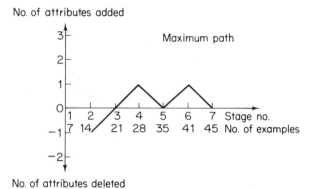

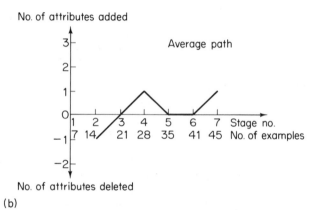

(b)

Fig. 3.13. Specific control criteria: total attributes added or deleted at *j*th stage and *i*th path versus number of examples. (a) Coincidental selection; (b) random selection.

for individual types of paths and attributes. There are three distinguished types of paths, two monitored changes, and *n* attributes. Therefore for a given learning process $3*2*n$ single-attribute criteria can be used. Several relationships of these attributes (for a specific rule) versus number of examples are shown in Figs 3.15 and 3.16. As before, in the case of LCAC, we observe that when a coincidental selection of examples is used changes in attribute values occur in earlier stages of the process than for random selection.

3.7   CONCLUSIONS

Computer learning from examples is becoming an area of interest not only to computer scientists, but also to researchers and practitioners in different areas of engineering. From the engineering point of view the crucial question is how to use individual inductive tools in the most effective way to extract decision rules from a given body of examples. The research the results of which are presented here was intended to address this question, and to develop the methodology of inductive learning. This methodology is defined as a subarea of inductive learning, dealing with the process of generating decision rules from examples, and methods of control and optimization of this process in order to minimize the time required to extract an equivalent set of decision rules from a given body of examples.

Our research has an experimental character and the results obtained are initial. However, even these limited results confirm our hypothesis that an inductive learning process can be identified as a new engineering process. Its improved understanding from the user's point of view is important, considering all expected engineering applications of inductive systems.

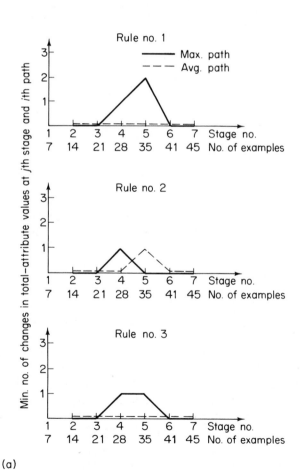

(a)

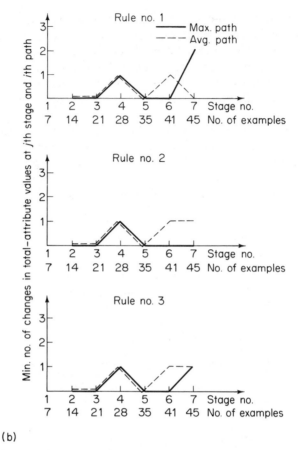

(b)

Fig. 3.14. Specific control criteria: minimum number of total attributes changed values at *j*th stage and *i*th path versus number of examples. (a) Coincidental selection; (b) random selection.

The proposed models of the learning process can be used for practical purposes, and our results indicate that multi-stage models should be particularly useful, and sometimes even feasible, when using a personal computer. Multi-stage models also enable the conducting of a monitored learning process whose by-product is an improved understanding of the problem being analysed.

Our research revealed that the selection of examples for individual stages of learning process is very important and that much better results are usually obtained using a coincidental selection rather than random selection of examples.

The developed system of control criteria has been verified in a number of tests, and these criteria were found sufficient for engineering purposes.

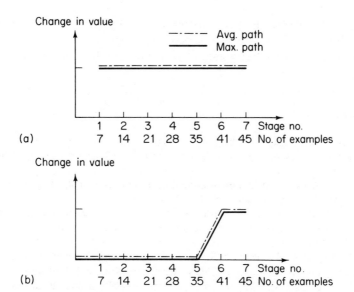

Fig. 3.15. Specific control criteria: single-attribute criteria added or deleted at *j*th stage and *i*th path versus number of examples. (a) Coincidental selection; (b) random selection.

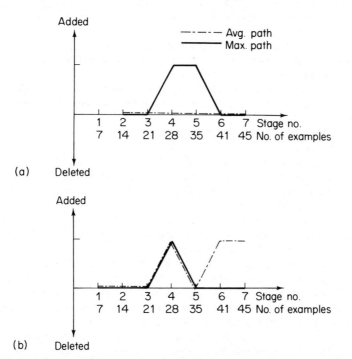

Fig. 3.16. Specific control criteria: single-attribute criteria, changing at *j*th stage and *i*th path versus number of examples. (a) Coincidental selection; (b) random selection.

The research described in this chapter is a first step in the process of developing inductive learning from the user's point of view; work is still in progress. Therefore, any comments, suggestions or advice would be most appreciated.

3.8 REFERENCES

Adeli, H. (1987) Knowledge acquisition in expert systems for structural design. *Proc. of the International Symposium on Fuzzy Systems and Knowledge Engineering,* Guangzhou, China, July.

Arciszewski, T. (1987) Mathematical modeling of morphological analysis. *International Journal of Mathematical Modeling,* **8** (1), 52–6.

Arciszewski, T., Mustafa, M. and Ziarko, W. (1987) Methodology of design knowledge acquisition for use in learning expert systems. *International Journal of Man–Machine Studies,* **27**, 23–32.

Arciszewski, T. and Ziarko, W. (1988) Adaptive expert system for preliminary design of wind bracings in *Second Century of Skyscrapers,* Van Nostrand Publishing Company.

Arciszewski, T. and Ziarko, W. (to appear) Verification of morphological table based on probabilistic rough sets approach. *International Journal of Particulate Science and Technology.*

Asgari, D. and Modesitt, K. L. (1986) SSME test analysis. A case study for inductive knowledge-based systems involving large data bases. *Proc. of the IEEE Computer Society COMPSAC '86,* Chicago, Illinois, October.

Daumann, A. and Modesitt, K. (1985) Space shuttle main engine performance analysis using knowledge-based systems. *Proc. of the ASME International Conference on Computers in Mechanical Engineering,* Boston, Mass., August.

Dietterich, T. G. and Michalski, R. S. (1981) Inductive learning of structural descriptions: evaluation criteria and comparative review of selected methods. *Artificial Intelligence,* **16**, 257–94.

Forsyth, R. S. (1981) Beagle: a Darwinian approach to pattern recognition. *Kybernetes,* Vol. 10, pp. 159–66.

Forsyth, R. S. (1987) Seminar Materials, Machine Learning Seminar, Learned Information Ltd, Oxford, and Machine Learning Research Ltd, Nottingham, London.

Forsyth, R. S. and Rada, R. (1986) *Machine Learning Applications in Expert Systems and Information Retrieval,* Ellis Horwood, Chichester.

Hajdo, P., Arciszewski, T., Ziarko, W. and Aktan, H. (1988) Inductive shallow approach for generation of engineering models. *Proc. of the Ninth Europe Meeting on Cybernetics and Systems Research,* Vienna, Austria, April, pp. 933–40.

Michalski, R. S., Carbonell, J. G. and Mitchell, T. (1983) *Machine Learning: An Artificial Intelligence Approach,* Morgan Kaufmann, Los Altos, Calif.

Michalski, R. S. and Larson, J. B. (1978) *Selection of Most Representative Training Examples and Incremental Generation of VL1 Hypotheses: The Underlying Methodology and Description of Programs ESEL and AQ11,* Report 867, University of Illinois.

Michie, D. (1984) *EX-TRAN7 User Manual,* Intelligent Terminals Ltd, Oxford.

Modesitt, K. L. (1987) Space shuttle main engine anomaly data and inductive knowledge-based systems: automated corporate expertise. *Proc. of the Conference on Artificial Intelligence for Space Applications,* Huntsville, Alabama, November, pp. 1–8.

Pawlak, Z. (1982) Rough sets. *International Journal of Information and Computer Sciences*, **11** (5), 145–72.

Quinlan, J. R. (1983) Learning efficient classification procedures and their application to chess end games in *Machine Learning: The Artificial Intelligence Approach* (eds R. S. Michalski, J. G. Carbonell and T. Mitchell), Tioga Press, Palo Alto, pp. 463–82.

Shannon, C. E. (1948) A mathematical theory of communication. *Bell System Technical Journal*, **4** (2), 379–423.

Sillen, R. V. (1987) *Building PC-hosted Expert Systems Using Induction Methods*, Research Report, Novacast Expert Systems AB, Sweden.

Software Review (1985) EXpert-ease makes its own rules. *PC Magazine*, **16** (April), pp. 119–24.

Spiehler, E. J. (1987) Application of machine learning to classification of glass fragment evidence in forensic science. Seminar Materials, Machine Learning Seminar, Learned Information Ltd, Oxford, and Machine Learning Research Ltd, Nottingham, London.

Turing, A. (1950) Computing machinery and intelligence. *Mind*, (59).

Wong, S. K. M. and Ziarko, W. (1986) INFER – an adaptive decision support system. *Proc. of the Sixth International Workshop on Expert Systems and their Applications*, Avignon, France, pp. 713–26.

Ziarko, W. (1987) On reduction of knowledge representation. *Proc. of the Second International Symposium on Methodologies for Intelligent Systems* (Colloquia Program), Charlotte, NC.

Part two

Biologically inspired systems

4

The evolution of intelligence

RICHARD FORSYTH

> It is highly unlikely that any system we can build will
> be able to undergo the kind of evolutionary change (or
> learning) that would enable it to come close to the
> intelligence of even a small worm, much less that of a
> person.
>
> Winograd and Flores (1986)

Artificial intelligence (AI) scientists, as part of their training, are taught to love
precision, logic and elegance. They see intelligence as the ability to find short cuts
and to avoid obvious, brute-force solutions. Thus they are predisposed against
any method that relies on random trial and error. This is one of the reasons why
the Darwinian approach to learning has had to struggle to make any headway as
an AI technique.

Yet, as we shall see, the characterization of learning methods based on
evolutionary principles as blind trial-and-error search is a misconception. In fact
evolutionary learning often offers an effective alternative to more traditional
induction methods, and deserves to be better known within the AI community,
and outside it.

4.1 THE EVOLUTION OF IDEAS

All evolutionary learning systems are based on the premiss that it is a good idea in
this age of high technology to look back about 4 billion years into the past and
consider the process that gave rise to the blob of grey meat with which you are
now interpreting these words – the process of evolution. As a natural model for
computer-based optimization, it has a number of advantages. It is robust,
relatively well understood (at least in broad outline) and it has been very
extensively field-tested. But AI scientists have tended to overlook it, believing that
it does not work, or rather that it could not form the basis of a workable computer
algorithm.

They have based their pessimism largely on a book by Fogel *et al.* (1966) which reported a series of attempts to design learning programs on an evolutionary model. The trouble with the Fogel *et al.* experiments was that they used mutation as their primary genetic operator. Thus they restricted themselves, in simple terms, to asexual reproduction. As we shall see, mutation is not the primary genetic operator in abstract genetic algorithms, nor in the living world for the vast majority of species which indulge in sexual reproduction.

While the AI community, with few exceptions, dismissed the whole concept of evolutionary systems, workers in other domains got on with the job of building self-improving computer systems based on a Darwinian approach. As early as 1964 (before the supposedly definitive study by Fogel *et al.*) Ingo Rechenberg had employed an evolutionary algorithm in an engineering context. He used it as a way of finding shapes that minimized drag in a fluid flow (Rechenberg, 1965). Since then his methods have evolved (to coin a phrase) and been used successfully in aircraft design and structural engineering. They have also been successfully adopted by the West German automotive industry as a practical, money-saving design technique (see Rechenberg, 1985; see also Chapter 5).

More recently, Rechenberg's ideas have had a spin-off in an entirely different application – computer art. Richard Dawkins (1986) has created the 'Biomorph' system which follows a quasi-evolutionary approach and creates pleasing shapes on a graphical display screen. The Biomorph program is also used as a teaching aid in biology.

But Rechenberg is an engineer and Dawkins a zoologist. Moreover they are Europeans. So, since AI looks largely to the USA (and mainly to the West Coast at that), most AI researchers are unaware of their work. It was not until the mid-1970s, with the publication of *Adaptation in Natural and Artificial Systems* by John Holland (1975) at Michigan University that a reappraisal of the promise of an evolutionary approach to learning began in the AI community; and even Holland's work took about a decade to gain acceptance. Only recently has the subject become respectable again. Holland's theoretical treatment has in recent years led to the development of practical evolutionary learning algorithms (e.g. Smith, 1980; Goldberg, 1983).

In any evolutionary learning scheme there is a population of structures which are treated like simulated living organisms. Each of these structures defines a potential (or partial) solution to the problem under consideration. They are also used to generate new structures in ways that are explicitly designed to simulate the main attributes of biological reproduction. If the structures are rules, which is the normal case, then we have an evolutionary rule-induction system.

Selection of which rules survive longest and have greatest likelihood of 'breeding' is governed by their performance on the task. This has been called **naturalistic selection** (Forsyth, 1981). It corresponds to the popular phrase (due to Herbert Spencer, not Darwin) 'survival of the fittest'.

A groundplan for a genetic/evolutionary algorithm can be outlined as follows:

1. Create an initial population of rules at random;

2. Evaluate the rules and if the overall performance level is good enough halt and display the best of them;
3. Compute the selection probability of each rule as $p = e/E$ where e is its score and E the sum total of all rule scores;
4. Generate the next population by selecting according to the selection probabilities and applying certain genetic operators; then loop back to step (2).

Each pass round this loop corresponds to a single generation in a population of living creatures. Clearly generations are not so well synchronized in the animal kingdom; but despite its many simplifications, the basic genetic algorithm is a robust, general-purpose optimization procedure, applicable to a wide variety of problem domains.

Most people think they understand biological evolution very well, even when they do not, and on that basis regard the genetic algorithm as a crude, brute-force approach to learning. It is of course a highly simplified version of what goes on in nature; but it is by no means synonymous with brute-force trial and error. The reason people underestimate its subtlety is that they think only of mutation; but the key genetic operator is cross-over, not mutation (which is a 'background operator' serving only to prevent the system sticking on a local optimum).

Mutation involves making a few haphazard alterations in the genetic information, and is usually (though not always) detrimental. Evolution, in nature and in the computer, is greatly speeded up by sex, because sexual crossing produces variety without mutation: genetic information is chopped up and respliced. As Holland has proved in the abstract, and as the huge energy expenditure of animals and plants on sex should lead us to expect, the hybridization resulting from applying the cross-over operator is a fundamentally more efficient way of searching the space of possible structures than random mutation. Its power lies in the implicit parallelism of the process (coupled with explicit parallelism in the real world). (See Holland, 1986.)

The inherent parallelism of the evolutionary process should alert us to another important property of genetic algorithms: they are tailor-made for the new generation of highly parallel computer architectures which almost everyone in the industry is expecting to revolutionize computing by the turn of the century. To put it simply: genetic algorithms are ready for the future. While a number of well-established computing techniques (such as Quicksort and the A* search algorithm, to name only two) will cease to look clever once processors are two-a-penny, genetic algorithms will come into their own.

Genetic algorithms did not appear from nowhere: in fact they are a special class of the 'Monte Carlo' methods employed by statisticians and operational researchers on problems which defy analytical solution. Monte Carlo methods employ controlled randomness to achieve optimal or near-optimal solutions to difficult problems. But, as mentioned earlier, AI workers have traditionally frowned upon randomness: somehow it does not fit with the profoundly rationalist world-view in which AI has grown up – although it was a prominent theme in the early cybernetic days of machine intelligence.

In a pure Monte Carlo method, solutions are generated at random for as long as there is time and the best solution found is kept. Each trial generates a completely fresh potential solution with no reference to what has gone before. If the problem under attack, for example, is the travelling salesman problem (TSP), then each trial will create an entirely new route for the salesman, measure it, and – if it is the shortest so far – retain it.

This is indeed a blind search procedure, and does justify the description brute-force trial and error. A genetic algorithm, however, modifies this basic procedure to make use of information about the distribution of values in the solution space. Instead of throwing away the structures generated on each trial, it maintains a population of candidate solutions. Sub-patterns that have been found useful are recombined in various ways. Thus the search is guided through the enormous multidimensional space of possible solutions towards regions where good results have been found on previous trials. In the example of the TSP, new routes would be generated by small modifications of existing, shorter-than-average routes (see also Greffenstette *et al.*, 1985; Oliver *et al.*, 1987).

Looking at evolutionary algorithms as Monte Carlo procedures, we can usefully distinguish four levels of complexity:

0. simple Monte Carlo methods
1. mutation-only methods
2. the basic genetic algorithm
3. the 'élitist strategy'

Each level is characterized by a different answer to the question:

How is the next candidate solution to be chosen?

Method (0) simply hops from one random point in the search space to another. This is the basic Monte Carlo technique. It takes no account of any regularity which that search space almost certainly possesses. Method (1) modifies existing structures to produce new ones for testing. It will do better than Method (0) provided that the value of potential solutions varies smoothly with their location in the search space, as is often the case. Method (2) generates new structures by recombining portions from old ones that have proved valuable. It can be shown to be more efficient that Method (1) by virtue of exploiting implicit parallelism. Method (3), the élitist strategy, differs from biological evolution in preserving the best-ever structure until it is displaced by a better one in the breeding population. It confers effective immortality on the best structure so far. Thus it approximates more closely to the brave new world of artificial genetic engineering than the classical Darwinian scheme of nature.

We have been applying the élitist strategy to our livestock and crops for a long time. In the near future we may apply it to human beings as well. The ethics of doing so are questionable, but we need have no ethical qualms about cutting up rule structures in a computer's memory.

4.2 WORKING EXAMPLES

The acid test of any computing method is whether it works in practice. We present here two example applications in two different domains using two different variants of the basic algorithm to give a flavour of the evolutionary strategy in action.

4.2.1 Gas flow

Goldberg (1983, 1985) reports the application of a genetic algorithm to two engineering problems, both connected with flow optimization in natural gas pipelines.

His first test was to apply the genetic algorithm to a steady-state natural gas pipeline problem. This was a model of a system with an alternating sequence of ten compressors and ten stretches of pipeline. The inlet was a fixed pressure source; gas was delivered at the outlet at line pressure. The objective was to minimize the summed horsepower of the ten compressor stations, subject to minimum and maximum pressure constraints.

A coding scheme was required to represent the state of the system in a form suited to the genetic algorithm, i.e. as fixed-length bit strings (Goldberg, 1985):

> In this study, the full string is formed from the concatenation of ten, four-bit substrings where each substring is a mapped fixed-point binary integer (precision $=1$ part in 16) representing the difference in pressure across each of the ten compressor stations. This rather crude discretization gives an average precision in pressure of 34 psi over the operating range 500–1000 psia.

Three separate trials were initiated with a population of fifty random strings, running the genetic algorithm for sixty generations. In each of the three experiments near-optimal performance was achieved after twenty generations. There was little further improvement between twenty and sixty generations. Thus the genetic algorithm reached a near-optimal solution with only 1050 function evaluations. This compares very favourably with more conventional function-optimization procedures (Goldberg, 1985):

> To put this in perspective, with a string of length 40, there are 2^{40} different possible solutions in the search space ($=1.1 \times 10^{12}$). Therefore, we obtain near-optimal results after searching only 0.0000001% of the possible alternatives. If we were, for example, to search for the best person among the world's 4.5 billion people as rapidly as the genetic algorithm we would only need to talk to four or five people before making a near-optimal selection.

The optimal solution, for comparison purposes, was known from a dynamic programming study on the same test case (Wong and Larson, 1968).

Goldberg's second experiment was more ambitious. He devised a Learning Classifier System (LCS), consisting of three components:

1. A message-passing production-rule interpreter;
2. An apportionment of credit system;
3. A genetic algorithm.

This three-part architecture follows Holland's treatment (see Holland, 1986). The LCS receives environmental information through detectors which pass it on in a standard message format. This input data (as well as internally generated information) is placed on a message list, which is the system's working memory. On each action cycle, messages in this list are scanned and may activate classifier rules in a rule store. An activated classifier puts new messages on the list. Some of these messages may cause external actions via the LCS's effectors.

For the gas-flow study, the input messages were fourteen-bit strings, and the classifier rules were fixed-length strings using the alphabet $\{0, 1, \pounds\}$ where £ is the wild card, matching either a 0 or a 1. Input messages gave information about inlet pressure, outlet flow, time of day, time of year, and so on in a detailed simulation of the pipeline's behaviour.

The apportionment of credit module was based on Holland's 'Bucket Brigade Algorithm' (BBA), which is modelled after a competitive service economy. The essential idea behind the BBA is that each classifier rule must (in a sense) pay to fire. Rules that lead to successful effector actions receive a reward, a fraction of which is passed back to the rule that posted the message enabling the rewarded rule to fire. Thus reward can propagate backwards along a chain of co-operating classifier rules, as in a simplified cash economy.

Rules that grow rich can afford to bid more, and will fire more often; rules that grow poor have very few chances of firing. This is the first level of adaptation (tuning by a strength parameter). The second level of adaptation is more important, and is provided by the third component of the LCS, the genetic algorithm. Rules that lose almost all of their 'cash' in this pseudo-economic model are deleted periodically and replaced by using the genetic algorithm to recombine elements from fitter rules. It is capitalism in its purest form: survival of the richest!

The pipeline simulation was run with and without occasional leaks (inserted at random) (Goldberg, 1985):

> The LCS, consisting of a syntactically simple rule and message system, an apportionment of credit mechanism based on a competitive service economy, and a genetic algorithm, was taught to operate a gas pipeline under winter and summer conditions. It also was trained to alarm correctly for leaks while minimizing the number of false alarms.

Thus the LCS as a whole proved itself a competent control system on an economically important task. According to Goldberg, the pipeline simulation was detailed and realistic enough (making allowance for turbulent flow, peaks and troughs in demand, and so on) to indicate that a controller based on the LCS could operate successfully under field conditions.

It should be noted that only one component of this tripartite LCS, the new-rule generator, employed an evolutionary algorithm. The message-passing architecture and the BBA are conceptually separate. Indeed, Goldberg was able to turn off the rule-modifying component and run the system without introducing new rules, to demonstrate the effectiveness of the genetic algorithm.

Because of Holland's influence, especially in the USA, it is sometimes thought that all genetic algorithms have to be embedded within a system employing classifier rules and a message-passing control cycle, together with a credit-assignment strategy based on the BBA. But this is emphatically not the case, as our next example clearly shows.

4.2.2 BEAGLE

The BEAGLE system (Biologic Evolutionary Algorithm Generating Logical Expressions) displays the essential ideas of the genetic algorithm in an entirely different context. It is one of the few commercially available software packages employing evolutionary rule induction (Forsyth, 1987). It consists of six main modules:

SEED	Selectively Extracts Example Data
ROOT	Rule-Oriented Optimization Tester
HERB	Heuristic Evolutionary Rule Breeder
STEM	Signature Table Evaluation Module
LEAF	Logical Evaluator And Forecaster
PLUM	Procedural Language Utility Maker

A diagram of how they link together is shown as Fig. 4.1.

We shall concentrate on HERB, which is the heart of the system – the program that actually performs the evolutionary induction process. It works by running through the following procedure, expressed below in 'Pidgin Pascal':

```
REPEAT
  mainloop: = mainloop + 1;
  runs: = 0;
  REPEAT
    runs: = runs + 1;
    reset(datafile); {start at beginning of training data}
    FOR nx: = 1 to samples do begin
      {for every training instance}
      {get the next sample case}
      {try all rules on it}
      end;
    scoring; {apply the Critic}
    culling; {get rid of sub-standard rules}
```

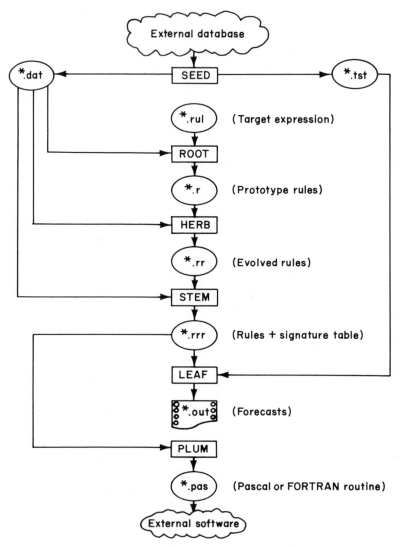

Fig. 4.1. The BEAGLE software modules.

BEAGLE contains six main components which are generally run in sequence. SEED (Selectively Extracts Example Data) puts external data into a suitable format, and may append leading or lagging data-fields also. ROOT (Rule Oriented Optimization Tester) tests an initial batch of user-suggested rules. HERB (Heuristic Evolutionary Rule Breeder) generates decision rules by naturalistic selection. STEM (Signature Table Evaluation Module) makes a signature table from the rules produced by HERB. LEAF (Logical Evaluator And Forecaster) uses STEM's output to do forecasting or classification.

Finally PLUM (Procedural Language Utility Maker) can be used to convert a BEAGLE rule file into a language such as Pascal or FORTRAN. In this form the knowledge gained may be use in other software.

eugenics; {mate the survivors}
mutation; {clobber a few rules at random}
tidying; {clean up the mess}
UNTIL (runs ⩾ gens); {enough done}
savebest; {keep the top-scoring rule}
wipeout; {eliminate the variables it used from further use}
UNTIL (mainloop ⩾ maxloops) OR (varsleft < 2);
{dump saved rules on to a file}

This is in fact an outline of the HERB main program, with comments to explain what is going on. It is also the basis for Fig. 4.2.

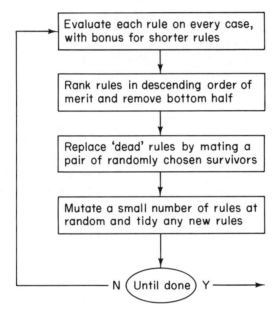

Fig. 4.2. HERB main program flowchart. Differences from real genetics: genotype = phenotype; male = female; no recessives; no chromosomes.

The mating procedure picks out random sub-trees (sub-expressions) from the two 'parents' and simply glues them together with a random connective. Thus if the parents were the two rules

((GREEN − ORANGE) > 0.33456)

and

((LANDMASS > 4) & (AREA < 600.00))

a possible descendant could be

(LANDMASS > 0.33456)

or

$$((GREEN - ORANGE) \geqslant (AREA < 600.00))$$

where the latter involves a comparison between a numeric value and a logical value. This is resolved in BEAGLE's rule language by treating TRUE as 1.0 and FALSE as 0.0 where context demands.

BEAGLE can be said to use a non-parametric version of the genetic algorithm: the survival of rules is determined by their rank order of merit. Its original contribution lies in resolving the apparent contradiction between a flexible rule language modelled on that found in procedural programming languages such as C and Pascal, and the demands of the genetic algorithm for fixed-length strings. BEAGLE does occasionally come up with rules that are very hard to interpret (some might say that is part of its charm), but compared to a stretch of DNA they are as clear as crystal. Prior to BEAGLE, most computer scientists had presumed that genetic algorithms could only work with fixed-length, position-independent rule strings, i.e. with a write-only description language. BEAGLE shows that a hierarchically structured rule language can also be subjected to quasi-genetic recombinations.

To give an idea of how the system works, we will briefly run through an example where it learns discrimination rules on a training set describing nations and their flags. The objective given to the system in this case was to discriminate between Spanish-speaking and non-Spanish-speaking countries on the basis of information about colours and designs in their flags, geographic location, population, area and so forth. It is a contrived example, for tutorial purposes; but it has the merit of being real, not made-up, data. Also it fits squarely within the concept-attainment framework (Quinlan, 1985) in which the majority of rule-learning systems work:

Given: a collection of objects or events (countries in this case), and their
        descriptions, whose class membership is known;
Find: a classification rule, expressed in terms of the attributes used in the
        descriptions, that will assign objects to their class.

Each country was described in terms of thirty attributes. To save space, only those eventually used in the BEAGLE rules are explained below.

LANDMASS	1 = N. America, 2 = S. America, 3 = Europe, 4 = Africa, 5 = Asia, 6 = Oceania
ZONE	Geographic quadrant, based on the Greenwich meridian (E/W) and the Equator (N/S): 1 = NE, 2 = SE, 3 = SW, 4 = NW
AREA	Area in thousands of square km
POPULATION	In rounded millions
LANGUAGE	Coded as: 1 = English, 2 = Spanish, 3 = French, 4 = German, 5 = Slavic, 6 = Indo-European, 7 = Chinese, 8 = Arabic, 9 = Japanese/Finnish/Magyar/Turkish, 10 = others

RELIGION	Coded as: **0** = Catholic, **1** = other Christian, **2** = Muslim, **3** = Buddhist, **4** = Hindu, **5** = ethnic, **6** = Marxist, **7** = others
GOLD	1 if gold/yellow in the flag, else 0
WHITE	1 if white in the flag, 0 otherwise
QUARTERS	no. of quartered sections in the flag
STRIPES	no. of horizontal stripes in the flag

It will be seen that numeric coding has been used for all these variables. In practice, the success of BEAGLE, like other induction programs, can often depend critically on exploiting happy coincidences in the data-encoding scheme. So it is wise in tasks such as this to spend a good deal of time on decisions about data encoding (see also Chapter 3).

The first step in running BEAGLE is normally to split the main database, using SEED, into a training and a test set; but in this case all the 194 countries (from Moore and Ross, 1986) were used to form the rule. The next step is to run ROOT and create an initial population of random rules for the breeding process. Having done that, the main evolutionary learning module, HERB, was run for thirty-five generations, to produce the rule file listed below.

(LANGUAGE = 2.0000)
$

((WHITE ⩽ POPULATION) − RELIGION)
$ 71.29   20   13   1   160
(LANDMASS ⩽ 2.5000)
$ 56.17   20   28   1   145
((ZONE ⩽ 2.6000) < (((ZONE ⩾ 2.0000) ⩾ GOLD) < AREA))
$ 54.08   21   32   0   141
((QUARTERS + STRIPES) > 2.0000)
$ 33.26   17   49   4   124

This file starts with the 'target expression' (LANGUAGE = 2) which is the definition of the concept that the user wants the system to acquire. (The coding scheme adopted, see above, assigns no. 2 to those countries where Spanish is the official language – about 11% of the total training set.) After the target expression come four different rules for distinguishing Spanish from non-Spanish countries. Let us take the simplest, to explain the format:

(LANDMASS ⩽ 2.5)
$ 56.17   20   28   1   145

This says that countries in North and South America are more likely to speak Spanish. (1 and 2 are the LANDMASS codes for the Americas; 3 to 6 are the other continents; hence LANDMASS ⩽ 2.5 is true for North and South America, and false elsewhere.) The dollar sign $ is merely a rule terminator. The number **56.17** is the score that this rule obtained as a discriminator in its own right, based on a statistical measure of association known as the phi coefficient. The other numbers are:

20	True positives
28	False positives
1	False negatives
145	True negatives

In other words: 20 countries within the Americas (LANDMASS ⩽ 2.5) speak Spanish and 28 do not; 1 country outside the Americas speaks Spanish (Yes, it's Spain) and 145 do not.

Four separate rules have been generated, on the assumption that one single rule is unlikely to give perfect results. After saving the first rule, involving variables **WHITE, POPULATION** and **RELIGION**, HERB repeats the same process, but does not allow itself to use the attributes in previously saved rules.

Interpreting rule number 3

$$((\text{ZONE} \leqslant 2.6000) < (((\text{ZONE} \geqslant 2.0000) \geqslant \text{GOLD}) < \text{AREA}))$$

is left as an 'exercise for the reader'. It shows that BEAGLE does not always produce perspicuous rules. (If you attempt this exercise, you will need to know that logical expressions, such as (ZONE ⩾ 2) yield a value of 1.0 when true and 0.0 when false, and that this numeric truth value can be compared with other numeric values, such as **AREA**.)

The final step in the rule-generation process was to run STEM in order to tie the independent rules together into a rule set. Additionally, STEM suggests discarding the one rule which gives least additional predictive power in the context of the other rules. In this case the last rule was dropped, leaving the following rule set:

(LANGUAGE = 2.0000)
$

((WHITE ⩽ POPULATION) – RELIGION)

$	20	13	1	160

(LANDMASS ⩽ 2.5000)

$	20	28	1	145

((ZONE ⩽ 2.6000) < (((ZONE ⩾ 2.0000) ⩾ GOLD) < AREA))

$	21	32	0	141

() $ — from flag.dat on 25/11/1987 at 20:29:08

	0.1082	194		
000	0.0000	118	0.0009	0.0000
001	0.0000	16	0.0064	0.0000
010	0.0000	15	0.0068	0.0000
011	1.0000	12	0.0852	8.3333
100	0.0000	8	0.0120	0.0000
101	1.0000	4	0.2216	25.0000
110	0.0000	0	0.1082	
111	19.0000	21	0.8686	90.4762

After the rules themselves comes something called a **signature table** (Forsyth and Rada, 1986). This is BEAGLE's way of combining rules into a forecasting or classification procedure. Each of the three rules can be true or false, giving eight possible rule status combinations. The signature table simply tallies the frequencies of positive examples to total cases for each combination. Thus the 001 line records the frequency of Spanish countries (0/16) when the first two rules were false and the third one was true.

The two most interesting 'signatures' are 000 (all false) and 111 (all rules true). The relevant lines of the table are repeated below:

000	0.0000	118	0.0009	0.0000
111	19.0000	21	0.8686	90.4762

The order of items is: signature code, no. of positive examples, total no. of examples, probability estimate, actual percentage frequency. Thus, there were 118 cases (out of 194 training examples) when all rules were false, of which none at all were Spanish-speaking. This gives a 0% frequency, but on future occasions, when BEAGLE encounters a new unseen case, it would estimate the probability of a country that fails all three tests being Spanish-speaking as 0.0009 (i.e. slightly more than zero). This small bias towards conservatism is obtained by adding the average frequency (0.1082) to the positive cases and 1 to the total number of cases; thus $0.1082/119 = 0.0009$. (With a large sample, it makes very little difference, with smaller samples the effect of the bias is more marked.)

When all three rules were true, on the other hand, there were 19 out of 21 Spanish-speaking countries. (The two errors in this group were Brazil and Haiti.) This is a rate of 90.4762%, giving a probability estimate of 0.8686. Thus BEAGLE considers that a country that passes all three tests has a 0.8686 probability of speaking Spanish. We cannot put this rule set to the test on another planet in a parallel universe, so the exercise must terminate there.

However, it would be a mistake to think that BEAGLE can only be used for unrealistic exercises. It has already been applied to tasks as diverse as estimating the profitability of different types of property investment and forecasting the winners of horse-races. One of its more successful applications was in forensic science (Evett and Spiehler, 1987), where a rule set developed with the aid of PC/BEAGLE was found to discriminate among glass fragments better than standard statistical procedures. The problem was to distinguish different types of glass fragments on the basis of laboratory tests, including an elemental analysis derived from an X-ray fluoroscope. The determination of glass type (e.g. after a break-in or an automobile accident) often plays a crucial part in the assessment of evidence in court. The results are given in Table 4.1.

It is gratifying to note that in every case the evolutionary method outperformed a commonly used statistical technique. Moreover, the BEAGLE rules were comprehensible, and were later incorporated into an expert system for glass identification – not something that would be possible with the NNC or other common statistical methods.

The figures in Table 4.1 were obtained by retesting the rule(s) on the training data, which, as we have seen, tends to underestimate the true error rate. Because

Table 4.1 Discrimination of glass fragments. PC/BEAGLE versus nearest neighbour classification (NNC) of microscopic glass fragments based on element composition and refractive index

		% Correct	
Source	*Samples*	*NNC*	*BEAGLE*
Building window (float)*	70	85	87
Building window (non-float)*	76	69	74
Vehicle window	17	73	94
Container glass	13	56	77
Tableware	9	67	78
Headlamps	29	83	86

*'Float' and 'non-float' refer to two different glass-making processes.

glass analyses are not cheap, the number of example cases available to the authors was small; so they were all used in the rule-generation process. However, they later arranged a blind trial on ten fresh samples of several glass types, using BEAGLE-derived rules, the NNC method and a linear discriminant function. The BEAGLE rules made one mistake, the NNC algorithm made two mistakes, and the linear discriminant function made three mistakes. (One sample was misclassified by all three methods as window glass when it was from container glass: the authors surmise that it was actually made from recycled window glass.)

> Overall these results are interesting because they show that BEAGLE performs as well as, if not better than, conventional statistical methods at the chosen tasks. In addition, the fact that BEAGLE rules tend to misclassify different samples confirms that it can provide a fresh insight of existing problem areas. (Evett and Spiehler, 1987)

The NNC method is not the last word in statistical discriminant analysis; but it does provide a reasonable bench-mark. Bench-marking inductive systems is, in fact, a vexed question. A start has been made by Clark and Niblett (1987), who were aided in their comparative study by the fact that all the systems they tested came from two different families (AQ11-based or ID3-based).

In general, with the variety of induction methods (including possibly some statistical methods, as above), the variety of rule formats, and the variety of acceptable input data, the whole issue of meaningful comparison is problematical. So I would not wish to claim – especially as I have a commercial interest in it – that the results given show that using BEAGLE is better than doing a statistical data analysis or than using an alternative induction system. They do show, however, that the evolutionary strategy is a viable method for a wide range of concept learning tasks.

4.3   CONCLUSIONS

We have considered just two programs exemplifying an evolutionary approach to learning. This does not show the breadth of the field. (But see also Chapter 5.)

To convey the range of applicability of evolutionary/genetic algorithms, a sample of applications known to the present author is listed in Table 4.2. They encompass several different programs, implemented by different people, for different tasks in different countries.

The list in Table 4.2 is not by any means exhaustive. It is presented only to show that genetic algorithms have many applications – not all of them within the pattern-recognition paradigm.

Genetic algorithms do have commercial pay-offs: so much for the good news. But they have drawbacks as well. There are two areas in particular where problems can easily arise:

1. The fitness or quality function;
2. Representation issues.

Table 4.2   Applications of genetic algorithms

Task	Organization involved
Engineering and manufacturing	
Propellor blade design	Technical University Berlin, W. Germany
Vehicle shape optimization	Volkswagen, W. Germany
Gas-flow control	University of Alabama, USA
Job shop scheduling	Bolt, Beranek and Newman, USA
Electronics	
Layout of LSI chips	Texas Instruments, UK
Electronic circuit design	Brunel University, UK
Pattern recognition	
Identifying glass fragments	Home Office, UK
Sonar signal interpretation	Admiralty Research Stn, UK
Visual recognition	Rowland Institute, USA
Visual recognition	Itran Corp., USA
Games and puzzles	
Draw poker bidding	University of Pittsburgh, USA
Travelling salesman problem	Vanderbilt University, USA (and many other sites)
The bin-packing problem	Texas Instruments, USA
Finance	
Trading-rule generation	Inforem, UK
Horse-race forecasting	Warm Boot, UK

The quality function is the way the system evaluates rules. It is used to decide which rules will 'die' and which will remain 'alive' to contribute to the next generation. In many real-life tasks, this is inevitably a multidimensional measure, combining various features of the rule into an overall score. To give a simple example, BEAGLE modifies the raw success rate of each rule by deducting a penalty which increases with the length of the rule, thus favouring shorter rules. This is its version of Occam's Razor – a preference for simplicity. However, the weighting of success as opposed to brevity is not at all obvious from first principles.

To move on to a more realistic example: in a rule generator for trading on the London currency markets, it might be thought that the objective would be clear-cut, namely to make as much money as possible in a given time. However, one system known to the author which used profit rate as its sole fitness function came up with rules that were dismissed out of hand by the traders who were supposed to use them. Among other faults, the computer-generated rules would have traded too frequently – every few minutes – and thus completely out-stripped the capacity of the back office to cope with the volume of transactions. It required careful tuning of the fitness function before the system developed rules that were both profitable and acceptable to the users of the system. And this lesson is quite general: the ideal quality function for any given application of a genetic algorithm is not likely to be obvious at first, except in toy examples.

The second main deficiency of genetic algorithms is their reliance on an opaque description language, typically a sequence of 0's and 1's such as 101010001000 . . . . It is impossible to devise a lower-level rule language than this! Naturally, rules expressed in such a low-level notation are hard for people to comprehend; and this goes against the whole philosophy of knowledge-based systems.

There are two ways over this obstacle: one is to provide a translation mechanism between the underlying bit-string representation and a more user-oriented format; the other is to modify the basic evolutionary algorithm so that it knows about the structure of the rules, and therefore only breaks them up at points that are valid junctions in the syntax of the rule language. The second approach is that employed in BEAGLE. The first approach is employed by, for example, Smith (1985) who used a genetic algorithm for packing arbitrarily sized rectangular boxes as tightly as possible into an orthogonal bin (known to be a computationally intractable problem). Smith's solution was to represent the bin packing as a list of boxes plus an algorithm for decoding that list into a legal packing. Thus the genetic operators were applied to a string representation which was used to guide the performance of a bin-packing procedure. In effect, the bin-packing procedure was parameterized and the genetic algorithm optimized the parameters. Similar methods are used in applications of the genetic algorithm to very large-scale integration (VLSI) circuit design: the genetic algorithm is applied to a fixed-length string which is used to guide the operation of a layout program.

Both solutions have their drawbacks. Modifying the genetic algorithm to work on a higher-level language means that the cross-over and mutation operators have to be somewhat *ad hoc*, therefore there is no guarantee that the revised algorithm searches the rule space as efficiently as the classic genetic algorithm. Building an interpreter between the bit-string representation and the task it represents still leaves the underlying knowledge representation opaque, and is therefore only suitable when performance is more important than perspicuity.

Having made these cautionary remarks, it should be said that the evolutionary strategy is a robust general-purpose method that is likely to pay dividends where:

1. There is a reasonable quantifiable quality function;
2. There is no analytic solution;
3. The issues of representation can be resolved satisfactorily.

The message of this chapter is that users should start availing themselves of these techniques, and programmers should think about incorporating evolutionary methods into their 'kitbag' of conceptual tools, and in their software.

4.4 REFERENCES

Clark, P. and Niblett, T. (1987) Induction in noisy domains, in *Progress in Machine Learning* (eds I. Bratko and N. Lavrac), Sigma Press, Wilmslow, pp. 11–30.

Dawkins, R. (1986) *The Blind Watchmaker*, Longman, London.

Evett, I. and Spiehler, E. (1987) Rule induction in forensic sciences, in *KBS in Government*, Online Publications, Pinner, UK, pp. 107–18.

Fogel, Owens and Walsh (1966) *Artificial Intelligence through Simulated Evolution*, Wiley, New York.

Forsyth, R. (1981) BEAGLE: a Darwinian approach to pattern recognition. *Kybernetes*, **10**, 159–66.

Forsyth, R. (1987) *PC/BEAGLE User Guide*, Warm Boot Ltd, Nottingham.

Forsyth, R. and Rada, R. (1986) *Machine Learning: Applications in Expert Systems and Information Retrieval*, Ellis Horwood, Chichester.

Goldberg, D. (1983) Computer-aided pipeline optimization using genetic algorithms and rule learning, PhD Dissertation, University of Michigan, Ann Arbor, pp. 8–15.

Goldberg, D. (1985) Genetic algorithms and rule learning in dynamic system control. *Proc. Internat. Conf. on Genetic Algorithms and their Applications*, Carnegie-Mellon University, Pittsburgh.

Grefenstette, J. J., Gopal, R., Rosmaita, B. J. and Van Gucht, D. (1985) Genetic algorithms for the travelling salesman problem. *Proc. Internat. Conf. on Genetic Algorithms and their Applications*, Carnegie-Mellon University, Pittsburgh, pp. 160–8.

Holland, J. (1975) *Adaptation in Natural and Artificial Systems*, University of Michigan Press, Ann Arbor.

Holland, J. (1986) Escaping brittleness: the possibilities of general-purpose learning algorithms applied to parallel rule based systems, in *Machine Learning: An Artificial Intelligence Approach*, Vol. 2 (eds R. Michalski, J. Carbonell and T. Mitchell), Morgan Kaufmann, Los Altos, Calif., pp. 593–624.

Michalski, R. and Chilausky, R. L. (1980) Learning by being told and learning by examples. *J. Policy Analysis and Information Systems*, **4**, 125–61.

Michie, D. and Johnston, R. (1985) *The Creative Computer*, Pelican Books, Harmondsworth.

Moore, E. and Ross, D. (1986) *Collins Gem Guide to Flags*, Wm. Collins and Co., Glasgow.

Oliver, I. M., Smith, D. J. and Holland, J. R. C. (1987) A study of permutation crossover operators in the travelling salesman problem. *Proc. 2nd Internat. Conf. on Genetic Algorithms and their Applications*, Cambridge, Mass, pp. 101–7.

Quinlan, J. R. (1985) *Decision Trees and Multi-Valued Attributes*, New South Wales Inst. of Technology Report 85.4, Sydney.

Rechenberg, I. (1965) *Cybernetic Solution Path of an Experimental Problem*, RAE Farnborough.

Rechenberg, I. (1985) The evolutionary strategy: a mathematical model of Darwinian evolution, Technical University of Berlin Report.

Smith, D. (1985) Bin packing with adaptive search. *Proc. Internat. Conf. on Genetic Algorithms and their Applications*, Carnegie-Mellon University, Pittsburg, pp. 202–6.

Smith, S. (1980) A learning system based on genetic adaptive algorithms, PhD Thesis, Computer Science Dept, University of Pittsburgh, Pa.

Winograd, T. and Flores, F. (1986) *Understanding Computers and Cognition*, Ablex Publishing Corp., Norwood, N.J.

Wong, P. J. and Larson, R. E. (1968) Optimization of natural gas pipeline systems via dynamic programming. *IEEE Trans. Auto. Control AC-13*, **5**, 475–81.

5

Artificial evolution and artificial intelligence

INGO RECHENBERG

5.1 THE EVOLUTION OF EVOLUTION

Living beings are the result of a large-scale experiment on earth, called biological evolution. This started about four thousand million years ago in the primeval ocean in the form of a living mass of slime. From that, fishes have developed. Some time later life crawled on to the land. Next, our ancestors were climbing up the trees. And finally we are looking at ourselves: Man meditating on how the method of evolution works (Fig. 5.1).

It may be worth reflecting on the effectiveness of the biological evolution strategy. Over the past years it has become obvious that the rules of biological evolution are the result of an evolution process themselves. Suppose a population of organisms existed with slightly modified hereditary rules compared with the existing norm. If these modifications help the population to adapt faster to their particular environment, then this population will have a better chance of survival in future than a population with less effective hereditary rules. Therefore it should be assumed that evolution, during its action over more than three thousand million years, gave itself an optimal mode of operation. In the end the evolution strategy in its optimal mode has developed fascinating systems including the

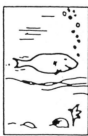

Fig. 5.1. Short version of biological evolution (Cartoonist Prehn, 1977).

human brain. This gives rise to the idea that strategic concepts of biological evolution may also be used with success to create machine intelligence.

5.2   FIRST EXPERIMENTS

It was in 1964 (Rechenberg, 1964), when I started my first experiment to imitate the method of biological evolution in a laboratory of fluid mechanics. An aluminium plate flexible at five positions was mounted in an open wind tunnel (Fig. 5.2). The articulated plate can be altered stepwise. There are 345 025 251 possible forms. The task was to find the shape with minimum drag. We all know that this is the flat plate, directed parallel to the air stream. But suppose we do not know that. Therefore the plate is set into a random starting configuration. To produce the random alternations of the five hinges (the mutations in biology) I used in this first experiment a mechanical apparatus (Fig. 5.3). Five balls, representing the five hinges of the plate, pass the pyramid of pins and land in the ground boxes. The box markings determine the alternations of angle.

The experimental arrangement makes it possible to measure the fitness of the mutated shapes. The technical fitness is the drag of the plate, which has to become a minimum. At the beginning of the wind-tunnel experiment the plate was folded

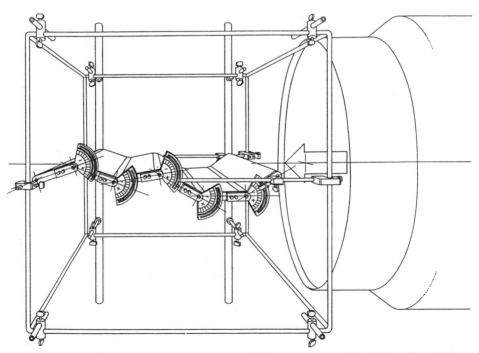

Fig. 5.2. The articulated plate: the experimental device was created to imitate Darwinian evolution in a wind tunnel.

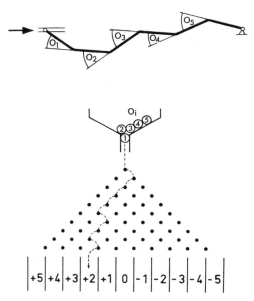

Fig. 5.3. Galton's pin board: this mechanical apparatus generates the random mutations for the evolution experiment in the wind tunnel.

into a zig-zag shape of high drag. The experimental scheme to imitate rules of biological evolution will be discussed later in detail. The basic idea is to reject all mutations with increasing drag (decreasing fitness). But if a randomly generated form has a lower drag, then it becomes the parental shape for the next generation. Figure 5.4 shows the result of my first evolution-like experiment. The drag of the plate is plotted versus the number of generations. Below the diagram the best form of the plate after every 10 generations is shown. We achieve the plain shape after 300 generations.

While the test with the articulated plate is more of academic value, the following three experiments in the field of fluid dynamics are of practical interest (Rechenberg, 1973). The next task was to find the form of a right-angled pipe bend with minimum flow resistance. Figure 5.5 shows the experimental arrangement. Two flexible plastic hoses are held by adjustable bars in the deflection zone. The position of the six bars of each pipe are the optimization variables. At the beginning of the experiment both pipe elbows were adjusted to a quarter of a circle. While one pipe bend was continuously varied according to the algorithm of evolution strategy, the second pipe remained unchanged as a reference system. Figure 5.6 shows the initial form and the optimum form one upon the other. The optimum pipe bend, having 10% less deflection losses, starts with a steadily increasing curvature (similar to Euler's spiral) and ends with a small reverse in curvature.

In another experiment a two-phase supersonic flow nozzle was developed using

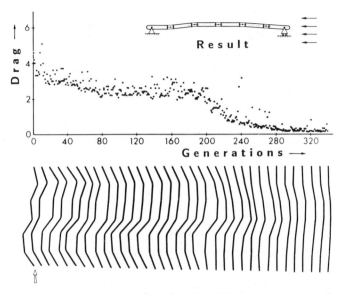

Fig. 5.4. The *experimentum crucis*: applying the rules of biological evolution, the articulated plate develops to the form of minimum drag.

an evolutionary strategy (Schwefel and Klockgether, 1970). Heated water vaporizes partly in the throat of a convergent–divergent nozzle. The expanding vapour forms the propellant for the remaining liquid. It is impossible to calculate the shape of the nozzle for maximum thrust. For experimental optimization the nozzle was made up of segments. A total of 400 segments with different conical borings were available. By continually exchanging segments in accordance with the rules of evolution strategy, an optimum nozzle form was found which looks

Fig. 5.5. Experimental arrangement for the evolution of a pipe elbow.

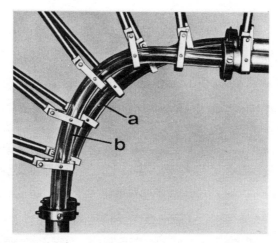

Fig. 5.6. Circular form (a) and optimum form (b) of the pipe elbow.

like a modern vase (Fig. 5.7). Here the evolution strategy has made two inventions: the first astonishing feature is a chamber in the diverging part of the nozzle enhancing mixing between liquid and vapour. And a second unexpected quality is the double chamber to the inlet of the nozzle, which helps to smooth the temperature profile. The energetic efficiency of the initial conical nozzle, calculated on the basis of supersonic theory, was 55%. The optimum nozzle has an efficiency of 79%.

It is a classical problem of fluid dynamics to find the minimum drag profile of an axisymmetric body. Recently this problem has been solved on a computer, combining boundary layer calculation techniques with evolution strategy. Figure 5.8 gives an example from this work (Pinebrook and Dalton, 1982). A body of revolution with constant maximum diameter and a given length evolves to a dolphin-like form with minimum drag. The computer run required 2400 generations to fit the 21 intensities of the variational problem.

Finally an application of the evolution stategy is presented in the field of structural engineering. A lattice frame with given loads has to be constructed for minimum weight. The variables of the structure are the plain co-ordinates of the six joints. Figure 5.9 shows the development of the frame. The initial design resulting from a linear optimization procedure has a weight of 922 kg. The optimum solution, which looks like a crane jib, weighs only 718 kg (Hoefler *et al.*, 1973).

5.3 EVOLVING AN INTELLIGENT VEHICLE

Evolution strategy, however, demonstrates its effectiveness just as much for systems of artificial intelligence. A question of immediate interest is how to

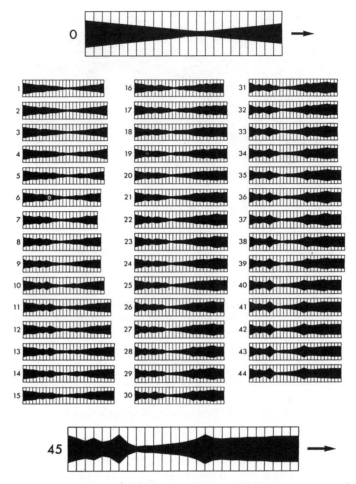

Fig. 5.7. Evolution of a hot-water flashing nozzle: a set of 400 segments, each conically bored, made it possible to build up different nozzle configurations.

control a number of vehicles in order to minimize energy dissipation due to acceleration processes and air resistance, while complying with the constraint that collisions are to be strictly avoided. Biological evolution, of course, has solved these problems. The flight of birds in formation as well as the arrangement of fish in schools contribute to a reduction of flow resistance while complying with collision avoidance. The mechanisms presumably ruling the co-ordination of distance and motion in swarms of animals are not known precisely enough that a transcription into algorithmic terms could easily be considered. Therefore we start with the heuristic formulation of algorithms for agglomeration and dispersion of vehicles which have to be developed and optimized by means of an artificial evolution process. The models to be considered are:

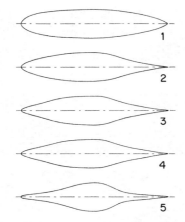

Fig. 5.8. Development of a body of revolution for minimum drag, shown at intervals of 600 generations.

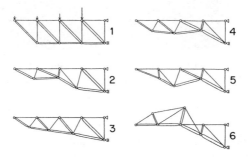

Fig. 5.9. Development of a lattice frame for minimum weight using the evolution strategy.

1. The potential model, which follows the physics of charged particles, assumes that the vehicles may attract or repel each other;
2. The facet-sensor model works with a number of discrete channels, the signals of which control the vehicle by means of production systems;
3. The laminar flow model, where vehicles are regarded as moving elements of a streaming fluid.

The facet-sensor model – believed to be the most promising of the three models – has been developed in more detail. In computer simulations, vehicles are initially equipped with a random number of sensors of arbitrary range and directions and with partially variable production systems. Subjected to certain traffic scenarios, the vehicles exhibit varying degrees of performance. The best adapted version of sensors and production systems is achieved by means of recurring mutation, recombination and selection (Fig. 5.10).

On one hand, the simulations will answer questions concerning the demands

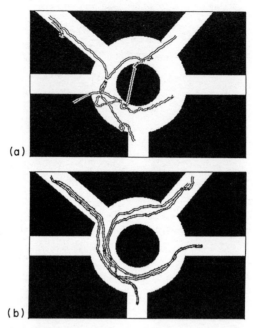

Fig. 5.10. Evolution of intelligent vehicles: (a) at first the vehicles crash with others or they leave the street; (b) applying the evolution strategy, traffic regulations are born.

placed on a system of sensors and production systems with respect to particular traffic situations. On the other hand, the behaviour of vehicles will be studied – and developed by the evolution strategy – in more complex traffic situations such as circular traffic or dense queues on motorways possibly involving traffic obstructions.

The criteria for developing and optimizing the models are determined by the idea of decentralized organization: any regulation model applicable in a future traffic system has to be capable of organizing a smooth traffic flow with each individual vehicle depending on no data but those which are locally available. The individual actions of the drivers are continuously supported by computer-controlled actions. Co-operative behaviour in a crowd of vehicles is achieved by gently correcting driver behaviour through continuous adjustment of direction and speed towards optimum performance. All vehicles, with and without computer-aided steering mechanisms, must be able to coexist in traffic situations.

5.4   SEQUENCE OF ES-OPERATIONS

The technical term 'evolution strategy' stands for a program: the objective is to copy rules of biological evolution in the most accurate form. So far the imitation of evolution in a simplified mode has proved to be very successful. Now the time has come to describe different styles of evolutionary operations.

The rules for evolutionary card games are summarized in Fig. 5.11. The nine symbols denote:

1. *Variable set:* On the data card – that is the genotype in biology – the instantaneous variable adjustments are noted down;
2. *Duplication:* The double arrow indicates that the information of a data card will be replicated;
3. *Mutation:* The broken arrow points to a random modification of the instantaneous variable settings;
4. *Population:* A pile of data cards represents a complex of information similar to the genotypes in a biological population;
5. *Selection:* The branching arrow below the circumscribed pile of cards indicates that the individuals are divided into good and worse ones;
6. *Realization:* The information on a card is materialized, such as setting the articulated plate for the historical wind-tunnel experiment;
7. *Random choice:* The w-symbol beginning with an arrowhead denotes that a card is randomly chosen out of the pool;
8. *Recombination:* Two (or more) variable columns are arranged side by side and the numerical values of the rows are randomly exchanged;
9. *Valuation:* The quality Q (fitness in biology), measured for the realized information, is noted on the data card.

It is useful to introduce at this point a universal nomenclature for the different modes of the evolution strategy. This will be done by the formal abbreviations:

$$(\mu/\rho + \lambda) - \text{ES} \quad \text{or} \quad (\mu/\rho, \lambda) - \text{ES}$$

We wish to call μ the number of parents of a generation and λ the number of

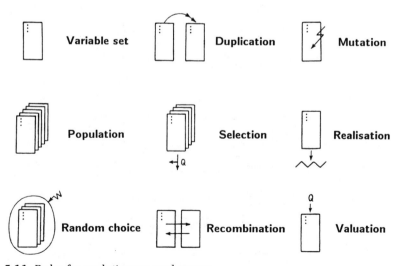

Fig. 5.11. Rules for evolutionary card games.

descendants (the children of the parents). The integer ρ is referred to as the mixing number. If three parents mix their variables (this is impossible in biology but possible in evolution strategy), the mixing number is 3.

Now we start with the simplest imitation of biological evolution. This is a $(1+1)-$ES. The game of cards (data cards) in Fig. 5.12 demonstrates how this algorithm works. A single data card represents the genotype. By card repeating the parental information will be doubled. DNA replication errors are introduced into our game by using a Gaussian random number generator. The randomly altered information of the offspring has to be realized. In our example, this is a slightly changed form of the articulated plate. We measure the drag of the plate within the airstream of the wind tunnel. The drag becomes the fitness of the offspring genotype. The parental card plus the offspring card are put into a ballot box. The best card holds the parental information for the next generation. This so-called two-membered evolution strategy has been applied in my first experiments.

A higher imitation level of biological evolution will be obtained with the algorithm of a $(1+6)-$ES (Fig. 5.13). Now the parent will produce six offspring. Random alternations are introduced and the information is translated into the phenotypes. After the drag has been measured all six offspring cards plus the parental card are put into the ballot box. The best of them will become the parent for the next generation.

The next scheme takes into account that the parents have a limited life-span. We set up a $(1, 6)-$ES (Fig. 5.14). The comma in this notation was first introduced by Schwefel (1977) in his doctoral thesis. The comma indicates that the parent is not included in the selection. With the exception of this modification

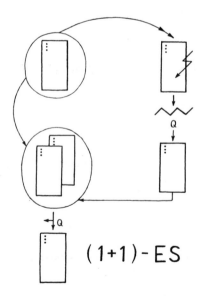

Fig. 5.12. $(1+1)-$ES.

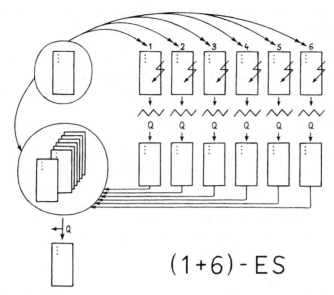

$$(1+6)-ES$$

Fig. 5.13. $(1+6)-$ES.

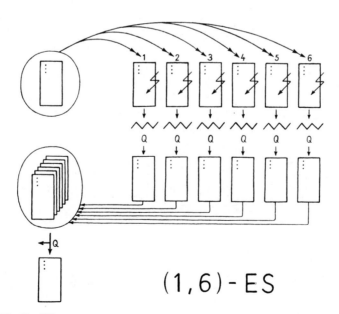

$$(1,6)-ES$$

Fig. 5.14. $(1, 6)-$ES.

the operations are the same as in the preceding algorithm. This kind of evolution strategy is preferred in our mathematical treatment today.

Next we introduce a population of three parents (Fig. 5.15). They produce in a random sequence nine offspring. Because it is the comma version of the evolution strategy only the nine offspring are put into the ballot box. The three best of them survive and become the parents of the next generation. This sort of evolution game will be named a $(3, 9)-ES$.

Last we introduce genetic recombination in our algorithmic notation (Rechenberg, 1978). For the given example of a $(6/2, 10)-ES$ there are six parents producing ten offspring (Fig. 5.16). Each parent, however, transmits only one-half of the information to the offspring. The parents producing an offspring are picked out by chance and their information will be mixed in the following way: homologous variables are chosen with even probability from one of the parental cards and transferred to the offspring card. This procedure will be repeated (with arbitrary parents) until ten offspring have been composed. All following operations have been described above.

5.5   THE DISCOVERY OF THE EVOLUTION WINDOW

The evolution strategy has proved to be of unprecedented efficiency for multivariable problems (Schwefel, 1977, 1981). In this case the mutation step size to get maximum rate of progress becomes very small. Parents and their

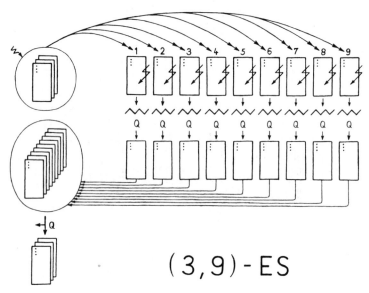

Fig. 5.15. $(3, 9)-ES.$

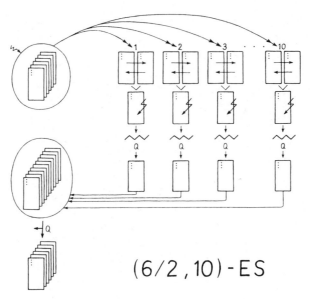

$$(6/2,10)-ES$$

Fig. 5.16. (6/2, 10)−ES.

offspring are diffusing along the gradient path to the optimum within a narrow passage. Therefore we may be allowed to interpret the method of biological evolution and its man-made analogy as a hill-climbing procedure. Hill climbing is a principle common to many optimization strategies. A hill-climbing strategy acts like gravity, forcing a ball to roll down the gradient of a hill, but it works in the opposite direction. The effect is that the vast space of possibilities is reduced to a narrow passageway, on which the optimum seeking takes place. Applying such a strategy one must make sure that a hill exists to climb up. This was the case for all our engineering experiments using evolution strategy. I claim there is no difference in biology: piecewise smooth relationships between the fitness of an organism and the structure of the variables form a genetic landscape with hills to climb up.

To demonstrate the gradient climbing of a (1, 10)−ES we look at an ordinary optimization problem in automobile engineering. The object is a carburetter with two adjusting screws (Cairns-Smith, 1982). The contour lines in Fig. 5.17 represent screw settings of equal efficiency. To find the optimum setting we start with the parent at a random position (a). This parent will produce ten children (b). Then the parent will die out (c). The offspring with the highest efficiency is declared to become the new parent (d). All other children die out (e). Obviously from generation to generation the parents will move up the hill with a certain speed φ (f).

We will now direct our attention on the calculation of the speed of progress. To do this we must know the local form of the quality function. A smooth quality

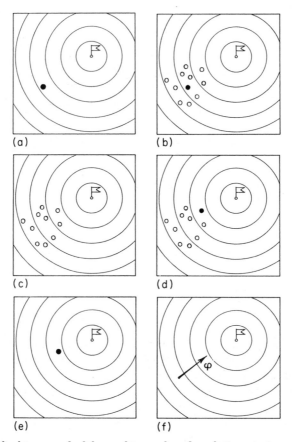

Fig. 5.17. Hill-climbing speed of the multi-membered evolution strategy.

function may be described by a general quadratic equation with the variables x_1, $x_2, \ldots x_n$:

$$Q = Q_0 + \sum_{k=1}^{n} a_k x_k - \sum_{i=1}^{n} \sum_{k=1}^{n} b_{ik} x_i x_k \qquad (5.1)$$

The variables are altered by random numbers satisfying a $(0, \sigma)$-normal distribution. Because the mutations are distributed in a symmetrical sphere around the parental point, a rotation of the co-ordinate axis will be allowed. The transformation of equation (5.1) to the principal axis gives the result:

$$Q = Q_0 + \sum_{k=1}^{n} c_k y_k - \sum_{k=1}^{n} d_k y_k^2 \qquad (5.2)$$

It is permitted to compare this general n-dimensional quality function with a

Taylor series expansion, breaking off after the quadratic term. For the general description (equation 5.2) of the local form of the quality landscape I succeeded in calculating the rate of progress in the case of a $(\mu, \lambda) - $ ES:

$$\varphi_{\mu,\lambda} = c_{\mu,\lambda}\sigma - \Omega\sigma^2, \qquad \Omega = \sum d_k / \sqrt{\sum c_k^2} \tag{5.3}$$

The term Ω measures the strength of non-linearity (complexity factor) of the quality function. All difficulties are concentrated in the evaluation of the progress coefficient. In the case of a $(1, \lambda) - $ ES one has to solve the integral:

$$c_{1,\lambda} = \sqrt{(2/\pi)} \, \lambda \, 2^{1-\lambda} \int_{-\infty}^{\infty} z \exp(-z^2)[1 + \mathrm{erf}(z)] dz \tag{5.4}$$

Table 5.1 shows that fortunately the progress coefficient will not change very much.

Figure 5.18 shows the theoretical result in the form of a diagram. The climbing speed Φ (in a universal notation) is represented as a function of the mutation step

Table 5.1

μ \ λ	5	10	20	50	100	200	
1	1.16	1.54	1.87	2.25	2.51	2.75	
2	0.91	1.35	1.71	2.12	2.39	2.64	
5	0	0.90	1.37	1.85	2.16	2.43	$c_{\mu,\lambda}$
10	—	0	0.98	1.57	1.92	2.22	
20	—	—	0	1.19	1.62	1.97	

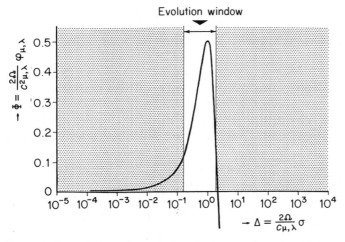

Fig. 5.18. The evolution window: the evolution strategy works only within a small band of mutation step length.

size Δ (also in a universal notation). It is a very remarkable result that the evolution strategy works only within a small band of the mutation step size. I have named this band the 'evolution window'. Out of this window no evolution occurs. This is a very exciting fact, because Schwefel (1977) has found in his doctoral thesis that the main difference between the evolution strategy and other problem-solving methods is the exponent by which the search effort will rise with increasing number of variables. This means that the result of the evolution window is of more general evidence. The existence of the narrow band of variational freedom is disconcerting, for the worker in artificial intelligence as well as for the designer of technical apparatus. However, it may also be useful to reflect on this fact for the development of economic and social systems. Right of the window you may locate the field of revolution with negative values of Φ. Left of the window you will have the region of conservatism with no progress. The logarithmic scale for Δ has been chosen, because this quantity (mutation rate in biology) will change in a decimal power mode.

5.6 THE TWOFOLD ALGORITHM OF THE EVOLUTION STRATEGY

The existence of the narrow evolution window gives rise to a new problem. How can the evolution strategy find the window in order to be effective? The answer is: the multi-membered evolution strategy is a twofold optimization procedure. In this case the mutation step size adapts itself to the local topology of the quality function to get maximum rate of progress. To demonstrate this very important feature of the multi-membered evolution strategy we look at a similar situation in the life of man.

Suppose you are an alpinist climbing a difficult mountainside. You have picked out an appropriate climbing technique. You cannot, however, decide if it is the best, because there is no standard of comparison. Next day you are climbing in a group. Each member of the group is using a slightly different climbing technique. After a short time it becomes evident which technique is the best and you may copy it.

The same procedure can be implemented using a $(1, \lambda)-$ES. Suppose the parent produces ten offspring, but five of them with a small step size and the rest with a large step size. After that the offspring with the highest quality is declared to become the parent of the next generation, while all other children die out. The all important point is: most probably these children will win the selection game having a step size to be located nearer to the centre of the evolution window. In biology the mutation step size (strictly speaking the mutation rate) is related to the precision of the error correcting DNA-polymerases. Therefore the mutation step size is a hereditable character. Extended to the evolution strategy, the step size of the surviving offspring has to be transferred to the corresponding parent of the next generation. The best step size of the foregoing generation will be declared to be the norm of the current generation. Creating the new set of children, however, we must not forget to mutate the norm step size.

The $(1, \lambda) - \text{ES}$, taking step length mutations into account, can be formulated as follows:

$$\delta_1^g = \delta_e^g \xi_1$$

$$o_1^g = o_e^g + \delta_1^g z_1 \quad \text{(offspring 1 of generation g)} \tag{5.5}$$

$$\vdots$$

$$\delta_\lambda^g = \delta_e^g \xi_\lambda$$

$$o_\lambda^g = o_e^g + \delta_\lambda^g z_\lambda \quad \text{(offspring } \lambda \text{ of generation g)}$$

Let b denote the best offspring:

$$Q(o_b^g) = \text{max/min}\{Q(o_1^g), \ldots, Q(o_\lambda^g)\}$$

$$\delta_e^{g+1} = \delta_b^g$$

$$o_e^{g+1} = o_b^g \quad \text{(parent of generation } g+1)$$

In this algorithm the random vectors z_i have $(0, 1/\sqrt{n})$ normally distributed components. In the case of $n \gg 1$ the total length of the random vector is then 1. Therefore the factor δ may be interpreted as the total step length of the mutation. In accordance with the logarithmic scale of the mutation step length in the evolution window, the deviates ξ_i are obtained from log-normally distributed numbers.

5.7   HILL CLIMBING IN HYPERSPACE

What is the optimum mutation step length of the evolution strategy adapting itself to maximum rate of progress? To give a feeling for it we look to the most simple non-linear quality function. This is the n-dimensional quadratic form giving the minimization problem:

$$Q = \sum_{i=1}^n o_i^2 \rightarrow \text{min!} \tag{5.6}$$

The functional landscape of Q in the n-dimensional hyperspace may be viewed in two-dimensional sections. In these plain sections the contour lines are circles. Let r denote the radius of curvature of these contour lines. Then the complexity factor turns out to be

$$\Omega = n/(2r) \tag{5.7}$$

According to the theory of the evolution window the mutation step length to give maximum rate of progress can be evaluated:

$$\delta_{\text{opt}} = \sigma_{\text{opt}} \sqrt{n} = c_{\mu,\lambda} r / \sqrt{n} \tag{5.8}$$

At this point it has to be stated that the formulae (5.3) and (5.8) are the result of an asymptotic theory ($n \to \infty$). The general solution becomes more complicated. However, workers in artificial intelligence are just interested in complex systems having many degrees of freedom (variables). Now, if the number of variables is increasing, the optimum step length to get maximum rate of progress will decrease. If it were possible to look into the multidimensional Euclidean space designed by the n variables of the problem, then one would observe that an evolution process looks like a one-dimensional diffusion process winding up the gradient path of the quality function. The picture of an evolution process to find the optimum is not that of a concentrating cloud of points. It is an elongating chain of points following the gradient line of the quality function (Fig. 5.19). The gradient acts as a guiding thread from the starting-point to an optimum of the functional landscape. The evolution strategy will not scatter into the vast space of possibilities.

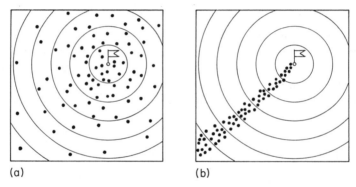

(a)   (b)

Fig. 5.19. Hill-climbing picture of the evolution strategy in many dimensions (a) false: shrinking cloud of random points; (b) true: diffusion along the gradient line.

Many people extrapolate the two-dimensional view of the problem into n dimensions. This turns out to be a fatal error. You can poke around in a two-dimensional manifold to find the optimum. Of course, applying pure random search you can jump from a local to a global optimum in two dimensions. However, you have no chance to repeat this in n dimensions. There is only one way to overcome the curse of dimensionality: to follow the gradient line. All optimum seeking methods act in this way. The evolution strategy, however, will do so with a minimum of search effort.

5.8   CODING THE EVOLUTION STRATEGY

The quality function to test the evolution strategy may be given by equation (5.6). Let us work out a simple BASIC program of a $(\mu/\mu, \lambda)-$ES. The special feature of this most effective evolutionary algorithm at present is the multi-recombination. It means that the variables of all parents are mixed. This procedure, of course, is uncommon in biology. Multimixing, however, has proved to be more effective than mixing only two variable sets.

We start the ES-program with the computation of the quality Q:

100 Q=0:FOR I=1 TO V:Q=Q+O(I)^2:NEXT I

Before doing line 100 we have to generate the offspring. The ith variable originates with equal probability from one of the μ parents. In the same line the mutation is added. For the generation of $(0, 1/\sqrt{n})$-normally distributed random numbers we use the well-known transformation formula of Box and Muller (1958): BOX=SQR(−2∗LOG(RND))∗SIN(6.2832∗RND)/SQR(V)

90 FOR I=1 TO V:R=1+INT(M∗RND):O(I)=E(I,R)+D∗BOX:NEXT I

We must go back further. The mutation step length D for each offspring has to be calculated. In the original algorithm (5.5) this is done by multiplying the norm step length DN with log-normally distributed random numbers. Another proven method of changing the step length is to multiply or divide it equally, probably by the factor 1.5.

80 IF RND<0.5 THEN D=DN∗1.5 ELSE D=DN/1.5

Averaging the step length of the winning offspring in the present generation we get the norm step size for the next generation. The analogue in biology is the intermediate heredity.

70 DN=0:FOR J=1 TO M:DN=DN+DE(J)/M:NEXT J

To begin with the sequence of operations (70–100) we had to define the starting mutation step length as well as the initial values of the variables for the μ parents.

40 FOR J=1 TO M:DE(J)=?:FOR I=1 TO V:E(I,J)=?:NEXT I:NEXT J

The task is to generate λ offspring. Therefore we had to repeat the operations 70–100 λ-times. This is done by designing the following program loop. The lines up to 130 are reserved.

60 FOR K=1 TO L
130 NEXT K

A temporary storage contains the data OB (variable setting), DB (mutation step size) and QB (functional quality) of the μ best offspring at present. In the next operation the index J of the worst offspring is picked out.

110 W=1:H=QB(1):FOR J=2 TO M:IF QB(J)>H THEN H=QB(J):W=J
111 NEXT J

If the offspring, created in the loop, is better than the worst one picked out, then the data in the storage belonging to the index W are exchanged by the better ones.

120 IF Q<QB(W) THEN QB(W)=Q:DB(W)=D:FOR I=1 TO V:
     OB(I,W)=O(I):NEXT I

After leaving the generation loop the index F of the first offspring is picked out of the temporary storage. This is the inverse operation of the lines 110, 111.

    140 F=1:H=QB(1):FOR J=2 TO M:IF QB(J)<H THEN H=QB(J):F=J
    141 NEXT J

Printing of the generation number G, the functional quality QB of the first offspring and the mutation step length DB of the first offspring, is done on line 150.

    150 PRINT G,QB(F),DB(F)

In the following line the selection takes place. Strictly speaking the μ best offspring of the generation, stored in the temporary memory, will be declared to become parents for the next generation.

    160 FOR J=1 TO M:DE(J)=DB(J):FOR I=1 TO V:E(I,J)=OB(I,J):
         NEXT I:NEXT J

As long as the generation number does not exceed a given limit we jump back to the starting line of the program.

    170 IF G<? THEN 50

Going into line 50 a new generation will be counted. We put μ imaginary offspring into memory having the fictitious worst quality of 10^{10}.

    50 G=G+1:FOR J=1 TO M:QB(J)=1E+10:NEXT J

This is the head line of the program. Because the evolution strategy proves its real advantage in the case of many variables, we start the minimum seeking process with 30 variables.

    10 V=30:M=4:L=12:DIM O(V), OB(V,M), E(V,M), QB(M), DE(M),
        DB(M)

5.9   REFERENCES

Box, G. E. P. and Muller, M. E. (1958) A note on the generation of random normal deviates. *Ann. Math. Stat.*, **29**, 610–11.

Cairns-Smith, A. G. (1982) *Genetic Takeover and the Mineral Origins of Life*, Cambridge University Press, Cambridge.

Hoefler, A., Leyssner, U. and Wiedemann, J. (1973) Optimization of the layout of trusses combining strategies based on Michell's theorem and on the biological principles of evolution. *AGARD Conference Proc.*, **123**, A1–A8, Milan.

Pinebrook, W. E. and Dalton, Ch. (1983) Drag minimization on a body of revolution through evolution, in *Computer Methods in Applied Mechanics and Engineering*, Elsevier Science Publishers BV (North-Holland), pp. 179–97.

Rechenberg, I. (1964) *Cybernetic Solution Path of an Experimental Problem*, Royal Aircraft Establishment, Library Translation 1122, Farnborough.

Rechenberg, I. (1973) *Evolutionsstrategie – Optimierung technischer Systeme nach Prinzipien der biologischen Evolution.* Frommann-Holzboog, Stuttgart.

Rechenberg, I. (1978) Evolutionsstrategien, in *Simulationsmethoden in der Medizin und Biologie* (eds B. Schneider and U. Ranft), Springer, Berlin, pp. 96–110.

Rechenberg, I. (1984) The evolution strategy – a mathematical model of Darwinian evolution, in *Synergetics – from Microscopic to Macroscopic Order* (ed. E. Frehland), Springer Series in Synergetics, Vol. 22, Springer, Berlin–Heidelberg, pp. 122–32.

Schwefel, H. P. (1977) *Numerische Optimierung von Computer-Modellen mittels der Evolutionsstrategie*, Birkhäuser, Basel and Stuttgart.

Schwefel, H. P. (1981) *Numerical Optimization of Computer Models*, Wiley and Sons, Chichester.

Schwefel, H. P. and Klockgether, J. (1970) Two-phase nozzle and hollow core jet experiments. *Proc. 11th Symposium on Engineering Aspects of Magnetohydrodynamics*, Pasadena, California Inst. Tech., pp. 141–8.

6

Learning and distributed memory: getting close to neurons

IGOR ALEKSANDER

6.1 LEARNING: A COMPLEX CONCEPT

Among the many words in everyday speech, 'learning' belongs to that set which is easily said and used, but implies a wide variety of phenomena in the brain. The early learning of an infant who is beginning to recognize simple repetitions of patterns, the learning of language and the handling of human relationships, the acceptance of cultural values, schooling and higher education, are all encompassed by the word 'learning'. In some ways learning never stops. It may get more difficult with age but, as many a septuagenarian freshman has shown, it does not become impossible.

The problem for the anatomist or the 'neural engineer' is to explain, first what the common ground between these different modes might be, and second to speculate on the differences between them. There is also some responsibility for explaining the difference between 'learning', 'knowledge acquisition' and 'memorizing'. It may be appropriate to start with some definitions of these levels so as to avoid ambiguities later. These definitions are idiosyncratic to this chapter and may not be generally accepted.

6.1.1 Some definitions

Memorizing, knowledge acquisition and learning are a bit like a stacking Russian doll, with memory at the centre. Memory may be defined as the mechanism which allows one to label experiential events. Seeing a friend and saying 'Fred' or being able to recall a sequence of events (say remembering a poem) point to this simplest level in the learning nest. So, memorizing is the setting in motion of the associative process which underpins the labelling of experiential events. This could be direct such as recognizing Fred, or indirect such as completing the sentence 'Mary had a . . .'. 'Little lamb' could be seen as a label associated with the first part of the phrase, which is, as it were, an internal experiential event.

Knowledge acquisition goes with statements such as 'I know how to fit your car radio' or 'I know where you can buy inexpensive wine'. This again relies on associative memory based on a chaining of internal events (e.g. 'you go down the King's Road towards Putney, turn left at the first set of traffic lights after Chelsea Fire Station and the shop called White's Wine Store is just on your right'). Note that this is much the same mechanism as memorizing poetry, but has an added degree of complexity as it 'imagines' contingencies such as 'if you are coming from Putney turn right just before the fire station . . .' or 'you may need a special tool to cut a hole for the aerial'. The notion that this level of learning includes learning and remembering the 'poetry' as well as the contingencies that cause 'branching' is important at this stage.

At the highest and least well-defined level is learning not only based on ideas, etc. (mathematics is a good example of this) but learning how to reason for its own sake. Here the structures are even more complex and interactive: think of 'knowing how to prove Pythagoras' theorem'. This most general level of learning also encompasses the complex relationship between 'understanding' (another simple word with a lot of hidden meaning) and further learning. This division into levels does not address the question of innate ability – what is learnt and what is instinctively known. There are controversies about this, particularly as expressed about the learning of language (see Piattelli-Palmerini, 1980).

Our main objective in arguing that some learning takes place at each of these levels is to show that the provision of a 'neural' or distributed memory type of explanation gives insight into the nature of these levels and the difference of the mechanisms between them.

6.1.2   The neuron as an atom of memory

Those who are familiar with computers will soon agree that the atom of memory in any digital system is the 'bit'. Physically, this exists in the computer as the state of a flip-flop or (for older computer scientists) as the state of magnetization of a ferrite core.

But the brain neither contains flip-flops nor ferrite cores. Its memory is thought to reside in its neurons – the synaptic contacts between neurons to be precise. Basically, a neuron stores more than one bit – exactly how many is not known. But in order to discuss the hierarchy of learning we must resolve the problem, albeit in a stylized way.

A neuron we assume, has N inputs from which it can receive messages from other neurons. We assume further that the neuron either fires or does not fire. We represent these two states as 1 and 0. In addition we allow the neuron to say 'I don't know' by firing or not firing at random. When a neuron 'knows' what to do it always responds in the same way (with 0 or 1) to an input pattern of 0's and 1's. There is a total of 2^N such patterns each of which needs to store 0, 1 or d (d for don't know). One could say that the neuron input addresses a storage location which contains 0, 1 or d, which it outputs as its response to that input.

It has been shown elsewhere that this is a general representation of the operation of a neuron (Aleksander, 1987). Its simplicity allows one to discuss the neural basis of important phenomena: learning in this case.

One more point needs to be covered: how does this neuron learn what to do? There are several learning modes. The first is a direct setting of the neuron to the desired output with the appropriate 0/1 pattern at the inputs. This is a mode used in practical systems such as the WISARD (Aleksander *et al.*, 1984), of which more will be said later.

In another mode signals are applied to the node indicating that a change is required which, should the current input be causing an output of 1, will be changed to 0 and remain so for future presentations of the same input pattern (clearly this goes for changing from 0 to 1 too). This mode is particularly useful with systems that use nodes with the 'don't know' state. In such cases it is also possible to confirm that a randomly chosen output is correct and should be associated with the input pattern. Other rules (as in Aleksander, 1988) can cause outputs that are deemed to be wrong to revert to the 'don't know' state.

6.1.3   A note on naming objects

It is often said in the literature on child development that the naming of objects is the starting-point for more sophisticated forms of learning. Indeed this has been implied earlier in this chapter. But when viewed as a task for a neural net or a distributed memory system, the ability of a human being to name objects turns out to be a sophisticated task which has more in common with the higher levels of learning mentioned earlier than may be apparent at first glance. We shall approach it in stages.

6.2   HOW WISARD LEARNS TO RECOGNIZE PATTERNS

The **WISARD** (WIlkie Stonham and Aleksander's Recognition Device) is a commercial pattern recognition system based on neural principles. This is discussed in full elsewhere (Aleksander *et al.*, 1984). Here we state its principle briefly so as to discuss its mode of learning both in terms of its adequacies and its inadequacies. The image to be recognized is presented as K bits (set in a frame-store). Typically these bits form a 512×512 ($= K$) binary image. A group of K/N 'neurons' (each being part of WISARD's random-access memory, with N a variable to be determined by the user) is called a 'discriminator' and is devoted to the recognition of a particular class of pattern. There are no 'd' states.

The basic mode of learning and remembering in such a discriminator is well known, but will be restated here for completeness. The 'neurons' are connected to the K points purely at random. Imagine that K represents an image T_1 of unit area. Starting with all its storage locations set at zero, the discriminator is taught T_1 by being made to store a 1 at the storage locations addressed by T_1. Say that this is repeated for a second training image T_2. The question is, how will the discriminator respond to some unknown pattern T_u which on a point-by-point basis has in common a total area h_1 with T_1 and h_2 with T_2 (due to the insistence on unit area for K, $0 < h_1$, $h_2 < 1$).

Choosing arbitrarily just one memory, say the jth one, the probability of all N inputs being connected in the common area between T_u and T_1 is $(h_1)^N$. Similarly for T_2, $(h_2)^N$. Under both these conditions the chosen neuron will respond with a 1. To calculate the total probability of responding with a 1 we have

$$p_j = (h_1)^N + (h_2)^N - (h_{12})^N \qquad (6.1)$$

where the third term is the probability of the jth neuron being connected to the common area between T_1 and T_2, h_{12} being the proportional of overlap between T_u, T_1 and T_2: this has to be subtracted so as not to be counted twice. A similar equation can be obtained for any number of training patterns.

This equation has the form:

$$p_j = (h_1)^N + (h_2)^N + \cdots (h_s)^N - (h_{12})^N - (h_{13})^N \cdots (h_{s,s-1}) + (h_{123})^N + (h_{124})^N \cdots$$

The response of the discriminator, as a proportion of its neurons firing with a 1 is precisely p_j, as the law of large numbers can be involved. The behaviour of such a system can be gleaned from equation (6.1). First consider $ih_1 = 1$. This means that the response of the discriminator will be 1 if a training pattern is presented to it. The key difference between this and storing $T_1 \ldots T_s$ in a conventional computational system is that the neuron net responds with the delay time of just one neuron, whereas in the conventional computer, a comparison would have to be made with each stored pattern.

A second feature of the discriminator is that it is both capable of accepting that two similar objects require a strong response as well as two very different ones. In the former case the discriminator acts as a broadly tuned filter over similar interpolates. Imagine T_1, T_2, T_u to be as shown in Fig. 6.1. The discriminator responds strongly whenever T_u is in between T_1 and T_2. However, were T_1 and T_2 a horizontal and a vertical bar the system would have learnt to respond strongly to T_u when it is nearly horizontal or nearly vertical, but give a low response when it is between the two.

The degree of 'tuning' of the discriminator depends on N. Given only one training pattern a 10% change produces the following changes in responses depending on N:

N	p_j	
1	0.90	
2	0.65	Two decimal places
8	0.43	

The WISARD contains more than one discriminator. Assume that discriminator 1 is trained on T_1 and discriminator 2 on T_2. When T_u is presented we have

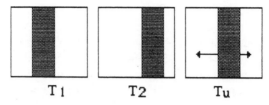

Fig. 6.1. Training patterns T_1 and T_2; test patterns T_u.

$$p_1 = (h_1)^N; \ p_2 = (h_2)^N$$

hence the nearest match can be obtained simply by comparing p_1 with p_2, the greater of the two providing the recognition. Several parameters now enter the argument:

1. The absolute confidence is given by p_{max}, where p_{max} is the strongest response from a set of discriminators. The decision may be rejected if this confidence is not high enough.
2. The relative confidence

$$(p_{max} - p_{next})$$

where p_{next} is the second strongest response. Again the decision can be rejected if the relative confidence is not high enough.

Groups of discriminators may also be used to interpolate precisely between two (even badly defined) objects. The WISARD is often demonstrated with one discriminator trained on a smiling face and another on a serious face. A relative confidence of zero between these two indicates a 'half smile'.

6.3   WHY WISARD DOES NOT LEARN TO NAME OBJECTS

In what has just been described, we discover a process which in many ways could be said to be 'learning'. The system has the ability to group things together as directed by the teacher and to generalize from this training process by putting similar images into the appropriate category. Indeed this is a perfectly adequate regime for the industrial applications among which the WISARD finds a market. The main advantage of this type of learning is that it enables an operator unskilled in the art of computer programming to describe to what is undoubtedly a computing machine how that machine should behave. The application domains are plentiful in industrial inspection tasks and security work (intruder detection, face and signature verification, etc.).

But how close is this to the learning exhibited by a child when he first starts to name correctly his mother (ma ma . . .) and, maybe a dog (do . . . do)? 'A long, long way' is the answer to this question – the problem lies with the fact that in human learning, or true learning as one could call it, even at this very low level, the teacher cannot exert the same power over the process as the operator can in WISARD. A mother's voice, face, the retinal image of a dog, the sound of one's own voice – this is all bewildering perceptual input to a child, and long before any naming of objects takes place, this mass of data has to be distinguished and mastered. We shall take some of these steps using the 'neuron as the atom of memory' concept as virtually the only axiom.

6.4 MENTAL IMAGES

It is unlikely that a child is born with a built-in package of mental images that neatly represent the real world. These are clearly part of the learning process and need to be seen as a feasible property of a system of distributed neurons.

Consider the system in Fig. 6.2. This shows a three-neuron net. Initially the neurons are all in the 'don't know' state. We can draw a 'state diagram' which relates all the possible patterns of timing to one another. Because of the initial 'don't know' state stored in response to all inputs in all the neurons the probability of moving from any state to any other is the same: one-eighth. So the diagram is not worth drawing in full – part of it is shown in Fig. 6.3 – just to get some practice in looking at such probabilistic state diagrams.

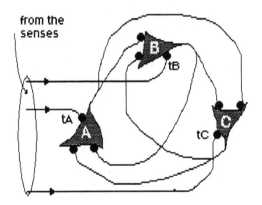

Fig. 6.2. A simple neural net.

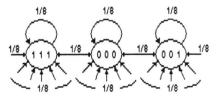

Fig. 6.3. Part of state space of untrained net.

It is now necessary to cheat a little and postulate a way in which sensory inputs might impinge of the neurons. 'Cheat' because not much is really known about the way this happens in real neurons. We assume that the synaptic connections from the sensory inputs act in a special way, different from that of the other synaptic inputs.

First, these neuron inputs (t_A, t_B, t_C) are thought to have three states, 1, 0 and neutral (π). In the 1 state it forces its neuron to fire, in the 0 state it prevents it from firing and in the π state it allows the neuron to use its own decision mechanism to decide whether to fire or not.

A further mechanism must be at work and that is the change in the logic of the neuron. We postulate that through some other control the neurons can be in a 'plastic' or 'fixed' state. In the plastic stated they are influenced by the t_j inputs in the way suggested earlier. This may be best expressed by a table (Table 6.1). In the fixed state t_j has no effect on the association – it merely overrides (if 0 or 1) the firing of the neuron. We now 'expose' the net to the environment which consists only of patterns with two zeros and a one. To simplify matters it can be assumed that the system goes plastic while an environmental input is present. In this case, the environment consists only of patterns 001, 010 and 100.

Table 6.1   Influences upon neurons in the plastic state

t_j input	Current association for neuron input state	New association for neuron input state
0	0	0
0	d	0
0	1	d
1	0	d
1	d	1
1	1	1
π	0	0
π	d	d
π	1	1

Assume 001 is present at the input just before the system goes plastic. The system is forced to fire 001 on ABC. If it now goes plastic it will 'auto-associate' pattern 001. That is, even if the input connections go to 0, 001 will regenerate itself as A has learnt to output 0 for an input of 01 from BC, B outputs 0 for an input of 01 from AC and C outputs 1 for an input of 00 from AB. Repeating this performance with 010 and 100 gives rise to the state diagram in Fig. 6.4. If the

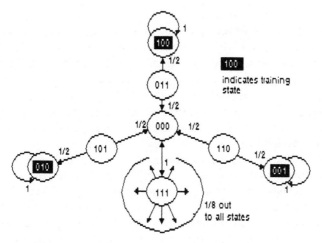

Fig. 6.4. State space after training.

probability of being in a state at some (discrete) time t is $p\,(a)_t$, the probability of being in state j at time $t+1$ is

$$p(j)_{t+1} = \sum_i p(i)_t x\,(i,\,j)$$

where $x\,(i,\,j)$ is the transition probability from state i to state j. This is mentioned because this simple equation enables us to work out what state the system is likely to inhabit as time goes by. Assume that to start with the probability of being at any state is equally $1/8$ (in other words we do not know what state the system is in). Table 6.2 shows how these probabilities develop with time.

Table 6.2 shows that with time there is equal probability for the system to 'live' in one of the true learnt states. These are the only mental images the system is capable of. In fact, this can be observed directly from the state diagram: the learnt

Table 6.2 Developmental progression of probability states

State	$p(i)0$	$p(i)1$	$p(i)2$	$p(i)3$	$p(i)\infty$
000	0.125	0.203	0.041	0.054	0
001	0.125	0.203	0.242	0.271 ...	0.333
010	0.125	0.203	0.242	0.271	0.333
011	0.125	0.016	0.017	0.027	0
100	0.125	0.203	0.242	0.271 ...	0.333
101	0.125	0.016	0.017	0.027	0
110	0.125	0.016	0.017	0.027 ...	0
111	0.125	0.141	0.221	0.068	0

states are the only ones that are certain to re-enter themselves: once the system falls into them it cannot get out. Contrast now the state of affairs before and after learning. Before learning, the external image enters the 'internal' world of neuronal interconnections through the forced action of the t_j synapses. This is a perceptual act. We would not be breaking the rules governing the meaning of the word by saying that the net perceives which input pattern is present. But as the input lines return to π the perception is lost. After learning, an input from one of the learnt patterns is not only perceived but retained in mental imagery even when the input is lost (eyes are closed, say).

The important factor in the discussion is that the mental image occurs in the same place in the net as the perceived image. This is a function of learning. Images not part of 'knowledge' do not leave a trace in memory. It would be difficult to recall mentally a totally new image (say a complex wiring diagram), but there would be no difficulty in perceiving it. The model net also throws some light on an old argument about vision: the idea that the eyes throw a picture on an inner screen which the rest of the brain can 'look' at. The model shows that this is indeed a description of what is happening except that there is added sophistication. The screen is active and holds (and indeed recalls as we shall see) known images and loses unknown ones. Further, the screen encodes the image in neural signals so that it can be read by the rest of the brain without needing a new pair of eyes (transducers).

We now discuss another interesting property: what happens if the net sees only part of an image at its input? Imagine that input line to unit A only is firing (1) while the other two are inactive π. This modifies the state diagram of Fig. 6.4 by forcing a 1 into the A position. This reduces the diagram to four states with probabilities of transition as in Fig. 6.5. This time there is only one recurrent state: 100. Again, it is clear that sooner or later this state will be entered and held. So, the presentation of a clue which matches only one trained state leads to that trained state. This is a kind of *Gestalt* – an important mechanism whereby the net

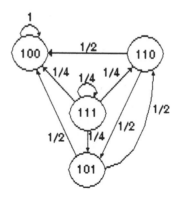

Fig. 6.5. A clamped to 1.

copes with partially specified inputs: it recognizes them in the best way it can. Now, consider what happens if A perceives a 0. Using a similar technique as for the 1, the state diagram in Fig. 6.6 is generated. If the net happens to be in one of the two compatible states, it will not be disturbed, but should the input $0\pi\pi$ arrive when the system is in the third state 100 which is not compatible, it will enter an inner 'confusion' between states 000 and 111 and switch backwards and forwards between the two. In summary, therefore, we have shown that a simplified neural net can have the following properties:

1. *Perception.* Entering a state directly related to the input. This is not dependent on learning;
2. *Learnt mental images.* The creation of stable images internally, at the same locations in the net as the perceived images;
3. *Recognition of learnt images.* The net enters appropriate stable states and knows it has recognized its input as the image is a firm rather than passive perception;
4. *Completion* of partly seen images but those that correspond to learnt mental images. Ambiguity in the input leads to an uncertain completion;
5. *Association.* This is merely another aspect of completion. If A and B are two parts of a trained pattern and A is fragmented, B should be generated as part of the completion process and vice versa. This assumes that A and B are uniquely coupled in the learnt state (i.e. there is no other pattern such as AC).

6.5   THE POWER OF PATTERN COMPLETION: NAMING OBJECTS

It is the process of pattern completion that is the secret computing tool of neural nets. Armed with this, it is now possible to show the following crucial step in learning to name objects: saying 'mah' when mother's face appears. It is a known fact that early utterances such as 'mah' 'pah' are naturally produced by a child as part of a 'babbling' process which, when appropriate, is reinforced by parents. But words such as 'reinforced' and 'appropriate' are not explanations of what may be going on among the neurons. For this we return to the pattern completion property possessed by such nets.

Consider another example of a net with three major components as shown in Fig. 6.7. (*Note:* here there is no attempt to describe how the human brain works:

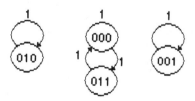

Fig. 6.6. A clamped to 0.

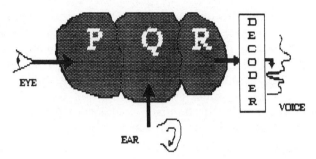

Fig. 6.7. A three-component net.

this is a hypothetical creature we are describing, but one that acts as an existence theorem.)

P's neurons are driven from vision sensors as in our previous example. Q's neurons receive their perceptual inputs from the hearing organs. R, however, is different. It generates signals which when decoded in some way drive the mouth and vocal chord muscles.

In its random wanderings through state space, R causes this creature to emit random, short sounds. This in itself is not so useful, until one begins to realize that the creature given ears will hear its own babblings. This means that net Q and R become correlated, and the pattern in Q could be said to be 'mental images' of the sounds made by the creature itself. Let us consider a concrete example, with very limited capabilities, but considerable explanatory power. Let each of P, Q and R consist of three neurons roughly interconnected as in the previous example, but with some cross-connections across these groups. So, we have said that group Q forms 'mental images' of the sounds generated by R. Say that in R

$$100$$

causes the muscles, etc. to emit the accidental sound 'mah'. As there is no order in the way the things are connected, it may be that in area Q, 'mah' stimulates the pattern 101. If this state goes through a learning phase, the pattern in Q, R

$$101 \quad 100$$

becomes a stable one. The same would occur for other spontaneously generated utterances. The implication of this is that it may be possible for similar sounds from other sources to stimulate, via the auditory channels, the same 'mental image' as generated by the creature's own production.

The way we have left things at the moment is that on stimulating the inner image of a sound, completion implies that there would be an automatic repetition of the sound by the vocal mechanism. It is clear that living creatures have simple ways of appraising such outward action – but the mechanism of such inhibition is beyond the needs of the current discussion.

Say now that the mother's image stimulates pattern 111 in net P. But there is as yet no link between this and the creature's ability to emit a particular sound. This is where it is known that parents are very helpful. The mother does not impose sounds on the child, but uses the ones that she knows the child is capable of emitting. This is an observed fact. Through this she may stimulate the crucial 101 in net Q to form the complete association 111, 101, 100 in P, Q and R. Of course, she is helped in this endeavour as, whenever she gets close to 101 in Q she will get a response from the child – even a fully developed 'mah'. This completes a suggestion for a mechanism for learning to produce one, appropriately selected utterance, upon seeing the face of the mother: through the completion of pattern

$$111 \qquad 101 \qquad 100$$

in P, Q and R given only 111 in P.

6.6   CORRECTING THE WORDS

It so happens that in the above example the word 'mah' or 'mah mah' corresponds more or less to a complete word. Here we raise the question of the way a child may learn to correct an utterance from baby talk to a real word. Take 'ball' or, phonetically /bol/. Say that the creature's nearest 'natural' approximation to this is 'boh'. Take again the PQR net and the learnt recognition of an image of a ball as 'boh' (say 010 in R, 110 in Q and 000 in P). Now, the parent in showing the ball says 'ball', which is a bit like 'boh' and sets up an association between P and Q

$$000 \qquad 111-$$

111 in Q being a bit like 110. The problem is that the creature does not 'know' what coding in R will produce 110 in Q – i.e. it does not know how to produce the right sound. But here too, it must trust to luck. As observers we know that 'ball' is in the creature's repertoire of sounds – we've heard other creatures do it – it would not be in the language otherwise.

So, all that has to happen is that the slight modification from 'boh' to 'ball' should happen at some time. The image of the ball will be recalled and the appropriate coding in R (say 011) has been learnt. Now the pattern

$$000 \qquad 110 \qquad 011$$

will become to firmly established state in the net, which means that the creature will have had its pronunciation corrected.

Many of us have, as children, seen people who are capable of rolling up their tongues from the sides inwards. This seems an impossible task until at some point we manage it – and then never forget it. Learning to speak must make quite a heavy call on such random but not unlikely events.

6.7   PREDICTION

By going back to the simple net of Fig. 6.2 we can illustrate that prediction is a capability that is not only additional to pattern completion but works hand in hand with it. To remove net idiosyncrasies from our argument, we assume that the net is slightly modified so that each neuron also receives an input from its own output. It may be shown that for this net any transition may be learnt without affecting the others. In larger nets this condition can be approached by increasing the input size of the neurons but not necessarily to the extent that each neuron 'sees' what every other neuron is doing.

Let 000 be the only trained stable state. Let some outside agency induce a 1 in the leftmost neuron and keep on putting it back should that neuron ever fire with a 0. Outside agency no. 2 now induces the following sequence whenever the 100 state is entered

$$100 \rightarrow 110 \rightarrow 111 \rightarrow 000$$

(000→000 exists already).

The state diagram is now shown in Fig. 6.8. Because the learnt sequence 100→110→111→000→000–mimics external events following 100, it can be said that 110→111→000→000 . . . is a prediction of 100. We can now use this property to show that our 'creature' can learn to call its mother when, say, hungry.

6.8   WANTING AND LEARNING TO ASK

Say that our creature is capable of getting hungry and that this is registered as a 1 in the leftmost bit as in the last three-neuron example. It is likely that such a signal would be linked innately to a crying reflex. This would bring the mother to the creature who would proceed to feed it. At the end of this the hunger will have been removed and the mother can leave. This is mirrored by the state sequence shown

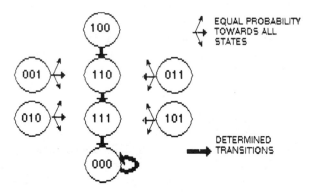

Fig. 6.8. Learning to predict.

in Fig. 6.8 if the centre bit is interpreted as 'the presence of the mother' and the rightmost bit as the sensation of the feeding implement (breast?) with 000 being a 'rest' or 'contented' state. Imagining now a juxtaposition of Figs 6.7 and 6.8, the centre bit of Fig. 6.8 could, in fact, be the three image bits of Fig. 6.7. The learnt sequence could still be as in Fig. 6.8, the hunger and the breast being merely other parts of the net.

Having learnt the likely sequence of events now simply leads to the situation where on getting hungry, the creature will run through the predictive sequence and, possibly replace some of the crying by saying 'mah' when the mother's mental image is present. Stepping to an anthropomorphic description, the creature has learnt that when hungry it is the mother who provides the feeding implement which leads to satisfaction. Also, the creature has earlier learnt to call 'mah' when it 'thinks' of mother so now it can call its mother when hungry.

Note that only actual, rather than mental feeding will lead to satisfaction, so that if the mother does not come, the system in Fig. 6.8 reverts to state 100 due to the continued presence of hunger. The process starts again and the creature tries to call for its mother again.

In general, the sequence

$$100 \rightarrow 110 \rightarrow 111 \rightarrow 000$$

could be divided up into 100 being the problem, 110 and 111 being intermediate steps and 000 being the solution and goal state.

So what we have shown for our fictitious creature, equipped only with four neurons, is that suitably structured neural nets with access to external inputs and outputs can learn to predict events as they occur in their environment and learn to 'know' what action (calling 'mah') is required of them to achieve the solution. So what we earlier labelled as being a simple task of memorizing turns out to have a reasonable processing structure at the neural level. In fact, most of the apparatus has now been explained to take a brief look at knowledge acquisition – the process we have said to involve branching.

6.9 BRANCHING AND PREDICTION

So far, the property of prediction was seen to reside in learning a sequence of states where an inner image of the first would lead to, or predict the last. The only missing ingredient is the branching effect. To discuss this imagine driving down a road R1, coming to a fork F. Taking the left fork leads to Acme town (A) via road R2, while taking the right fork goes to Blankville (B) via road R3. The vehicle in which our creature is situated can either be driven straight S, left L, or right R. It can also halt, H. Again it is equipped with a field for visual images, whether externally driven or internal, and another field which in this case is not related to inner images of utterances, but images of driving actions. Having 'learnt' the above routes by trial, we can show the state diagram that has been created. Instead of showing the firing patterns of the neurons we can now express ourselves entirely in terms of state diagrams labelled as follows: X, Y refers to X in the visual field and Y in the action field. The learnt state structure is shown in Fig. 6.9.

The branching occurs at the very first state where in the absence of a decision a mental run provides an uncertainty in the neuron which signifies L or R. The situation so far may be that if the real input is R1S the mental run can end in either H, A or H, B with equal probability. This, assuming a description of the neural trajectory could be extracted from the creature, represents the statement

> 'I know that if I am in RI, and drive straight I can either turn left when I reach the fork and end up in A or right and end up in B.'

While this fulfils our definition of knowledge acquisition it raises another question. How can the creature decide to go L or R (i.e. use its knowledge). In terms of formal logic this acquired knowledge must express itself as: A implies F, L; B implies F, R. Getting a conventional computer to extract such history from simply stored traces of the actions in Fig. 6.9 would be relatively easy. But it is not the way the brain does it, so we are under some obligation to postulate a neural mechanism that does this type of translation as an emergent property. This is not only an obligation in the pursuit of brain science, but also (and it may be worth restating) an engineering pursuit as the brain – given more complex inferences than those in the above example – operates much more efficiently than a conventional computer when it comes to learning. Many neural mechanisms could have the same effect, so here is one which is simple.

We again have to cheat a little since neuroscience fails to inform us. We assume that the fields of the neural net are not directly connected to specific inputs, but

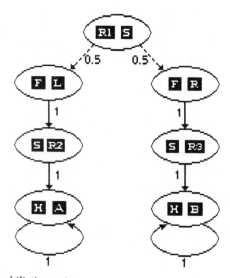

Fig. 6.9. Learnt probabilistic routes.

'fill up' as perceptual inputs come in. Figure 6.9 is now transformed into Fig. 6.10. Instead of creating chains of states in a narrow field we have only created two stable states which are distinguished by LA and RB, and are the same otherwise.

Now using 'd' for 'don't know', given say dd FL dddd will deliver

R1S FL R2S AH,

or more pertinently given

R1S dd dd AH

which effectively says: If I start in R1S and want to get to A where I halt what do I need to do? Pattern completion yields

R1S FL R2S AH

which effectively says: 'You have to turn left at the fork then drive straight along R2 to get to A where you must stop.' Whereas given R1S ('I am driving along R1, Straight') the system will deliver

R1S FF R2S AH

or

R1S FR R3S BH

with equal probability (. . . if you turn left . . . you will get to A).

This goes some way towards showing that neural, distributed memory schemes can deal with branching and so fulfil our definition of 'knowledge acquisition'. Now for the broadest aspects of learning: abstraction.

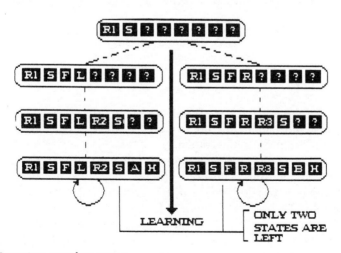

Fig. 6.10. Learning complete states.

6.10   HIGHER LEVELS OF LEARNING

There is no doubt that this is where we run into trouble with neural explanations. It may well be that even simple things like learning to count and learning to do arithmetic on numbers require the co-operative action of a wide variety of neural mechanisms where interaction does the trick. As Donald Norman (1985) points out, the science of neural nets (or parallel distributed processing as he and other workers in this field call it) has as yet not got to the stage where such general ideas may be framed.

There is no reason to believe that this is not possible, and to this end we will give an example in which neural nets might capture an abstraction, without explaining exactly how it gets there nor how it gets to be used – this is just not known. Perhaps a few speculations could be admitted later. The abstraction we tackle is 'A is greater than B'. Assume that a neural net such as shown in Fig. 6.11 is to represent this concept.

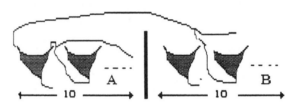

Fig. 6.11. 'A is greater than B?'

In this specific example we assume that there are twenty neurons equally divided into two fields. For the sake of being specific we assume that each neuron has four inputs. Quantities are represented as the number of 1s in each half. The extremes of

A is greater than B

and

B is greater than A

are with ten 1's in A and ten 0's in B and vice versa, respectively. These two can be learnt as stable states in an attempt to represent the concept. We first show that this amount of learning is inadequate.

Assume that just one 1 appears in the B group with all 1s in the A group. This implies that four neurons will receive inputs they have not been trained on. Assuming that they respond arbitrarily, on average half will get it right and half will get it wrong. This means that if the 1 in the 0 group is seen as an 'error' there will now be two errors. This effect propagates and instead of associating the original state with one of the taught ones, the net ends up in confusion.

But now assume that the net is taught on all the near misses represented by the twenty possible single errors. Clearly, the above no longer happens. Now take the example of five 1's in the A group and four 1's in the B group as an initial state. The question is what does the net do next and where does it end up? Take a neuron in the A group. Being in the majority group, we would see it as doing the correct thing were it to respond with a 1. There are five distinct conditions that the neurons will respond to correctly (with a 1) assuming that i_1, i_2, i_3, i_4 are the inputs to the neurons and we know that i_1 and i_2 are connected to the A group and i_3, i_4 to the B group. These are indicated in Table 6.3 with their probabilities.

Table 6.3 Input conditions to neurons which result is a correct response

i_1	i_2	i_3	i_4	*Probabilities*		
1	1	0	0	$0.5 \times 0.5 \times 0.6 \times 0.6$		$=0.09$
0	1	0	0	$0.5 \times 0.5 \times 0.6 \times 0.6$		$=0.09$
1	0	0	0	$0.5 \times 0.5 \times 0.6 \times 0.6$		$=0.09$
1	1	1	0	$0.5 \times 0.5 \times 0.4 \times 0.6$		$=0.06$
1	1	0	1	$0.5 \times 0.5 \times 0.4 \times 0.6$		$=0.06$
					Total	$=0.39$

The total in Table 6.3 means that about four out of the ten neurons will be 'properly' addressed and output 1. Of the remaining six, about half will output a 1 making a total of seven neurons on the A side outputting a 1. Similarly it may be calculated that on the B side only three neurons will output a 1. So the most likely event is that starting in a state such as

A   B

0101101010   0101110000

the next state will be something like

1101010111   0100010001

It is clear that this approaches one of the foundational training states. In fact, were one to do the calculations repeatedly we would discover that the foundational state could be reached within, on average, about six steps. A general analysis of this type of progression may be found in Aleksander (1988).

Taking an anthropomorphic view, an explanation of what has happened is the following:

1. The net was shown the correct example of 'A is greater than B' and 'B is greater than A';
2. The net has also shown some very near misses (all twenty of them);
3. Subsequently given any version of 'A is greater than B' and vice versa, the net

changes states, getting closer to and eventually reaching the defined standard state of 'A is greater than B';

4. Hence the net can 'tell' whether A is greater than B or B is greater than A by associating any one of the possible 2^{20} (10^7) patterns with the appropriate state after only having been shown 22 examples of these. This is an impressive emergent property!

So, in summary, the possibility of representing an abstraction in a neural net has been demonstrated. But this is only the first step on an enormously difficult road. Some of the difficulties have already been resolved. For example in Aleksander (1987) I have discussed the representation of parity, which is a notoriously difficult problem and requires the action of hidden neurons which form intermediate concepts on which the major concern is built. Also, in the same publication, it has been shown that the near misses may be automatically trained into the system through the use of noise.

6.11 EPILOGUE: THE FASCINATION AND THE CHALLENGE OF DISTRIBUTED MEMORY MODELS

Before the domination of cognitive science by the serial computer and, in particular, the design of models of cognition using formulations from artificial intelligence (AI), it was common for those interested in neural networks in the brain to work together with mathematicians and engineers. This is how the now-famous model of the neuron of McCulloch and Pitts (1943) was conceived. But AI changed much of that – being rule based – and practitioners saw neuronal arguments as being 'low-level' while neuroscientists could not express what they found in neural structures in terms of production rules or search trees which are so much a part of AI methodology. There was an over-reaction to Minsky and Papert's (1969) book on neural nets. They rightly showed the limitations of a narrow class of such systems; it remained for Hopfield (1982) to revive the interest in such systems, much of the current excitement being documented by Rumelhart and McClelland (1986). The contribution made by my colleagues and myself has, over the last twenty years, taken a very direct logical approach to the modelling of the neuron. This is reflected in this chapter. But independently we have discovered that while learning is at the centre of these systems (as opposed to the programming of rules), the distributed memory concept puts the word 'learning' under the microscope in a way that no other discipline has done before.

I have tried to convey some of this through discussing the limitations of learnt labelling as in WISARD, through higher forms of knowledge acquisition and learning of abstractions. But we have only scratched the surface – an enormous amount of work needs to be done to pursue in a precise and systematic manner, plausible, neural, distributed-memory architectures which reach the subtlest aspects of learning.

Artificial intelligence has so far not had an impact on engineered products. I feel that distributed memory methods on their own would suffer from the same drawback. But there might be considerable engineering benefit in bringing the two together – AI to handle logically based symbol processing, and distributed processing to handle the learning tasks. Whatever our aspirations for the competence of artificially intelligent systems, it may be worth remembering that even the greatest thinkers do their thinking over a distributed net equipped only with experiential knowledge gathered by learning.

6.12 REFERENCES

Aleksander, I. (1988) The logic of connectionist systems, in *Neural Computing Architectures* (ed. I. Aleksander), North Oxford Academic Publishers Ltd, London.

Alexander, I., Thomas, W. and Bowder, P. (1984) WISARD, a radical step forward in Pattern Recognition. *Sensor Review*, July, 120–4.

Hopfield, J. J. (1982) Neural networks and physical systems with emergent computational abilities, *Proceedings of the National Academy of Sciences, USA*, **79**, 2554–8, 1982.

McCulloch, W. S. and Pitts, W. (1943) A logical calculus of the ideas immament in nervous activity. *Bull. Math. Biophys.*, **5**, 115–133.

Minsky, M. and Papert, S. (1969) *Perceptions: An Introduction to Computational Geometry*, MIT Press, Boston, Mass.

Norman, D. A. (1986) Reflections on cognition and parallel distributed processing. In D. E. Rumelhart and J. L. McClelland (eds) Vol 2, pp. 531–46.

Piattelli-Palmerini, Massimo (ed.) (1980) *Language and Learning*, Routledge and Kegan Paul, London.

Rumelhart, D. E. and McClelland, J. L. (eds) (1986) *Parallel Distributed Processing*, Vols 1 and 2, MIT Press, Cambridge, Mass.

Part three

Automated discovery

7

Automated discovery

KENNETH HAASE

> 'Odd!' he repeated. 'The men who have advanced the
> theory of gravitation can practically be named on one
> hand! Aristotle, Galileo, Newton, Einstein, Hoyle – and
> now Colossus! This is NEW, Charles! Colossus has gone
> on where Hoyle left off over thirty years ago!' Fisher
> banged his fist on the desk, snatched up the roll of
> paper and waved it at Forbin. 'New! Do you hear? Do
> you realize what it means?'
>
> D. F. Jones, *Colossus: The Forbin Project*

Scientific discovery is the crossroads of two of our culture's great mystiques: the mystique of creativity and the mystique of scientific understanding. For practising scientists, the mystique of scientific understanding diminishes but the mystique of creativity – if anything – grows more pronounced. By attempting to build models and programs directed at the process of discovery, researchers are assailing this mystery with the tools of a constructive science; they are attempting to make programs which make discoveries.

The standard organization approach to machine learning places discovery at one end of a continuum whose opposite end is 'learning by being told'. What characterizes these computer programs which do 'discovery' can be seen in Fig. 7.1; various approaches to machine learning are ordered based on how much explicit 'organization' exists in the data they are given. Discovery programs – at one extreme – begin with completely unorganized data and from this seeming chaos produce order.

But the continuum of Fig. 7.1 is slightly misleading, because though the program is given as imput a disorganized mess, it is also given (in its implementation) a set of principles which implicitly organize this mess. Consider a simple 'discovery' program in the form of a robot which builds a map of a maze. While this robot may acquire a map which its creator could not foresee (a simple counter-example to the 'Computers can only know what they're told' fallacy), its creator did foresee the general nature of mazes and operations within them. In some sense, this embedded knowledge organized the mass of maze 'experience'

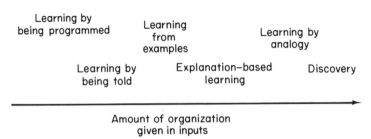

Fig. 7.1. If we organize learning programs by the amount of order given in their inputs, discovery programs are at one extreme of this continuum.

into structures which could be 'learned' by the program. Discovery programs usually have within them learning algorithms which are heuristically applied to potential organizing schemes.

In examining a discovery program, the important things to identify – outside of the technical innovations involved in its implementation – are the organizing principles by which the program imposes structure on unstructured inputs. As I survey some existing discovery programs in the rest of this chapter, I will try to make their organizing principles transparent.

In the sections which follow, I will present three sorts of discovery systems: programs which invent categories, programs which invent laws, and programs which invent domains.

Programs of the first sort take examples from a described domain and produce general categories which organize the example. I describe the GLAUBER program (Langley *et al.*, 1987) and the CLUSTER/2 program (Michalski and Stepp, 1983) as instances of this sort of program.

Programs of the second sort also take examples from a described domain but generate laws characterizing relations in the domain; these laws are generalized descriptions of phenomena in the domain. In describing the discovery of physical laws, I take my examples from the BACON programs (Langley *et al.*, 1987) devised at Carnegie-Mellon University by Pat Langley, Herbert Simon, Gary Bradshaw and Jan Zytkow. These programs each invent or rediscover fundamental physical laws from relevant experimental data.

Programs of the third sort begin with a described domain and – based on regularities or structure noted among examples in the domain – create new sorts of descriptions which constitute a new domain for the program. In this category, I will discuss Doug Lenat's AM and EURISKO programs, which perform discovery in mathematics and several other domains. I will also discuss my own CYRANO program, which began as a thoughtful reimplementation of AM and EURISKO.

For each program, I will briefly describe its representation (the form of its inputs and outputs and internal descriptions) and its control structure (the steps it takes in producing outputs from inputs). These descriptions will set the stage for discussing the organizing principles each program applies.

Before I begin presenting individual programs, it is worth while to make a point about discovery programs in general. In Haase (1986), I introduced the notion of a 'cycle of discovery' with a figure much like Fig. 7.2. The cycle of discovery reveals the constraint or requirement that a program be able to build on its own results. Without this capacity, no program can go beyond simple 'inductive learning' to full-blooded discovery. In Fig. 7.2, we see a discovery process which takes inputs described in a particular way and produces as outputs which constitute new modes of description for the given data. Ryzsard Michalski (1987) has recently introduced a similar distinction of 'closed-loop learning' and the BACON programs (as we shall see) also implement 'levels of description' for the phenomena they operate on. We also find in philosophy, the enchantingly similar notion of a 'hermeneutic circle' which underlies all the ways we (as rational creatures) understand or perceive the world.

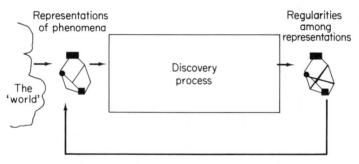

Fig. 7.2. The design of discovery programs is constrained by the cycle of discovery. A discovery program must not only be able to discover regularities or structure in a domain, it must be able to use those regularities to generate new inputs to the discovery process.

7.1   INVENTING CATEGORIES

The opening section of this chapter was an example in category application. I began by dividing learning programs along a continuum based on how much organization was present in their inputs. I then took one extrema of this continuum (discovery programs) and further divided it based on the 'outputs' of the program: whether it produced categorizations, law-like characterizations, or whole new domains of description.

The categorization presented in the introduction (like most categorizations) is fuzzy and overlapping: a program which discovered laws might also discover categories to which those laws applied; in turn, a program which discovered new domains might specify those domains in terms of categories or laws it had discovered. But having a categorization introduces terms and distinctions which allows us to concentrate on differences and similarities within or between categories. Categories also give intelligence much of its generality: methods or knowledge which have worked on past situations may well apply to future situations in the same category.

The general notion of a category requires little more than an applicable test and a collection of inferences from the test's result. In particular, a category need not be an abstract description of the properties possessed by a class of objects. For instance, we could form categories by mapping object descriptions into an *n*-dimensional space and specifying structures within that space; for instance, the spheres determined by distances from particular prototypes might define a collection of categories.

But in this chapter, I only examine programs which form precise categories; their definitions are characterizations of particular properties of the category's members or of particular sorts of relations in which the category's members participate. I begin with the GLAUBER program (Langley *et al.*, 1987) implemented at Carnegie-Mellon University, which learns simple chemical categories from examples of reactions; I then move on to the CLUSTER/2 program implemented at the University of Illinois by Ryzsard Michalski and Robert Stepp (1983).

7.1.1   The GLAUBER program

The GLAUBER program takes a set of event descriptions as inputs and organizes these events' constituent parts into categories which support the formation of general laws based on the descriptions. In this sense, GLAUBER is a law discovery program, but I focus on how GLAUBER creates categories supporting the expression of general laws.

Figure 7.3 illustrates a sequence of GLAUBER's invented categories and statements. It describes an example given in detail (Langley *et al.*, 1987). Each input has a type (e.g. REACTS) and a set of properties (e.g. INPUTS and OUTPUTS) which are each sets of terms (e.g. NaOH, KCl). From these inputs, GLAUBER produces a set of categories (e.g. ACID is the category containing the terms HCl, KCl) and a set of generalized laws expressed in terms of these categories (e.g. ACIDs and BASEs REACT to produce SALTs). A law is just like one of GLAUBER's inputs (having a type and properties) except that the elements filling the properties are now the general categories invented by GLAUBER.

GLAUBER produces its categories by selecting a type of input (for instance, REACTS) and picking one particular property and element (for instance, INPUTS and HCl) for that type of input. It then constructs classes based on the values taken by other properties (or other elements of the same property) when the selected property contains the selected element. If considering instances of REACTS with INPUTS containing HCl, GLAUBER would form the classes: 'Things I've seen react with HCl' and 'Things I've seen produced by HCl reactions'. With the inputs given in Fig. 7.3, these classes are {HCl, KCl} and {NaOH, KOH} respectively.

For a given set of inputs, there may be many sets of categories which GLAUBER

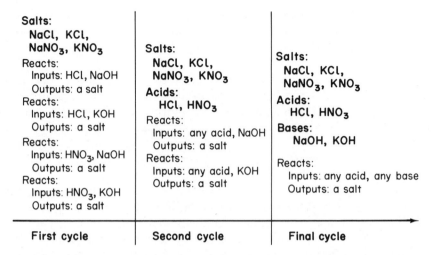

Fig. 7.3. GLAUBER begins with a single category and a set of reaction descriptions. It proceeds by generating new categories which allow the generalization of reaction descriptions to reaction laws.

could define; GLAUBER chooses the set whose categories are the largest (these categories will also cover the largest number of examples). Generated categories are included in laws by substituting categories for elements in observed events. This replacement is accompanied by a quantification of the category. If only one category is being introduced, the generalization is valid for every element of that category. If more than one category is being introduced, one of the replacements can be universal (holding for every element of the category) while the other must be existential (holding for only some elements of the category.

In the original data given to GLAUBER, the 'atomic' terms (NaCl, KOH, etc.) are (in some sense) already categories. The generalized forms of GLAUBER's observations are identical in form to the original observations; they can be used again as events for further category formation and law generalization. In this way, GLAUBER can proceed again to find categories and laws which organize and characterize its own generalizations. Here we see the cycle of discovery described in the introduction; the outputs of one stage of discovery provide inputs to the next.

For instance, to extract a fragment from Langley *et al.* (1987), suppose that GLAUBER were given the inputs in Fig. 7.3 with the right-hand sides (the products) already generalized to the category salts (perhaps by taste). GLAUBER would look at these and produce the single category acids by 'fixing' one input at NaOH and noting that the other input might be either HCl or HNO$_3$ (the same category is produced if we fix one input to KOH). When GLAUBER uses these terms to generalize the input events, it derives the general law that every acid combines with a particular substance to produce a salt. And with another iteration (fixing either an input as an acid or a product as a salt), GLAUBER forms the category bases consisting of KOH and NaOH, whose application in generalization yields the general law that any acid and base combine to produce a salt.

GLAUBER searches for category definitions which support the statement of general laws. In the sense presented in the introduction, the 'organizing principles' to which GLAUBER attends are co-occurrence in observed events. This co-occurrence leads to effective generalizations because a generalization tries to combine several instances based on co-occurring terms. GLAUBER's method of selecting these co-occurrences selects one particular as a focus and considers the co-occurrences among events containing it.

The next program I shall describe, CLUSTER/2, produces clusterings based on objects and their properties rather than events or relations involving the objects. This representation and GLAUBER's representation are reducible to each other, but the important point in GLAUBER is that the new categories are based on how terms relate, rather than simple properties of terms. But the simplicity of GLAUBER's representation may be a contrivance. One important part of scientific progress is determining precisely what constitutes events and relations; GLAUBER is given these things implicitly in its representation.

7.1.2   CLUSTER/2

The CLUSTER/2 program takes a collection of examples and produces a taxonomic organization which divides the examples into disjoint clusters at several levels.

CLUSTER/2's approach is called 'conceptual clustering' and can be contrasted with a rich literature on 'geometric clustering' which organizes objects into clusters based on distance in a similarity space. In contrast, CLUSTER/2 receives a set of symbolic descriptions and produces a set of abstract descriptions which organize the inputs into disjoint partitions. The generation of these descriptions is parameterized by various 'quality criteria' which constrain the search for an acceptable clustering.

The inputs given to CLUSTER/2 are either single inputs (called events) or more abstract descriptions which characterize whole classes of events. This generality permits CLUSTER/2's algorithm to be applied recursively to generate a taxonomic hierarchy; a first clustering produces a set of descriptions which can be further clustered; this clustering can also be clustered and so forth.

(a) The representation of CLUSTER/2

CLUSTER/2 stores events as sets of variable bindings; an event space is determined by a set of variables each of which accepts a declared range of values. A particular event specifies particular values for some or all of these variables.

For instance, if the event space is determined by variables colour (which must be one of red, blue or yellow), size (which must be one of small, medium, large or huge), and age (which must be an integer between 0 and 100), a large red octogenarian event would be described:

[colour = red] [size = large] [age = 80]

Abstract descriptions which specify parts of this event space are constructed by specifying sets of values the variables may take. The set of small red or green events older than 55 could be described:

[colour = red V green] [size = small] [age > 55]

CLUSTER/2 incorporates a 'learning from examples' module which generates abstract descriptions from sets of examples. This module works by determining the most specialized description which satisfies all the examples and then generalizing this description.

(b) The algorithm

The algorithm used by CLUSTER/2 is complicated and this section presents only a sketch of it. A more detailed exposition (with examples) by the authors may be found in Michalski and Stepp (1983) and readers interested in theoretical background should also consider Michalski (1980).

CLUSTER/2 consists of two modules: a clustering module and a hierarchy-building module. The clustering module takes a set of input events/descriptions and a number of clusters (*k*) to produce. Figure 7.4 illustrates how the hierarchy-building module applies the clustering module to generate a hierarchy of descriptions. The clustering module is applied over a range of *k* values to find a best clustering of the input data. The abstract descriptions characterizing this clustering then become data for a further clustering whose terms are the clusters of the original space.

The basic loop of the clustering algorithm is shown in Fig. 7.5. Beginning with a set of *k* seed events, the loop produces a disjoint clustering around these seed events and then evaluates this clustering. The result of the evaluation is used to 'hill climb' in the search space of cluster seeds; as long as the quality of the clustering keeps improving, the algorithm selects new seeds from the centre of the defined clusters; however, if the quality of the clustering drops off, the algorithm picks 'border events' far from the centres of the current clustering. The algorithm terminates on a threshold of clustering quality; if some generated clustering surpasses a particular standard of quality, the clustering is returned as a result.

A clustering is generated from a set of seed events by first characterizing the differences distinguishing each seed event from every other seed event. These clusterings are called the 'stars' of each seed event against the others; a first-pass algorithm constructs a potentially overlapping clustering which is pruned by a second process. This algorithm uses a 'learning by examples' module to generate its cluster descriptions.

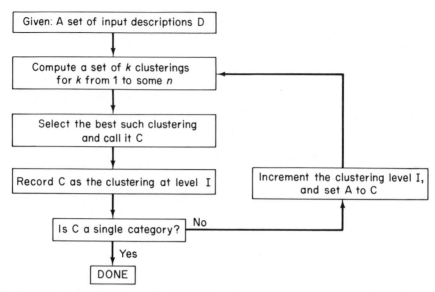

Fig. 7.4. The loop of the hierarchy-building module in CLUSTER/2 recursively applies the clustering module to higher and higher level descriptions. It begins by constructing a clustering (a set of abstraction descriptions) at the lowest level and then constructs a new clustering at the next higher level. In this way, CLUSTER/2 closes the cycle of discovery.

The pruning process constructs a disjoint clustering by removing all conflicting events (events in more than one cluster) and then restoring each removed event (one at a time) to a single cluster. The cluster awarded the event is chosen to enhance the quality of the overall clustering.

(c) Judging clustering quality

The criterion used to produce the pruned clustering is the same as used to judge the final clustering. This measure of clustering quality is a parameterized function (called the LEF criterion) which takes into account the following properties of an abstract clustering:

1. The fit between the clustering and the data;
2. The simplicity of the cluster descriptions;
3. How different the clusters are from one another;
4. The number of parameters which occur (with different constraints) in every cluster;
5. The dimensionality of the clustering. This is too involved for detailed description here, but it can be roughly summarized as the amount of information necessary to place an event firmly in one cluster or another.

The clustering module takes a set of parameters determining how much each of

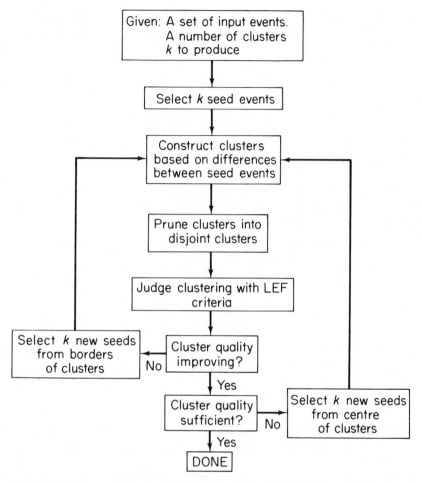

Fig. 7.5. CLUSTER/2 generates a particular clustering of size k by searching through a space of 'seeds' for clusters. One can think of this process as attempting to find the right 'representative' elements for an effective clustering. The steps in this search space are based on previous clusterings; if cluster quality is improving, new seeds near the centre of the current clusters are chosen; if cluster quality is diminishing, new seeds near the borders of the current clusters are selected.

these properties matters in the final clustering to be produced. Based on these parameters, a 'score' for a particular clustering can be generated and various clusterings compared to one another based on this score.

These comparisons guide CLUSTER/2's search through 'seed-space'. If a newly produced clustering is worse than the last clustering produced, new seed events are chosen at the edges of the current cluster. If the newly produced clustering improves on the last clustering, new seeds are chosen from near the 'centre' of the new clustering. The 'edges' and 'centre' of a category are determined by a syntactic distance function. In practice, some conservatism is introduced by only choosing border events when the cluster quality has been consistently declining.

7.1.3   Conclusions about category discovery

We have seen two somewhat different approaches to category discovery. GLAUBER formed categories based on perspicuous ways of casting event descriptions as laws. CLUSTER/2 formed clusters based on the properties of individual events in an abstract space of semantic descriptions. The 'organizing principles' of GLAUBER were based on the transformation – by straightforward generalization – of particular instances into general laws. CLUSTER/2, on the other hand, was driven by an emphasis on describing differences between instances and consolidating those differences into disjoint clusters. CLUSTER/2 also emphasized forming taxonomies of descriptions; keeping clusters disjoint is necessary for maintaining the fidelity of these taxonomies.

Both of the programs described here make an effort to close the cycle of discovery described in the introduction. The GLAUBER program produces new categories which can be applied to generalize events into 'half-laws' which provide input for further category formation. The CLUSTER/2 program is able to cluster not only concrete events, but also the abstract descriptions it produces. Both of these programs discover or invent categorizations which can be used again in further efforts at category formation.

7.2   INVENTING LAWS

If categories are the way we divide the universe, laws might be described as the way the universe connects our categories. Of course, this is over-simplified: the process of specifying categories is not independent of the process of discovering laws; indeed, it is often the case (as we saw in GLAUBER) that the formation of categories and the specification of laws go hand in hand.

This section describes programs which invent or discover laws. Broadly construed, a law enables an inference about the world; a gravity law allows me to predict what will happen if I leap out of the window, a homicide law allows me to predict what will happen if I push a troublesome guest out the window. In both cases, laws are applied deductively to generate consequences. In the first case, the law is presumably 'in the world' and acquired inductively; in the second case, the law is created socially and acquired (one hopes) from the culture. There are other sorts of laws, but these two classes emphasize the deductive application of laws of any sort. In the programs described below, I will only examine programs which discover physical laws of the first sort.

In talking about the discovery or invention of laws, I will use examples from the BACON series of programs, developed at Carnegie-Mellon University by Pat Langley, Herbert Simon, Gary Bradshaw and Jan Zytkow. These programs emerged for the same research programme as the GLAUBER program described above. As with the GLAUBER program, the BACON program is described with detail and clarity in Langley *et al.* (1987). Much of the description in the sections that follow summarizes the detailed examples in this text.

The BACON program reproduces some of the great discoveries of science, ranging from Kepler's laws of planetary motion to Snell's law of optical refraction to Black's formulation of the law of specific heat. In describing BACON, I begin with how an early version of BACON rediscovered Kepler's laws. I then describe how a later version repaired some flaws in the earlier version. This new version is then the basis for describing how BACON rediscovers Snell's laws of optical refraction.

7.2.1 BACON's architecture

The representation of BACON is quite similar to the representation we described for CLUSTER/2; its essential objects consist of 'data clusters' (which, despite the similarity of name, are quite different from CLUSTER/2's derived clusters) which specify a set of properties (variables in CLUSTER/2); for instance, a data cluster describing the Earth's orbit might look like this:

Orbit of: Earth
Distance (D): 1.0 (in astronomical units)
Period (P): 12 (in months)
D/P: 0.0833
D^2/P: 0.0833
D^3/P^2: 0.0069

Properties are of two basic sorts: independent terms and dependent terms. The independent terms are the data originally given the program: 'Orbit of', 'Distance', and 'Period' in the example. Independent terms are combinations of other terms: D/P, D^2/P and D^3/P^2 are such terms. BACON's law-finding activities consist of noticing regularities among defined terms (independent or dependent) and defining new dependent terms based on these regularities. In much the same way GLAUBER sought categories with would allow the simple expression of qualitative laws, BACON seeks definitions of dependent terms which allows the simple expression of quantitative laws.

The control structure of BACON is a 'production rule' system (much like modern expert systems), where all the rules applicable to a given situation are collected and one rule selected. This rule is applied to the situation to produced a new situation which may differ by the specification of new attributes (for instance, filling in values of a dependent term like D/P) or the definition of new dependent terms (for instance, defining a term like D/P from D and P). After a rule has been applied, the rule selection and execution process begins again with the new situation. The selection of which rule to run in BACON is managed by a simple algorithm based on 'newness' of data in the situation; a rule which is applicable to recent changes in the situation (for instance, the filling in of dependent terms) will fire before rules which apply to older elements of the situation.

While production rules are used to manage the collection of independent values from the user and the computation of dependent terms, my descriptions will assume that these happen 'in the background' so as to focus on BACON's definition of new terms and identification of regularities.

7.2.2   Analysing planetary motion

Table 7.1 shows data which BACON might use to rediscover Kepler's third law of planetary motion; the data given is artificially exact, but BACON has some capacities for dealing with noisy data. Kepler's third law amounts (more or less) to the assertion that the D^3/P^2 column of Table 7.1 is constant; BACON's process of discovery involves inventing the terms D/P, D^2/P, etc. and noting this regularity.

BACON has one set of heuristics for discovering laws and another for inventing new terms; the heuristics for discovering laws identify constant and linear relations between terms:

IF the value of a term T is C in all data clusters,
    THEN infer (propose the law) that T is always C.
IF two terms Y and X are linearly related with slope M and intercept B
        across all data clusters,
    THEN infer (propose the law) that $Y = MX + B$, for constant M and B.

BACON's heuristics for forming new terms compare how terms vary with respect to one and other:

IF the term X rises whenever the term Y rises,
    THEN define the term X/Y.
IF the term X rises whenever the term Y falls,
    THEN define the term $X*Y$.

Table 7.1   The rediscovery of Kepler's third law consists of deriving the term D^3/P^2 in the table and noting that this term is constant

Planet	Distance (D)	Period (P)	D/P	D²/P	D³/P²
Mercury	0.387	2.889	0.134	0.0518	0.0069
Venus	0.724	7.39246	0.0979	0.0709	0.0069
Earth	1.0	12.0	0.0833	0.0833	0.0069
Mars	1.524	22.5766	0.0675	0.1029	0.0069
Jupiter	5.199	142.253	0.0365	0.19	0.0069
Saturn	9.539	353.538	0.027	0.2574	0.0069

These rules only apply if no regularities (such as linear or constant relations) are observed for the relevant terms. Also (though this is not relevant to the Kepler example) the terms 'rise' and 'fall' are taken in terms of their absolute values.

In applying these to the Kepler data, there appears to be no obvious law involving D and P directly (no constant or linear relations); however, it is noted that D and P seem to rise together. This leads to the definition of the term D/P which (BACON notices) falls as D rises; BACON thus defines D^2/P. Still, no obvious laws emerge, but it notes that its two derived terms run in opposite directions; D^2/P rises as D/P falls. Based on this observation, it defines a third term $(D^2/P)(D/P)$ or D^3/P^2. The term turns out to be a constant, yielding Kepler's third law.

In sketching this progression, we have gone straight to the target. The reader may be asking: why did the program not waste time defining $(D/P)P = D$, since D/P also fell as P rose. The answer is that in defining products and ratios, BACON is careful not to define terms equivalent to terms already defined. One important part of any discovery program is a sort of 'common sense' about what are useful or useless formulations. And in any case, this recursion could only proceed for one level, since the linear relation between $(D/P)P$ and D would have halted any further definition of terms using $(D/P)P$.

7.2.3 Closing the cycle of discovery

Examining the approach above with the 'cycle of discovery' in mind, we note one particular deficit; the program can infer that a linear or constant relation exists, but it cannot use that inference to define new terms. For instance, there might be certain situations where a linear relation exists and we would like the slope of that relation to become a new dependent term. In the scenario above, this deficit is revealed when dealing with more than two independent terms; since the approach above cannot say 'X and Y are linearly related when Z is constant', no complicated relations between more than two terms can be discovered.

Only the earliest versions of BACON suffer from this deficit; later versions introduce two innovations which resolve the problem. The first innovation is to close the cycle of discovery by introducing 'levels of description' at which regularities at one level of data become dependent terms at the next level of data. In order for these new dependent terms ever to be anything but constant, it is necessary to recognize regularities (constant terms and linear relations) in subsets of terms; if a linear relation or constant relation held for all values of all terms, it would not be interesting to define a regular term out of it.

BACON recognizes regularities in subsets of terms by an exhaustive search of term groupings; if the terms it is given are X, Y and Z, then it looks for regularities among X and Y for various Z, among X and Z for various Y, and among Y and Z for various X. These regularities each specify some term or terms which become dependent terms at the next level of description. So if Z is constant when X has some value, Z is carried to the next level; if X and Y are linearly related for some fixed Z, the slope and intercept of this linear relation are defined as new dependent terms on the next level.

This exhaustive search might be quite expensive, but its cost is ameliorated by using regularities discovered for some set of fixed values as expectations for other sets. When a linear relation between X and Y is discovered for $Z = Z_1$, it is expected for $Z = Z_2$, Z_3, etc. Having expectations about regularities greatly simplifies the search for laws in other contexts.

This extension to BACON closes the cycle of discovery we mentioned in the introduction; BACON's discovery of regularities provide the basis for a new level of description. The addition of levels of description to BACON enables the discovery of laws relating an arbitrary number of quantitative terms. In the next section, we consider how these mechanisms are extended to deal with qualitative terms.

7.2.4   Snell's law of refraction

In rediscovering Kepler's laws, BACON invented terms and noticed regularities among real-valued properties of 'objects' represented as data clusters. In this respect, the BACON program is 'just' doing sophisticated equation discovery: heuristically finding equations which fit some given data. In this respect, the inputs and outputs of the BACON program are entirely quantitative. However, BACON is not limited to this sort of performance. In this section, I show how BACON can deal with a mix of qualitative and quantitative descriptions to hypothesize intrinsic quantitative properties to go with particular qualitative inputs.

BACON's qualitative descriptions involve 'nominal' properties which take a fixed set of symbolic values instead of arbitrary numeric quantities. For instance, in the Kepler example above, the 'Orbit of' property of a data cluster took a range of values: Mercury, Venus, Earth, Mars, etc. BACON discovers 'intrinsic' properties of certain nominal values; these intrinsic properties are values for certain terms which are always associated with particular nominal values. For instance, BACON would notice that the term D is constant for fixed values of the 'Orbit of' property; thus, D is an intrinsic property of the various values this property may take.

The recognition of intrinsic properties falls naturally out of the search process in the 'closed cycle' version of BACON. In its search, BACON looks for regularities among some subset of terms within a context where all the other terms are fixed. When there are no numerical relations holding among a subset of quantitative terms, BACON proposes various intrinsic terms connecting qualitative terms with quantitative values. This is equivalent to saying 'Term A has the numeric value X because Term B has the symbolic value Y'; this claim, however, is limited to the context within which the intrinsic term was defined. In order to use intrinsic terms in perspicuous laws, BACON must generalize these definitions.

BACON's criterion for generalization has to do with explainability; an intrinsic term T is carried into a new context if the values in the new context are linearly related with the values in the old context. Suppose that T is an intrinsic term for values of D (a numerical term) corresponding with particular values for N (a symbolic term); if in a new context, the values for D are linearly related to the values of D in the old context, the term T is transferred to the new context with values from the old context. This constraint means that the difference between the contexts is 'explainable' by a linear relation. And once the term is generalized into a new context, the slope of this linear relation becomes a new dependent term alongside it.

For example, consider BACON's rediscovery of Snell's law of optical refraction, again taken from Langley *et al.* (1987). Snell's law describes an experimental arrangement like Fig. 7.6; Snell's law describes the equality of the ratios $\sin A_1/\sin A_2$ (the sines of the angles of incidence) and i_1/i_2 (of the refractive indices (i_1 and i_2) of the juxtaposed materials). BACON begins with the experimental data in Table 7.2 and notes a linear relation between the two sine terms when Medium$_2$ is one particular material; at the second level of description, this relations slope (the intercept is zero) becomes a new dependent term and an intrinsic term n_2 is associated with Medium$_2$ and based on the slope of the sines.

Though this intrinsic term is defined in a context where Medium$_1$ is always vacuum, BACON notes that changing Medium$_1$ prompts only a linear change in its values; based on this, it generalizes the intrinsic term, producing the second-level description of Table 7.3. The slope of this linear relation becomes a new dependent term $(\sin A_1)/(n_2 \sin A_2)$ which again (as with the original angle of sines) seems to yield no law-like regularities. This leads BACON to define another intrinsic term n_1 associated with Medium$_1$.

Here, BACON assumes that intrinsic terms whose symbolic associates are of the same type (e.g. mediums) will have the same values. The new term n_1 has the same values as n_2, but at a higher level of description given in Table 7.4. The new

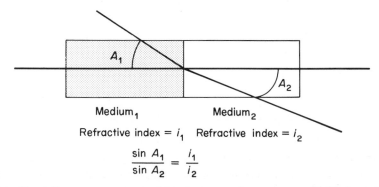

Fig. 7.6. The following experimental arrangement demonstrates Snell's law. For two materials with refractive indices i_1 and i_2 and an incident ray whose angle is A_1, the refracted ray will have an angle A_2 such that $\sin A_1/\sin A_2 = i_1/i_2$.

Table 7.2   In rediscovering Snell's law, BACON begins with the data in this table. The sin A_1 and sin A_2 terms are both contrivances that later versions of BACON can do without. (*Note:* The sine funtion was offset to range from 0 to 2 rather than -1 to 1.)

				$\dfrac{\sin A_1}{\sin A_2}$
Medium$_1$	Medium$_2$	sin A_1	sin A_2	
Vacuum	Vacuum	0.500	0.500	1.00
Vacuum	Vacuum	0.707	0.707	1.00
Vacuum	Vacuum	0.866	0.866	1.00
Vacuum	Water	0.500	0.665	0.75
Vacuum	Water	0.707	0.940	0.75
Vacuum	Water	0.866	1.152	0.75
Vacuum	Oil	0.500	0.735	0.68
Vacuum	Oil	0.707	1.039	0.68
Vacuum	Oil	0.866	1.273	0.68

Table 7.3   BACON synthesizes the new level of description based on assuming that the ratio sin A_1/sin A_2 is intrinsically related to the first medium in the experiment

		$\dfrac{\sin A_1}{\sin A_2}$		$\dfrac{\sin A_1}{n_2 \sin A_2}$
Medium$_1$	Medium$_2$		n_2	
Vacuum	Vacuum	1.00	1.00	1.00
Vacuum	Water	0.75	0.75	1.00
Vacuum	Oil	0.68	0.68	1.00
Water	Vacuum	1.33	1.00	1.33
Water	Water	1.00	0.75	1.33
Water	Oil	0.90	0.68	1.33
Oil	Vacuum	1.47	1.00	1.47
Oil	Water	1.11	0.75	1.47
Oil	Oil	1.00	0.68	1.47

and unexplained term (sin A_1)/(n_2 sin A_2) is also brought to this level, where BACON (as in the Kepler example) notes that n_2 rises while (sin A_1)/(n_2 sin A_2) falls. This leads to the definition of the term (n_1 sin A_1)/(n_2 sin A_2) which turns out to be constant. This law-like relation – given n_1 and n_2 as the reciprocals of refractive indices i_1 and i_{12} – is Snell's law.

Table 7.4 BACON synthesizes another level of description by assuming that there is an identical intrinsic term connected to Medium$_2$ as Medium$_1$

Medium$_1$	n	$\dfrac{\sin A_1}{n_2 \sin A_2}$	$\dfrac{n_1 \sin A_1}{n_2 \sin A_2}$
Vacuum	1.00	1.00	1.00
Vacuum	0.75	0.75	1.00
Vacuum	0.68	1.47	1.00

7.2.5 The invention of terms

In inventing terms which are not strict functions of observables, BACON imposes a certain structure on its experimental situation. This structure implies that objects have properties which 'mysteriously' affect certain experimental phenomena. But this is not any sort of flaw in BACON; it is what scientists do. Continuing in this spirit, BACON.5, the latest version of BACON, goes further with mechanisms for proposing terms which correspond to particular sorts of theories.

For instance, the example above made the assumption that intrinsic properties of the same 'type' have the same value. This would run into problems whenever there were two intrinsic properties of an object which interacted. BACON.5 does without the same-type/same-values assumption by explicitly defining new terms analogous to defined terms and checking if a symmetry exists between those terms. The definition of analogous terms also allows BACON.5 to do without the awkward use of sine functions as experimental inputs; instead, synthesized terms based on the ratio of physical distances (which are equivalent to sine terms) are used to make the discovery.

BLACK, a further result of work on BACON, defines theoretical conservation terms in order to generate conservation theories. In the same manner, the definition of new terms carries with it the definition of theories. In programs like these, an important place to look for 'organizing principles' is in the definition of new terms, for they reflect the biases of the theory-making process.

7.2.6 Conclusions about law discovery

We have seen the BACON program rediscovering many fundamental physical laws and properties; it is quite impressive that its simple mechanisms can discover so many laws. We also had an opportunity to see explicitly the organizing principles it applied in making its discoveries. In rediscovering Kepler's laws, it searched for divisors, products, and linear or constant relations among experimental data. With Snell's law, the notion that some numeric properties might be intrinsic to certain physical materials was explicitly proposed and tested. And we saw – in brief presentation – how more advanced versions of BACON explicitly seek symmetry or conservation in experiments by defining appropriate theoretical terms. The same mechanism – defining theoretical terms – is also used to attempt the formulation of conservation laws.

But by choosing famous examples from the history of science, the developers of BACON leave themselves open to the question: 'Is this what scientists really do?' It is curious that the designers of BACON, who stand out as experimentalists *par excellence* in artificial intelligence (AI), should so downplay the role of experiment design in their 'implementation' of science. The experimental 'inputs' given to BACON did not come to the scientists *ex nihilo*, but were the results of many failed apparati, sloppy metaphorical models, and extractions from the unscientific disorder of everyday life.

While the developers of BACON address these issues to some degree in Langley *et al.* (1987), it remains that BACON's discoveries appear to have much of the 'discovery' leached out and embedded in the experimental situations they are given. And then we may wonder 'Is this what progress in science was really like?'

In terms of the long-term progress of science questions like 'what questions do we ask?' and 'what do we count as answers?' count at least as strongly as any particular experimental results. As regards the 'truth' or 'accuracy' of scientific claims, particular results certainly matter; but as regards the long-term progress of science, these other questions are at least as important.

For today's 'hard' sciences, these questions and answers are embedded (partially) in the BACON program and their codification is an impressive achievement. But for the developing sciences of the past, these were open issues and their resolution arose as much from the dialogue with philosophers and mathematicians as from particular scientific results.

While these arguments suggest that BACON-like systems are not nearly complete scientists, BACON's impressive performance points to an important position for BACON as an assistant to scientists. It is easy to imagine programs like BACON as participants in the community of scientists, suggesting patterns and regularities which fit existing ways of organizing and casting scientific laws. The development and maintenance of such programs might well become a standard scientific activity, as central as publishing reports or providing experimental descriptions or samples to colleagues.

7.3 INVENTING DOMAINS

In the previous sections, we examined programs where the 'success criterion' was fairly well established: in GLAUBER, the program sought simple generalizations of events into laws; in CLUSTER/2 the program tried to organize objects disjointly with similarly simple and perspicuous definitions; in the BACON programs, there were descriptions of physical phenomena – experimental data – which needed to be described by simple mathematical relations.

The programs we examine in this section have much fuzzier notions of success. Part of the problem is that these programs invent – along with laws, categories and operations – new standards for success. For instance, Douglas Lenat's AM program (Lenat, 1976, 1982a) discovers regularities among operations on set-like structures; but the program's largest leap is defining new classes of structures where the standards of regularity are different. (And as we shall see, this changing of standards was crippling to many of the program's mechanisms.)

There is a sense in which talk of 'inventing domains' is merely a matter of perspective; it is possible to look at any of these programs as searching in a space of definitions using a criterion based on definitions previously generated or provided. But while this view of 'discovery as search' has its value, it suffers from the same super-generality as the characterization of computational processes as Turing machines. Speaking of 'inventing domains' adds useful structure to this search in a way that reduces its explosive potential. In particular, an invented domain is taken as 'primitive' in a way which changes the standards by which new definitions will be judged.

In discussing 'domain invention', my starting-point will be Lenat's AM program; it will remain a theme in my descriptions of the EURISKO and CYRANO programs, both of which were developed as successors to AM. The AM program begins in a domain of operations on set-like structures and invents the domain of arithmetic; from this basis of arithmetic it then invents some basic definitions in number (divisibility) theory.

The EURISKO program – also developed by Lenat – applied AM's methods to several domains, including the development of discovery programs (Lenat, 1983a,b). It was hoped that this self-application would remedy some of AM's shortcomings; unfortunately, this did not happen and many researchers in the field have been attempting both autopsy and revival (Lenat and Brown, 1984; Ritchie and Hannah, 1984; Haase, 1986).

My own CYRANO program was developed as part of such an effort; its primary domain is similar to AM's, but its methods and architecture are significantly different. An earlier implementation of CYRANO was much closer to Lenat's AM and EURISKO programs; experiences with this program led to many of the general observations of this section (and indeed, of this chapter). Work on CYRANO is still in progress; the description below offers a snapshot of an evolving program.

7.3.1   AM, an A____ M____

The expansion of the acronym AM is lost in relative antiquity; it has been variously suggested as 'Automated Mathematician' or 'Amateur Mathematician', but while that is in doubt, its reported results make it seminal in the history of AI. Given an initial description of set-like constructs and operations between them, AM innovations include:

1. Invention of the cardinal numbers;
2. Invention of arithmetic operations of addition, subtraction, multiplication and integral square root;
3. Invention of 'prime numbers';
4. The unique factorization of integers;
5. Goldbach's conjecture.

All of AM's work was empirical; it never produced proof of its claims. It 'merely' formed definitions it found interesting and used these definitions as a new inputs for the discovery process. Sometimes in defining new concepts, it 'proved' properties of its new definitions, but after being defined, the concept and its interaction with other concepts were only examined empirically.

In describing AM, I will begin (as with the other programs I have described) with a brief sketch of its representation and control structure. With this as background, I will present three 'highlights' from a 'good run' of the AM program: the discovery of cardinality, the invention of (the concept Lenat called) number, and the discovery and definition of prime numbers.

(a) AM's architecture

The basic representation of AM was quite similar to that of both CLUSTER/2 and BACON; AM's representations are CONCEPTS with particular PROPERTIES. In various versions of AM, these PROPERTIES were organized further into slots possessing facets, but I will refer to them simply as properties. For instance, an operation like APPEND might be represented by the APPEND-OPERATION concept with slots for IMPLEMENTATION, DOMAIN, RANGE, USED-IN-DISCOVERIES, etc.

Concepts are assigned numeric worths between 0 and 999; these worths are increased or lowered as concepts are found interesting or uninteresting by AM. Interestingness depends on a variety of factors; empirical regularities can make a concept interesting, as can increased interestingness of concepts created from or used to create a concept.

AM's control structure specifies TASKS which apply particular operations (like FILL-IN, EXAMINE, etc.) to particular properties of particular concepts. The worths of concepts are used to provide tasks with priorities; tasks are executed from a queue based on their priority and these priorities are updated with each task execution. A task is limited in the resources it may apply; if a task runs out of allotted memory or computation time, it is aborted.

AM's starting domain consisted of set-like concepts including sets, ordered sets, bags (unordered collections with multiple occurrences), and lists (ordered bags). AM's initial domain also had a variety of operations on and between these structures; structures could be intersected, unioned, compared and so forth.

New concepts were defined by AM using a variety of operators on operators. For instance, the COMPOSE operator-operator would take two established operators and compose their operation; for given operations f and g, COMPOSE defines $h(x) = f(g(x)))$. The COALESCE operator-operator takes an operation on two arguments (e.g. $f(x, y)$) and produces an operation on a single argument which applies the first operation to the single input twice (e.g. $g(x) = f(x, x)$).

The AM program has the virtue of being among the most documented and most criticized programs in AI. Lenat's thesis was a voluminous detailed work which gave many glimpses into the inner workings of AM; unfortunately, these glimpses were taken from instances of a developing program and the resulting document suffers from inconsistencies. Ritchie and Hannah (1984) call for more methodological approaches to AI research and heavily criticize AM's presentation as an example. Though their points are well taken, it is ironic that if Lenat had not attempted so detailed a presentation (unusual at the time), there would have been little to criticize.

(b) Discovering cardinality

AM was initially given the operation OBJECT-EQUAL for comparing two structures; an English-language version of this operation's implementation appears in Table 7.5. Much of AM's power came from its ability at examining and manipulating definitions just like this one; AM was an automatic programmer of significant power. In applying the comparison of Table 7.5 AM found (empirically) that very few pairs of objects passed the test; this suggested generalizing the definition by removing the italicized section and creating the definition of Table 7.6. This new definition – which Lenat renamed SAME-SIZE – is equivalent to the notion of comparing the cardinalities or sizes of two sets.

In terms of AM's tasks and representations, the episode above began with AM executing a task to FILL-IN the EXAMPLES of OBJECT-EQUAL. When executing a task of CHECKing these EXAMPLES of OBJECT-EQUAL, AM noticed their

Table 7.5 This implementation of OBJECT-EQUAL was transformed by AM into a definition of cardinality

X and Y are the EQUAL **if** either:
>   X and Y are the same primitive element
> **or**
>   X and Y are both empty structures
> **or**
>   X and Y are both non-empty structures
>   **and**
>   *the first elements of both structures are EQUAL*
>   **and**
>   when these first elements are removed, the resulting structures are EQUAL

Table 7.6 By removing the italicized condition of Table 7.5, AM invents a definition which checks if two structures are the same size; this is the notion of cardinality

X and Y are the SAME-SIZE if either:
>   X and Y are the same primitive element
>
> **or**
>
>   X and Y are both empty structures
>
> **or**
>
>   X and Y are both non-empty structures
>   **and**
>   when these first elements are removed, the resulting structures are the SAME-SIZE

empirical rarity; this led to a task of FILL-IN the GENERALIZATIONS of OBJECT-EQUAL. This final task – applying AM's programming expertise – produced SAME-SIZE.

(c) Defining 'number'

AM's CANONIZE operator-operator produced canonical representations for comparison operators. Presented with a comparison, the CANONIZE operator found (or implemented) another operator which mapped any two objects passing the comparison into the same object. One of AM's first actions on the newly defined SAME-SIZE comparison was to apply CANONIZE to it; the result was a function which iterated over a structure and produced a bag with one element (the symbol T) for each element in the original structure. This function transformed any structure into a BAG-OF-Ts corresponding to the structures size; Lenat renamed BAG-OF-Ts to NUMBERS and the canonicalization function (which AM had called CANONICALIZE-SAME-SIZE) to STRUCTURE-SIZE.

With the definition of number, we see the construction of new 'domains' which characterizes AM, EURISKO and CYRANO. Given this new concept, AM quickly defined the basic operations of arithmetic by carrying APPEND and DIFFERENCE over to its new representation. Certain meta-operators applied to these new operations constructed definitions for TIMES, DOUBLING, SQUARING and so forth. With these definitions, AM advanced its explorations to the domain of arithmetic.

(d) Discovering the prime numbers

One of AM's meta-operations was inversion of operations; as implemented, this usually produced an inefficient 'blind search' for arguments which produced certain values. Experimentally, AM inverted the TIMES operation to get a 'ways to divide' operation; the output of this inverted operation was a set of BAGs of products. Based on the nature of its outputs, AM decided to compose this inverted times operation with the UNION operation to produce an operation which Lenat called DIVISORS.

This implementation was so horribly slow (due to the blind search AM had implemented) that AM asked for a more efficient implementation. Lenat provided it with one and AM proceeded to consider special cases of the DIVISORS operation; in particular it defined classes of numbers with zero, one, two or three divisors. The definition of numbers with two divisors was eventually renamed prime numbers by Lenat. (Strictly speaking, it was really 'all prime numbers but one'.)

Why did AM form these particular concepts? Why did it not form the concept of numbers with 213 divisors? The answer lies in AM's notion of worth or interestingness. DIVISORS was interesting because it was related to the inverse of a very interesting operation TIMES and TIMES was interesting because – as AM ran – it had defined TIMES four different ways (each of the four ways involved different sorts of structural recursion and iteration). Small sets became interesting because early on – when first looking at sets and simple structures – AM isolated the extreme cases of sets by taking the first few unwindings of their recursive definition (e.g. a set is either the empty set or the addition of one element to a set). Combining these interesting concepts coming from different directions, AM defined these classes of numbers based on their number of divisors. Once defined, primes were considered particularly interesting because (through a somewhat obscure path) numbers with three divisors were always perfect squares (a concept it had defined earlier in exploring TIMES) and their square roots were always numbers with two divisors. Thus, NUMBERS-WITH-2-DIVISORS was declared interesting and was brought to the attention of Lenat, who renamed it PRIMES.

After defining the notion of prime numbers, AM went on to conjecture – based on empirical analysis – the unique factorization of integers, Goldbach's conjecture (that any even number can be expressed as the sum of two primes), and briefly explored the concept of maximally divisible numbers, which was new to Lenat, but had been explored by the Indian mathematician Ramanujan. However, ultimately, the discoveries of AM dwindled, and the new concepts it defined and explored became less interesting (both to itself and outside observers). As AM warned Lenat after some time: 'Warning: No Task on the Agenda has Worth over 200.'

7.3.2   EURISKO: AM revisited

In examining AM's eventual malaise, Lenat came to the conclusion that the reasons for AM's failure lay in the way its concepts outgrew its heuristics; in particular, its heuristics knew a great deal about modifying LISP operations on structures like sets and bags. As the program came into a new domain (of its own invention), these heuristics were no longer effective. His solution, embodied in the EURISKO program, was to apply the discovery mechanisms of AM to its own heuristics, so that as the program shifted to new domains, its heuristics shifted as well.

The EURISKO program was much like the AM program in its general representation and control structure. Its novelty lay in its explicit representation and access to these aspects of itself. Lenat and others at Stanford developed RLL-1 (Representation Language Language 1) (Lenat and Greiner, 1980; Greiner, 1980) for describing both concepts and the ways that concepts are described. RLL-1 was also used to describe EURISKO's own control loop: the selection, execution and judgement of heuristics was explicitly represented and subject to modification by EURISKO.

The EURISKO program was applied to several domains: elementary mathematics (where it reproduced the discoveries of AM), the design of three-dimensional VLSI components, and the design of fictional space armadas in a competitive role-playing game called 'Trillion Credit Squadron'. In this last domain, EURISKO (with Lenat) twice won the national championship with bizarre space fleets based on unrecognized loopholes in the rules.

While working in these domains, it was also working to improve its own heuristics. This domain, which Lenat dubbed 'heuretics', proved the source of many valuable heuristics. In fact, it reinvented many of AM's heuristics from more general specification; for instance, it had a very general heuristic:

IF some concept has two properties whose fillers may overlap (i.e. may
  have the same value),
THEN consider the cases where those properties do in fact overlap.

EURISKO produced one special version of this which was identical to AM's COALESCE operation:

IF an operation is applicable to pairs of A's,
THEN define a new operation on a single instance of A which applies
  the operation to this instance twice.

But despite this reflective capacity, EURISKO did not avoid the malaise of AM. Applied to AM's domain, EURISKO went little further than AM did. Lenat, reporting on EURISKO, attributed this to elementary mathematics being 'mined out'; all the interesting concepts had already been discovered. (I have a different explanation.) What EURISKO did do, however, was demonstrate that the AM methodology could be applied effectively to other domains; and particularly, that this application could give initial structure to domains which had been previously unexplored by human beings. EURISKO was a far more interactive program than AM; it was designed to explore new domains with a human being.

While EURISKO was a success by the criterion of introducing a new sort of man–machine co-operation, it failed to remedy the problems of AM. Lenat and John Seely Brown have suggested that AM's success (and failure) came from the close matching of its representations (simple procedures and structures) to basic mathematical concepts; recent work on reproducing AM in languages even closer to mathematics (Backus' language FP), have borne this out. However, I – in my own work with the CYRANO program – have a slightly different story to tell.

7.3.3   CYRANO, AM revisited again

My work on discovery programs began with an effort to understand and reproduce the AM program. In working on this, I came upon the notion of the 'cycle of discovery' introduced earlier; what was exciting about AM was that it made discoveries which it then USED to invent new operations and make further discoveries. This revealed itself in AM's most spectacular success and its most grievous failure. These involved the invention of 'number' by the CANONIZE operation. This was arguably AM's most impressive achievement, but the CANONIZE operation was only applied once by AM due to its failure to close the cycle of discovery.

CANONIZE had what might be called an 'output' problem and an 'input' problem. The output problem lay in the canonical representation it invented for SAME-SIZE, bags of T's; this was not strictly a new representation, but rather the specialization of an old one. It might be fair to say that AM did not explore operations on numbers but rather operations on a particular sort of subset of BAGS. And unfortunately, it was difficult to specialize this class much further.

The input problem lay in how AM generated the canonicalizations it did; its mechanisms were intimately tied to operations on simple, relatively flat, structures. It constructed a canonicalization by trying – experimentally – random structural mutations on structures to see if they changed the results of the comparison it was producing a canonical representation for. One of these mutations consisted of changing structural elements at random; if this did not affect the comparison, the canonicalization of changing every element to some unique element was suggested. However, once AM's representation had moved beyond simple lists and structures, its implementation of CANONIZE could no longer apply. In other words, CANONIZE instantly obsoleted itself. It is revealing that AM only used CANONIZE once, for the revolutionary leap from list-like representations to numbers.

It can also be argued that by installing a test for element invariance and a corresponding canonicalization method, the representation of numbers 'discovered' by AM was actually built in; however, this would be unfair, since Lenat simply enumerated all the simple structural mutations and one of them happened to correspond to a reasonable representation for numbers.

My approach with the CYRANO program – after experience with more literal reimplementations of AM – has been to take the notions of 'inventing representations' literally; CYRANO really constructs wholly new terms and new operations on those terms. These terms are entirely new objects and constitute a new vocabulary for further discovery and invention.

CYRANO is given an initial domain in terms of a collection of categories and operations on instances of those categories. Based on regularities among these categories and operations, CYRANO defines new operations and categories which can be used to characterize a new domain. Sometimes this new domain – like AM's numbers – is simply a specialization of the original domain; but sometimes it involves a significant abstraction which divides the original domain in fundamentally different ways from its original categories.

All of Cyrano's concepts are represented in a lattice of types; categories are types and operations and relations between them are types of pairs of these objects. This representation is detailed in Haase (1987). CYRANO also abandons much of the control structure of AM and EURISKO; there are no numeric worths in CYRANO. Concepts are ranked as either uninteresting, potentially interesting or definitely interesting. CYRANO's moment-to-moment activity (pictured in Fig. 7.7) consists of generating potentially interesting concepts from definitely interesting concepts and determining whether (and how) potentially interesting concepts might be interesting.

For instance, in reproducing some of AM's discoveries, CYRANO begins with only the operations PAIR, LEFT and RIGHT. PAIR constructs a data structure of two elements which can be accessed as the LEFT and RIGHT of the structure. The LEFT and RIGHT of pairs are either other pairs or terminals.

CYRANO quickly notes that LEFT and RIGHT are deterministic operations (for a given input they always have the same output), while PAIR is not. (PAIR always constructs a new output for any set of inputs.) The determinism of LEFT and RIGHT suggest defining a distance relation based on them; checking if two points are the same 'distance' from a terminal. CYRANO then (after some experiments) determines that both of these relations (SAME-LEFT-DISTANCE and SAME-RIGHT-DISTANCE) are symmetric; this regularity suggests forming a vocabulary of terms corresponding to the relation's equivalence partitions: these

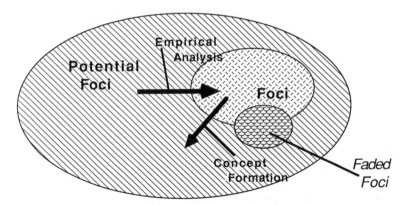

Fig. 7.7. CYRANO's control structure divides concepts into foci and potential foci. Empirical analysis converts potential foci into foci, while concept generation defines new potential foci from known-to-be-interesting foci.

are equivalent to the notion of numbers, since they count the number of pairs encountered in one direction along a structure. (There are other relations whose partitions are NOT equivalent to numbers.)

Operations on lists can be carried through this abstraction: LEFT through SAME-LEFT-DISTANCE and RIGHT through SAME-RIGHT become the PREDE-CESSOR operation. PAIR translated through either abstraction suddenly becomes RIGHT-DETERMINISTIC and a single-argument variant of this operation becomes SUCCESSOR.

Iterative versions of these operations become addition and subtraction, and further iterative construction produces multiplication and the remainder operations. While the CYRANO program has not proceeded so far, hand simulations have derived particular instances of modular arithmetic from the primitives CYRANO has devised.

7.3.4   Conclusions on discovering domains

The programs described above developed new domains from old based on regularities and structure identified in the original domains. These programs succeeded or failed based on whether or not their heuristics and operations could survive the transformation to the new domain. In the case of AM, they clearly did not, but this was partially due to the radical nature of the jump to numbers and the biases of the old heuristics towards structural algorithms and definitions. EURISKO, when it devised a new domain, made the jump fairly robustly; in some ways EURISKO's power came from being a self-optimizing system which accommodated its heuristics (by specialization and prioritization) to new domains.

EURISKO, however, had no real provisions for surviving the representational leap of AM; its self-modification heuristics could not reach inside powerful heuristics like CANONIZE to purge them of the list-specificity. CYRANO, while it currently lacks EURISKO's self-optimization capabilities, survives the sort of radical representational jump which crippled AM; upon discovering or being given a relation among its defined numbers, it can use that relation to define new categories and classes which further organize its representations.

An under-emphasized aspect of all these domain discovery programs is the role of example generation. They are all – for all their construction of definitions – primarily empirical: they note empirical regularities and use these as the basis of concept formation. In this sense, they do not work blindly from their definitions (like Descartes generating the universe from his armchair), but instead play with definitions guided by the structure and properties they impose on an experimental world.

Because of this interaction, the 'organizing principles' of these programs are hard to pin down. An interesting dynamic emerges in all these programs where inductive mechanisms seek useful regularities while generation mechanisms seek to reintroduce chaos by mutation and specialization. Curiously, this is exactly the way that Jean Piaget describes the psychological development of children: a continuing cycle of assimilation and accommodation (Piaget, 1954). Developing children go through stages of equilibrium where the world is easily assimilated to the regularities of their representations; but these periods are invariably followed by periods of disequilibrium where their representations must instead accommodate themselves to the world.

Programs like AM must work this way to keep the 'cycle of discovery' running beyond the limits of any initial conception; and like children (who are always discovering), they arrive in a world very different from that in which they began.

7.4   ACKNOWLEDGEMENTS

This chapter was written while I was visiting at the Vrije Universiteit in Brussels, Belgium. My research into discovery systems has been and continues to be supported by the Artificial Intelligence Laboratory at the Massachusetts Institute of Technology. The students and researchers at both of these locations have been a source of constant stimulation and education. With regard to this chapter, Jonathan Amsterdam and Walter Van De Velde both commented on early drafts of this chapter. In my explorations of discovery, I have been gifted by many insights from conversations with the members of my thesis committee: Marvin Minsky, Patrick Winston, Doug Lenat and Thomas Kuhn. Of course, any inaccuracies, errors or downright heresies are solely my own responsibility. And finally, I must thank my family and friends; their love has kept me relatively sane and happy throughout the last twenty-five years – thank you all.

7.5   REFERENCES

Greiner, R. (1980) RLL-1: a representation language language, Working Paper 80–9, Stanford Heuristic Programming Project.

Haase, K. (1986) CYRANO: a thoughtful reimplementation of Eurisko, *Proceedings of ECAI-86*, Brighton, England. Also available in *Advances in Artificial Intelligence II*, (eds B. Du Boulay, D. Hogg and L. Steels), Amsterdam, 1987.

Haase, K. (1987) TYPICAL: a knowledge representation system for automated discovery and inference, Technical Report 988, MIT Artificial Intelligence Laboratory.

Langley, P., Simon, H.A. Bradshaw, G.L. and Zytkow, J.M. (1987) *Scientific Discovery: Computational Explorations of the Creative Processes*, MIT Press, Cambridge, Mass.

Lenat, D. (1976) AM: an artificial intelligence approach to discovery in mathematics as heuristic search, Doctoral Dissertation in Computer Science at Stanford University.

Lenat, D. (1982a) AM: discovery in mathematics as heuristic search, in *Knowledge Based Systems in Artificial Intelligence* (eds D. Lenat and R. Davis), McGraw-Hill, New York.

Lenat, D. (1982b) The nature of heuristics. *Artificial Intelligence*, **19** (2), 189–249.

Lenat, D. (1983a) Theory formation by heuristic search. *Artificial Intelligence*, **21** (1) and (2), 61–98.

Lenat, D. (1983b) Eurisko: a program that learns new heuristics and domain concepts. *Artificial Intelligence*, **21** (1) and (2), 61–98.

Lenat, D. (1983c) The role of heuristics in learning by discovery: three case studies, in *Machine Learning: An Artificial Intelligence Approach* (ed. T. Mitchell), Tioga Press, Palo Alto, Calif, pp. 243–306.

Lenat, D. and Brown, J.S. (1984) Why AM and Eurisko appear to work. *Artificial Intelligence*, **23** (3), 269–94.

Lenat, D. and Greiner, R. (1980) RLL: a representation language language, *Proceedings of the First Annual Meeting of the American Association for Artificial Intelligence*, Stanford University (August) pp. 28–42.

Michalski, R. (1980) Knowledge acquisition through conceptual clustering: a theoretical framework and an algorithm for partition data into conjunctive concepts. *Policy Analysis and Informations Systems*, **4** (3), 219–24.

Michalski, R. and Stepp, R. (1983) Learning from observation: conceptual clustering, in *Machine Learning: An Artificial Intelligence Approach* (eds R. Michalski, J. Carbonell and T. Mitchell), Tioga Press, Palo Alto, Calif.

Ritchie, G.D. and Hanna, F.K. (1984) AM: a case study in AI methodology. *Artificial Intelligence*, **23** (3) (August).

Piaget, J. (1954) *The Construction of Reality in the Child*, Basic Books, New York (originally published in 1937).

8

The acquisition of natural language by machine

CHRIS NAYLOR

> He learns the language because he is shaped by nature
> to pay attention to it, to notice and remember and use
> significant aspects of it.
>
> Miller (1965)

For a long time psychologists have postulated the existence of a language acquisition device – to such an extent that this as yet unseen device has even managed to acquire an acronym of its own, the LAD. And, from a purely armchair point of view, the existence of such an LAD sounds eminently reasonable. After all, how else could so many otherwise disparate peoples in all four quarters of the globe manage to acquire their native tongues so easily and so naturally? It must surely be that they were born with the ability to acquire a natural language simply by being exposed to it. And that this ability probably exists in some specific human mechanism which we may as well call the LAD.

Well, from the comfort of an armchair that sounds all very well and good. But the next problem is rather more serious – for that is the problem of finding and catching the LAD. But, before we set about that, maybe a little motivation is in order.

Consider the problem of speaking to a computer. That is to say, the problem of speaking to a computer in the hope that the computer will recognize and act upon the words being spoken. We want to speak, not in an artificial language that has been specifically invented by man, but in the natural language that we were brought up to speak and which we learned by means of some mechanism that is, by now, almost totally unknown to us. What is more, we do not want to have to speak in discrete utterances in which the individual words are separated one from the other by a short pause. Instead, we want to be able to speak to our computer in a natural language and we want to be able to speak to our computer in a natural way – using continuous, unsegmented, speech.

And, at the end of our utterances, we want the computer to have understood, in some sense, what we have said to it.

Now, there is a very distinct difference between the problem of speaking to a computer in discrete speech and speaking to a computer in continuous speech and it is this that makes the former more or less possible using current technology and the latter more or less impossible. For the problem with continuous speech recognition by computer is that, with continuous speech, the sounds of individual elements of words become extremely variable at the word boundaries.

By way of example, consider the following phrases:

1. an ice blue
2. a nice blue

And now consider those two phrases spoken both with and without a pause between the words. Clearly, most speaker/listeners of the human variety can accurately convey the correct words to each other when the words are spoken with a pause between each one, as in discrete speech. But few speaker/listeners could distinguish between the two utterances if the message was conveyed using continuous speech. And one reason for this is because of the blurring that occurs at the word boundaries. The nature and shape of the words vary depending on the words that are adjacent.

But, of course, in that example both versions make semantic sense and it is more a case of different words sounding similar than of the same word changing its shape. So, consider the following two examples:

1. I told Helen or Dan
2. I told Dan or Helen

And now try saying those using continuous speech and, at the same time that you do, listen for the way the sounds of the words have changed due to the effect of the adjacent words on them. In particular, look out for the possible loss of the 'D' from Dan's name in the second example so that Dan is likely to turn into Ann.

Of course, if you sit down and contrive examples then it is not too hard to come up with something to illustrate a point, and something that will, also, confuse most speaker/listeners. But, possibly, this has at least demonstrated that words do change their sound quite dramatically at word boundaries depending on what happens to be next to them. And the problem then is: if words change their sounds like this how can we develop a mechanism that will recognize words at all when they are spoken continuously?

Well, it seems likely that it would help matters if we could define some central part of each word that was, more or less, invariant. A segment that was some way clear of the more variable boundaries yet still contained enough of the word to make a significant contribution to its recognition. All of which is a nice piece of armchair wishful thinking and much easier said than done in practice.

And it is at this point that the thought of the psychologists' LAD springs to mind and we begin to think of the possibility of some device or mechanism which could simply be exposed to a sample of natural language and would be able to start to acquire significant portions of it for itself. A machine learning system that, in some ways, mimicked the ability of the human infant and that might, at the end of a run, be able to decide for itself just which parts of an otherwise varying natural language were sufficiently invariant and significant to make a contribution to the understanding of that language.

And at this point the problem is getting a little more concrete than it was originally because what we have decided is that we want a mechanism which will acquire segments from a natural language simply by virtue of being exposed to that language. Essentially, we are saying that the most basic operation of language acquisition is the formation of some minimal elements into larger linguistic units. These larger linguistic units are the segments of natural language – segments which a competent user of a language would regard as psychologically real, but which are not necessarily provided as discrete segments to an infant acquiring that language. So, in this context, a segment might be a whole word, because whole words are regarded as psychologically real by a competent speaker of a language but, owing to the nature of continuous speech, whole words are not usually provided in isolation to the infant acquiring the language. Instead, they are provided to the infant surrounded by other words. Similarly, segments might be lesser units than words but a competent speaker would still allow these lesser units some psychological existence as linguistic units.

Hayes and Clark (1970) have demonstated an ability in adults to discover such segments by exposing them to a computer-generated artificial language whose 'words' were marked by no cues or stress or intonation. Subjective reports of the experiment suggest that the subjects acquired the segments of the language by the successive concatenation of smaller units into larger ones.

So, apart from the instance of the infant language-acquirer there is evidence that adult humans can start to acquire language in much the same way.

Wolff (1975) has written a computer program that attempts to simulate this process. In his experiment a stream of text was input which consisted of letters of the alphabet with all markers (spaces, punctuation) removed. The program proceeded by scanning the text for the most frequently occurring pair of letters which were then concatenated and regarded as a single linguistic unit. The next scan concatenated the next most frequently occurring pair of units. And so on. He found that the program did acquire words out of the stream of text in this way.

In a similar vein, Harris (1955) has worked from a continuous phoneme stream and shown that word boundaries may be detected by considering the two measures of predecessor and successor variety.

In many respects the paradigm of this approach can be illustrated by reference to Table 8.1. In this table a continuous stream of text is formed by removing all punctuation, spaces and indications of upper/lower case from some text. This text stream may then be entered into a two-dimensional matrix showing transitions from one minimal linguistic element to another in the stream. The task of the

Table 8.1   The basic problem of language acquisition

... This is a sunny day ...
can be represented as the continuous string of unsegmented text:
... T H I S I S A S U N N Y D A Y ...
and, then, in the two-dimensional transition matrix:

	T	H	I	T	S	A	U	N	D	Y
T		1								
H			1							
I					2					
T										
S			1			1	1			
A					1					1
U								1		
N								1		1
D						1				
Y									1	

Notes: This is a very small sample of text designed to show the basic principle of acquiring segments of natural language.

It should be made quite clear, since there has been some misunderstanding on this point, that the technique is not designed to illustrate the acquisition of a visually presented textual language but is intended to illustrate a possible principle for the acquisition of segments of continuous spoken speech.

It is suggested that continuous spoken speech may be approximately modelled by a textual string from which all spaces and punctuation and upper/lower case indications have been removed.

The problem faced by the LAD is gradually to acquire segments of language larger than the individual elements (letters, in this case) by means of concatenating these individual elements. The process is reckoned to be successful if the mechanism can acquire segments which tend to occur most commonly within words and least commonly across word boundaries.

Therefore, when faced with this example string the mechanism would be considered to have done well if it acquired the segment 'IS' and to have done badly if it acquired the segment 'YD', for example.

language acquisition mechanism is to select that pair of linguistic elements which seems most likely to form the basis of a larger linguistic element. Once a selection has been made a new matrix is formed out of the old elements together with the newly acquired linguistic element. The mechanism then has to apply itself to this new matrix in order to determine which larger linguistic element it should acquire next (see Table 8.2). And as the mechanism proceeds its acquired lexicon will grow.

An ideal language acquisition mechanism can, without prior knowledge of the

Table 8.2   The next stage of the problem

...T H I S I S A S U N N Y D A Y...
has led to the acquisition of the larger segment 'IS' so the continuous string can now be represented as:
...T H IS IS A S U N N Y D A Y...
which can now be represented as the modified two-dimensional transition matrix containing the new lexical item 'IS':

	T	H	I	T	S	A	U	N	D	Y	IS
T		1									
H											1
I											
T											
S			1			1	1				
A					1					1	
U								1			
N								1		1	
D						1					
Y									1		
IS						1					1

Notes: The problem here is exactly the same as in Table 8.1 except that the lexicon now contains one more item (one more minimal element, the segment 'IS') and the details of the transition matrix have now changed slightly to accommodate this new element and the loss of the individual elements which formed it.

language, acquire linguistic elements which occur mainly within words and which only rarely occur at word boundaries. Ideally, it will finally acquire whole words and phrases although these will not have been explicitly delineated anywhere in the text stream to which the mechanism was exposed. Like a human infant acquiring its native language, the mechanism will have acquired psychologically real elements of the language merely by being exposed to them in a continuous stream.

The only real problem that has to be solved with this model of language acquisition is that of deciding exactly by which criteria the mechanism shall choose to form a larger segment out of two adjacent, smaller, linguistic units.

Wolff used the criterion of the most frequently occurring pair; Harris used predecessor and successor variety; but is there a better way?

First, it seems reasonable to outline a brief criticism of the methods of Wolff and Harris.

It might, initially, seem as if Wolff's method, that of concatenating the most frequently occurring pair, makes sense – if only because one might argue that the greatest frequency of exposure to an occurring pair is likely to result in the greatest degree of learning of that segment which is created by concatenating that pair.

This does, however, have disadvantages. From a psychological point of view it is possible to argue that the degree of learning of a stimulus is not generally directly and solely related to the frequency of exposure to that stimulus. And, from a statistical point of view, one could also argue that the degree of association which exists between two objects is not usually measured solely by reference to the number of times they occur together but also has to take into account the statistical significance of these joint occurrences. Two objects which occur together one hundred times do not, after all, represent a particularly significant occurrence if those selfsame objects also occur together with every other object the same number of times.

It is this latter, statistical, point which Harris's work tends to address even though, chronologically, his work predates that of Wolff.

For Harris is arguing that predecessor and successor variety provides the clue to the association (or dissociation) of linguistic elements. In other words, it is the number of different things which might follow or precede any given linguistic element which determines whether or not two linguistic elements should be joined together.

Considering, by way of example, the two letters 'q' and 'u' in the English language, and disregarding the fact that Harris was working with phonemes rather than letters of the alphabet, we know that the successor to 'q' is always 'u' – there is little, if any, successor variety for the letter 'q'. And the predecessor variety for 'u' is pretty limited as well. All of which would tend to suggest that, even if they did not occur very often, the letters 'q' and 'u' could well be concatenated into a larger linguistic unit because when they do occur, they occur together. Whereas more frequently occurring pairs, because they have much greater predecessor and successor variety, might not be joined together with such certainty.

Obviously, neither the approach of Wolff nor that of Harris is entirely free from criticism although both approaches contribute something substantial to our consideration of the problem.

However, as a rationale for the approach I intend to adopt, I would like you to consider the LAD as it exists (if it exists) in people – together with the concept of evolutionary pressure.

Under this theory the following effects take place.

The LAD is able to acquire certain elements of the language to which it is exposed simply by virtue of being exposed to them. Because it is not a universal learning device but is specifically tailored to the learning of human natural languages there will be some aspects of the language which more nearly suit its language acquisition capabilities than others. These aspects of the language will, inevitably, be more readily acquired by the device.

Because of the survival benefits which language use can confer the LAD will, over an evolutionary time-scale, gradually improve, becoming better able to acquire the language to which it is exposed.

But, because some aspects of the language to which the LAD is exposed are more readily acquired than other aspects the language itself will, over an evolutionary time-scale, become modified in such a way that it becomes more 'acquirable' by the LAD. This process can be quite readily envisaged if we consider a subject only acquiring those aspects of the language which the subject found easy to acquire and, then, of necessity only passing on to the next generation that subset of the language which had in this way been acquired.

The overall result of this argument is that, over an evolutionary time-scale, the language and the LAD should grow together. In this way, the LAD becomes increasingly able rapidly to acquire the language simply by exposure to it and the language itself becomes increasingly modified so that, on being presented to the relevant LAD, it will be most rapidly acquired by that device. A kind of process of mutual survival more than anything else.

Anyway, the drift of this argument is that, over time, we should find that the LAD leaves some kind of imprint in the structure of the language itself and, consequently, if we want to know what the LAD looks like then all we have to do is to look at the language.

Not, of course, that the answer is likely to be staring us in the face. For what we are looking at is the language which is readily acquired by the device, rather than the device itself. But there should be remains there to be found, rather like fossil footprints.

But, at this point, we have to pause and work out just what we might by likely to find for we have to know approximately what we are looking for.

Well, by our earlier textual example based on Wolff's work what we are looking for is a mechanism which is able to join together two elements of the language such that the resulting whole segment is most likely to occur within a word rather than at a word boundary. So, clearly, what we are looking for is some sort of classification or discrimination mechanism that can distinguish between elements which occur within words and elements which occur at word boundaries.

And the next question we have to work out is what variables this mechanism can consider. In other words, what information it has to hand in making its decisions regarding the concatenation of two elements to form a new linguistic segment. And, in doing this, we have to bear in mind that the principle must be generally applicable to any human natural language and not just English.

At this point the approach used here differs from the approaches used by other authors inasmuch as the technique is no longer a matter of deciding on some criterion by which the mechanism might be reckoned to operate and investigating that criterion. Instead, the approach is to analyse the language looking for the mechanism which will acquire it.

The procedure essentially consists of using the linear discriminant function (see, for example, Kendall, 1975) in order to determine whether a given pair of linguistic elements is a pair which might occur within a word, and which can therefore be concatenated into one larger unit, or whether it is a pair which might cross a word boundary, in which case it should not be so concatenated.

The discovery of the LAD consists of determining the linear discriminant function for distinguishing these two cases.

The data used in deriving the linear discriminant function is a large body of text, arranged in transition matrices as per Table 8.1, and divided into two groups.

The first group consists of a transition matrix as per Table 8.1 for those letter pairs which occur within words.

The second group consists of a similar transition matrix for those letter pairs which occur between words.

With respect to these letter pairs five variables were identified as being of possible value. They were:

1. relative frequency of joint occurrence
2. relative frequency of occurrence of the first letter in the pair
3. relative frequency of occurrence of the second letter in the pair
4. successor variety of the first letter in the pair
5. predecessor variety of the second letter of the pair

Clearly, the first variable owes much to Wolff and the last two variables owe much to the work of Harris.

At this point it should be noted that all variables are measured on the pooled transition matrices and not on the individual within- or between-words transition matrices. So, for instance, if the letter pair 'IS' occurs five times within words and five times at word boundaries then the frequency of occurrence of that letter pair whether we are considering the within-words or between-words situation is ten, and not five, times. The rationale behind this is that the language acquisition mechanism, in considering a letter pair, does not, prior to the acquisition of that pair as a unit, know whether or not that pair is occurring within or between words. It only has a single figure for the behaviour of the pair within the body of the incoming language stream as a whole.

The reasons why these five variables were chosen for study is as follows.

They are all language independent in the sense that they are measures of the behaviour of the elements in the incoming language stream and not references to any specific part of any language itself. Therefore, a different language, or the same language described in a different way could by analysed and, hopefully, acquired in exactly the same way.

The combination of these variables enables one to envisage a mechanism which considers a particular pair of elements and, of this particular pair, is able to observe that the pair occurs together a given number of times. But that might not be remarkable if the individual elements themselves occurred frequently. So, how often do the individual elements occur? If the individual elements have a high measure of predecessor and successor variety (i.e. they occur with lots of other different elements) then any particular combination might not be remarkable. So, what is the predecessor and successor variety?

In order to use the linear discriminant function with these five variables the following restrictions should be borne in mind.

The variables under consideration should be approximately normally distributed and the covariance matrices for the five variables should be the same for both sets of data, i.e. the within-words data and the between-words data (Tables 8.3 and 8.4).

Table 8.3   The covariance matrix about means based on the within-words data

	x_1	x_2	x_3	x_4	x_5
x_1	6.643 963	2.359 701	1.984 242	−1.192 018	−0.712 209
x_2	2.055 390	−0.021 534	−0.931 014	0.017 444	
x_3	1.955 411	0.028 691	−0.720 688		
x_4	0.642 835	−0.020 271			
x_5	0.540 811				

No. of observations = 349.032 5

Notes: This is a covariance matrix about the means based on the within-words character transitions from a sample of 1 735 317 characters of text.
   The five variables shown are as described in the text.
   Note that the no. of observations refers to the number of cells within the transition matrix which are found to be filled by within-words entries. Cells containing both within-words entries and between-words entries are divided between the two types of entry.

Table 8.4   The covariance matrix about means based on the between-words data

	x_1	x_2	x_3	x_4	x_5
x_1	5.522 984	2.197 239	1.587 528	−1.030 506	−0.624 435
x_2	1.916 412	−0.171 855	−0.776 240	0.140 233	
x_3	2.040 265	0.116 598	−0.742 351		
x_4	0.521 626	−0.095 265			
x_5	0.587 970				

No. of observations = 307.967 5

Notes: This is a covariance matrix about the means based on the between-words character transitions from a sample of 1 735 317 characters of text.
   The five variables shown are as described in the text.
   Note that the no. of observations refers to the number of cells within the transition matrix which are found to be filled by between-words entries. Cells containing both within-words entries and between-words entries are divided between the two types of entry.

A brief examination of these five variables will reveal that none of them is normally distributed in the raw state, all of them exhibiting some skew.

Frequency of occurrence of the pair, frequency of occurrence of the first letter and frequency of occurrence of the second letter are variables which are all skew left. They all have a large number of items which occur with low frequency. Empirically, a log transformation corrects for left skew and it is possible to claim some theoretical justification for this particular transformation.

A part of this justification is that it is generally agreed that word frequency of occurence is a variable which is lognormally distributed (i.e. the log of the variable is normally distributed – see, for example, Carroll, 1967). These three variables are not, in general, words but as their concatenation proceeds they would ideally become words (in the case of items in the within-words group); or phrases (in the case of the items in the word boundaries group). If we allow the lognormal distribution to have some applicability to linguistic structures in general we might feel that a log transformation was an appropriate chance to take in this case. This transformation can also be justified on the basis of other, psychological, arguments which will not be expanded here.

The other two variables to be considered, predecessor and successor variety, are both skew right. The suggested transformation to normality in this case is the log of the number of items with which a given element does not connect. This may seem a little roundabout. However, from a pragmatic point of view we have a variable which is skew right and by subtracting it from a constant we transform it into a variable which is skew left and, then, by taking the logarithm we remove this skew.

By taking as our constant for this operation the total number of items with which a given element might connect (e.g. 26 in the case of the full English alphabet) and subtracting from it the number of items with which a given element does in fact connect in the sample under consideration we can argue that something real is still to be measured. Not predecessor and successor variety but, rather, the lack of it. This technique is, of course, open to criticism inasmuch as with the three earlier variables we are measuring something which actually occurs in the text. In this latter case, however, we are measuring something which does not occur and counting how many times it does not occur.

As a small practical point, the value 0.5 was added to each of these latter measures before the log was taken to avoid problems caused by any instances of the log of zero.

On inspection, the covariance matrices of these transformed variables appear to be substantially similar.

The linear discriminant function between the two sets of data was then calculated using the pooled covariance matrix of the two sets of data as an estimate of the common covariance matrix of the variables (Table 8.5).

The result is an equation based on the five variables.

A particular pair of elements can then be examined with respect to these five variables and regarded as being a pair of elements which occurs either at a word

Table 8.5   The mean vectors and the discriminant coefficients derived from this sample of 1 735 317 characters

	Mean vector		
	Within words	*Between words*	*Difference vector*
x_1	−7.826 984	−9.112 214	1.285 231
x_2	−3.782 778	−3.825 489	0.042 711 5
x_3	−3.643 328	−4.039 342	0.396 014
x_4	−3.556 74	−3.616 09	0.059 349 54
x_5	−3.436 589	−3.357 47	−0.079 118 97

Discriminant coefficients:
$b_1 = 0.600\ 307\ 1$
$b_2 = -0.347\ 464$
$b_3 = -0.248\ 209\ 4$
$b_4 = 0.801\ 139\ 8$
$b_5 = 0.378\ 003\ 4$

Notes: These are the mean and difference vectors for the data shown in previous tables. The discriminant coefficients define the language acquisition mechanism.

boundary or within a word according as the value of the linear discriminant function for that pair tends towards the mean value for one set of data or the other.

The second step of this analysis consists of regarding this linear discriminant function as an LAD and presenting it with a sample of unsegmented text from which it must form segments of language.

The procedure is to calculate the value of the discriminant function for each pair of elements within a text sample and then choose that pair of elements which has the greatest discriminant function value. In the present case that implies the greatest probability of the pair being from the within-words group rather than from the word boundaries group. This pair is concatenated and then treated as a new single element. Discriminant function values are recalculated and a second pair is chosen. And so on.

An example of some initial segments acquired from unsegmented text is shown in Table 8.6.

A variant on this procedure is to input text in a dynamic fashion.

In this case a pair of elements is still selected for concatenation but is only concatenated if the value of the discriminant function exceeds a given value, equivalent to a given probability of a correct choice.

If this given value is not attained, more text is input to the system until the maximum value of the discriminant function reaches the specified level. This might be considered to be analogous to the case described by Hayes and Clark

Table 8.6   Some linguistic elements acquired by the mechanism

The following is a sample of continuous unsegmented text consisting of 400 characters from a children's reader:

ITISSUMMERTIMESCHOOLISOVERANDTHELONGSUMMERHOLIDAYISHEREJANEAND
PETERTALKABOUTTHEIRLONGSUMMERHOLIDAYANDWHATTHEYAREGOINGTODOI
LIKESCHOOLSAYSPETERBUTIAMGLADTHEHOLIDAYHASCOMEYESIAMGLADTOO
SAYSJANEILIKESUNNYDAYSWHENWEHAVENOWORKTODOTHEREARESOMANY
NICETHINGSTODOINTHEHOLIDAYWHENITISSUNNYYESSAYSPETERANDDAD
THINKSITDOESUSGOODTOGETOUTINTHESUNWEWILLBEOUTEVERYDAYWHENTHE
SUNCOMESOUTDOYOUKNOWTHEREISANOLDDONKEYUPATTHEF

The language acquisition mechanism shown above acquired the following segments of text in the order shown:

Segment	Frequency of occurrence in original text	Segment	Frequency of occurrence in original text
TH	12	JANE	2
WH	4	PE	3
CH	2	PET	3
THE	10	PETE	3
THI	2	PETER	3
THIN	2	WHE	3
VE	3	WHEN	3
VER	2	ME	6
JA	2	MME	3
JAN	2	MMER	3

Applying that acquisition of linguistic elements to the original text suggests that the mechanism has acquired the following segmentation:

I T I S S U MMER T I ME S CH O O LI S O VER A N D THE LO N G S U MMER H O LI D A Y I S
H E R E JANE A N D PETER T A L K A B O U T THE I R LO N G S U MMER H O LI D A Y A N D
WH A T THE Y A R E G O I N G T O D O I LI KE S CH O O L S A Y S PETER B U T I A M G L A D
THE H O LI D A Y H A S C O ME Y E S I A M G L A D T O O S A Y S JANE I LI KE S U N N Y D A
Y S WHEN W E H A VE N O W O R K T O D O THE R E A R E S O M A N Y N I CE THIN G S T O
D O I N THE H O LI D A Y WHEN I T I S S U N N Y Y E S S A Y S PETER A N D D A D THIN K S
I T D O E S U S G O O D T O G E T O U T I N THE S U N W E W I L L B E O U T E VER Y D A Y
WHEN THE S U N C O ME S O U T D O Y O U K N O W THE R E I S A N O L D D O N K E Y U P A
T THE F

Notes: The above table illustrates the mechanism described working on a sample of only 400 characters from a children's reader. Before it makes a mistake of any description it has successfully acquired the names of the children in the story and a few other general-purpose words.

There is nothing about the mechanism which restricts it to the English language and it has, in fact, been tested on small samples of German with similar success.

The suggestion is that this is, in some respects, an analogue of a mechanism for learning the segments of a natural language when the elements of continuous spoken language are to be acquired.

(1970) for human subjects. A new segment is acquired when the probability of its being a segment in its own right is sufficiently high, but otherwise judgement is deferred while attention is paid to further examples of the continuous speech being input.

A further variation on the theme is to use the mechanism 'upside down' in which a very low value of the discriminant function is used to indicate a point in the text where some kind of word boundary is believed to occur. It is then assumed that the text between boundaries denotes the required linguistic segments.

In its present form there may well be applications for this LAD. However, while its working is confined to acquiring segments from a continuous stream of text these applications are likely to be limited. More interestng by far is the possibility that it does, in fact, demonstrate the existence of the remains of an LAD in our language itself and the possibility that by some means this technique might be usefully applied to spoken speech.

8.1   RESULTS

The following is an illustration of the analysis applied to a substantial sample of some 1 735 317 characters.

The variables considered were:

$$x_1 \qquad \log(a_{ij}/N)$$

where a_{ij} is the joint frequency of occurrence of a given character pair and N is the total number of characters.

$$x_2 \qquad \log(a_{i.}/N)$$

where $a_{i.}$ is the frequency of occurrence of the first item in a given character pair and N is the total number of characters as before.

$$x_3 \qquad \log(a_{.j}/N)$$

where $a_{.j}$ is the frequency of occurrence of the second item in a given character pair.

$$x_4 \qquad \log(L+0.5-k1)/L$$

where L is the total number of different items in the lexicon such that L would equal 26 if every letter of the English alphabet, and no other characters, occurred in the sample, and where $k1$ is the successor variety of the first element in a given character pair. It is the number of different lexical items which the first element is found to precede. The constant 0.5 is added to avoid the degenerate case when $k1 = L$.

$$x_5 \qquad \log(L+0.5-k2)/L$$

where $k2$ is the predecessor variety of the second element in a given character pair. It is the number of different lexical items which the second element is found to follow.

Variables were measured for two groups: those character pairs occurring within words and those character pairs occurring at word boundaries. Frequently, a given character pair occurs in both groups. In this case all measurements were weighted by an amount determined as follows:

$$a_{ij} = aw_{ij} + ab_{ij}$$

a_{ij}, defined as before, is made up of aw_{ij} occurrences within words and ab_{ij} occurrences between words. Then, within-words measurements were weighted by aw_{ij}/a_{ij} and similarly for ab_{ij}.

Covariance matrices were calculated for the two groups and the results can be seen in Tables 8.3 and 8.4.

The two matrices show marked similarities and they are pooled to form an estimate of a common covariance matrix. From this common matrix the inverse is calculated.

The two sets of means are calculated and their differences and these can be seen in Table 8.5.

By multiplying the difference vector with the inverse matrix we obtain the linear discriminant function coefficients. These linear discriminant coefficients are also shown in Table 8.5.

Denoting the linear discriminant function by F, we find F as:

$$F = b_1 x_1 + b_2 x_2 + b_3 x_3 + b_4 x_4 + b_5 x_5$$

The function would then classify a letter pair as coming from within a word or from a word boundary according as it was associated with a high value or a low value of F.

The variance of the function F may be calculated as the difference between F formed from the mean values of the x_i within words less the F formed from the mean values of the x_i formed between words. Dividing the b_i by their respective variances enables a more ready comparison to be made.

It should be noted that, due to the very large colinearities in the data, discriminant coefficients cannot strictly speaking be considered on a one-by-one basis.

However, the general picture is that, if the system searched among the letter pairs looking for a pair which maximized this linear discriminant function then it would be looking for: a frequently occurring pair (the positive b_1 coefficient), whose elements seldom occurred in any other combination (the positive b_4 and b_5 coefficients, related to low predecessor and successor variety); and, which was itself made up of fairly uncommon characters (the negative values of the b_2 and b_3 coefficients). Any pairs of elements tending to satisfy these criteria would be most readily learned by this mechanism.

The next step is to allow this mechanism to operate on a sample of unsegmented text.

A sample of 400 characters of text was used.

The program proceeded by scanning the text and identifying the individual characters which occurred therein. A joint occurrence (transition) matrix was built up for all letter pairs and the five variables calculated. The value of the discriminant coefficient was calculated for each pair. That letter pair which gave the maximum value for the discriminant coefficient was selected and concatenated into a new lexical item in its own right. The text was then rescanned to find the next highest value of the discriminant function including those items which co-occurred with the newly formed element. The process was repeated until an item was selected for concatenation which only occurred at a word boundary in the given sample.

The linguistic elements initially acquired by the mechanism are shown in order of appearance in Table 8.6.

8.2   REFERENCES

Carroll, J. B. (1967) On sampling from a lognormal model of word frequency distribution, in *Computational Analysis of Present-day American English* (eds H. Kucera and W. N. Francis), Brown University Press, Providence, R.I., pp. 406–24.

Harris, Z. S. (1955) From phoneme to morpheme. *Language*, **31**, 190–222.

Hayes, J. R. and Clark, H. H. (1970) Experiments on the segmentation of an artificial speech analogue, in *Cognition and the Development of Language* (ed. J. R. Hayes), Wiley, New York, pp. 128–44.

Kendall, M. (1975) *Multivariate Analysis*, Griffin, London.

Miller, G. A. (1965) Some preliminaries to psycholinguistics. *American Psychologist*, **20**, 20.

Wolff, J. G. (1975) An algorithm for the segmentation of an artificial language analogue. *British Journal of Psychology*, **66** (1), 79–90.

9

A computational model of creativity

MASOUD YAZDANI

9.1 INTRODUCTION

In this paper we propose a computational framework for creativity based on rule-based production of objects and meta-level reasoning about the rules. We have argued that a 'random by design' strategy could guide the exploration of rules in order to provide new and possibly more effective ones. We demonstrate the basic idea through the case study of our work on ROALD (Yazdani, forthcoming), a computer program for story-writing.

In order to generalize our experience of creative writing we have looked at two studies concerned with the art of picture-making. The first, AARON, already performs well in making pictures without any help from people. The other study by Edwards (1986) is primarily concerned with teaching people the skills involved in picture-making. We have argued that even a simple drawing package such as LOGO's turtle graphics could provide an effective means of teaching creativity to people.

9.2 CAN A COMPUTER WRITE A STORY?

The simplest way for a computer to write stories would be to:

1. Take any story you want;
2. Type it into the computer's memory;
3. Then a simple sequence of print instructions can easily produce a story.

This scenario can be, and indeed is, followed by people too. However, the scope of the scenario is limited to producing only one story.

The next scenario, although similar to the first, produces a larger set of stories as its output:

1. Take a TEMPLATE of any story made out of a mixture of 'low level' canned

sequences containing elements which can represent varying sequences (i.e. variables as in any programming language).
2. Work out the value of the variables in the TEMPLATE – out of a set of possibilities.
3. Reproduce the TEMPLATE filled with the worked-out values of the variables.

This scenario is limited to telling exactly the set of stories that have been put into it. However, it should be noted that the limits can be pushed towards an infinite number of possible stories as the combination of values for variables can be unlimited.

The main problem with variations of this scenario is that it tells us little about the creative nature of story-writing. Nevertheless it can be argued that a sophisticated version of it is actually used by some authors. It has been claimed that some authors produce a new story by varying a known story.

If people's memories are filled with detailed, but nevertheless, flexible representations of past events and past stories then there is no reason to doubt that they would use some of these as the bases of generating new ones. The work of Klein *et al.* (1973) and Klein (1975) seems to attempt to do this. It is claimed that structures identified by Propp (1968) are inherent in fairy-tales and are used to produce such tales. Klein *et al.*'s (1973) program based on this approach have produced '2100 word murder mystery stories in less than 19 seconds'! However, Klein has admitted (see Klein and Meehan, 1977) that in addition to more complex procedures, 'low-level canned sequences' have been used in producing those stories.

9.3   MEEHAN'S SIMULATION PROGRAM TALE-SPIN

Meehan (1976) has argued that the '. . . method, used by Klein, is to write some code which will produce each part of that particular story when the whole program runs'. A more general extension of this view would be that all the scenarios considered so far are generalizations of this approach.

Meehan (1976) attempts to 'model people making up stories'. The result is a 'theory' of story-writing, and a program called TALE-SPIN based on it, which actually generates some stories. Meehan's theory of stories is a clear and simple one: that 'a story is about a problem and how it gets solved'. TALE-SPIN is a computer program which writes stories based on the above theory; 'by simulating a world, assigning goals to some characters and saying what happens when these goals interact with events in the simulated world'. The program, however, is not totally independent of the reader.

'The reader (the user) gets to supply much of the information about the initial state of the world, such as the choice of characters and the relationships between one character and another.' Then the reader chooses the problem which the story is all about, out of a set of only four problems.

From then onwards the story generation is a report of a problem-solver. 'At the heart of TALE-SPIN is a problem-solver, a program which implements a new theory of planning. Accordingly, the stories TALE-SPIN produces are essentially accounts of what happens during the course of solving one or more problems. This is consistent with the theory that all stories are about problems.'

> Once upon a time George ant lived near a patch of ground. There was a nest in an ash tree. Wilma bird lived in the nest. There was some water in a river. Wilma knew that the water was in the river. George knew that the water was in the river. One day Wilma was very thirsty. Wilma wanted to get near some water. Wilma flew from her nest across the meadow through a valley to the river. Wilma drank the water. Wilma wasn't thirsty anymore.
>
> George was very thirsty. George wanted to get near some water. George walked from his patch of ground across the meadow through the valley to a river. George fell into the water. George wanted to get near the valley. George couldn't get near the valley. George wanted to get near the meadow. George couldn't get near the meadow. Wilma wanted to get near George. Wilma grabbed George with her claw. Wilma took George from the river through the valley to the meadow. George was devoted to Wilma. George owed everything to Wilma. Wilma let go of George. George fell to the meadow. The end.

The scenario which one could say Meehan's TALE-SPIN program follows is:

1. Identify a CHARACTER out of a predefined set;
2. Give that CHARACTER a PROBLEM out of a predefined set;
3. Create a MICRO WORLD out of a predefined set;
4. Input 1 to 3 above to a problem-solving simulator;
5. Either STOP or GOTO 1.

One of the problems with TALE-SPIN is that the program does not know what it is doing. 'TALE-SPIN does not "understand" the story it's telling'. The program does not have a notion of which stories are interesting or not. It is up to the programmer to categorize some as MIS-SPUN tales and some as correct ones. A MIS-SPUN tale is taken to be due to a bug in the program. The programmer changes the program in order to get what constitutes a correct outcome. The corrections are mostly *ad hoc*. The only time a radical change has followed the discovery of a bug is when the MIS-SPUN tale introduced the 'noticing' inference of 'Henry Ant' into the TALE-SPIN program.

> Henry Ant was thirsty. He walked over to the river bank where his good friend Bill was sitting. Henry slipped and fell in the river. He was unable to call for help. He drowned.

I find more interesting stories among the MIS-SPUN tales than among the boring correct ones.

> Once upon a time there was a dishonest fox and a vain crow. One day the crow was sitting in his tree holding the piece of cheese. He became hungry and swallowed the cheese. The fox walked over to the crow. The end.

The two stories above are interesting because they are different from Aesop's version of them. If a human writer were to rewrite Aesop's fables they would be different from the original as they would catch the flavour of the personality of the writer (see fables by James Thurber, La Fontaine . . .). The capability to generate stories similar to the MIS-SPUN tales would be a worthwhile exercise in its own right. However, these stories would be of use if the framework within which they are produced can recognize their interestingness. Unfortunately Meehan's theory of story-writing not only fails to appreciate this, but explicitly rules out these stories as 'wrong' stories.

9.4   BEYOND TALE-SPIN

TALE-SPIN at present deals with the case where there is only one character solving one problem at a time. However, if more than one character had goals which he actively tried to achieve simultaneously, then the simple problem-solver of the TALE-SPIN would not be able to cope with the situation.

It would be a challenge to produce a TALE-SPIN-like program which deals with more complicated situations (such as stories with two or more main characters) without having to change the theory that the stories are just about the problem-solving of the characters.

One solution would be to monitor the problem-solving of different characters, letting some achieve their goals and suppressing others. But the program then needs to have some other notion of what the story is about, to be able to produce a coherent story, rather than some unrelated accounts of different characters solving different problems. The monitor then starts becoming a complicated mechanism in order to manipulate the characters and their problems for the production of the story. At this stage the monitor needs to have goals of its own and plan the story.

My work on a story-writing computer program started in 1979 by a rational reconstruction of Meehan's (1976) program TALE-SPIN. As my theoretical model of story-writing had developed as an extension of Meehan's theory, I saw good reasons to believe that my program could also be built through modifications to his program. My program, ROALD, started becoming an independent entity as I attempted to use different story-worlds from those of Meehan's 'bear-world'.

Although TALE-SPIN is concerned with interpersonal interaction, the main problem seemed to be that the stories were always from the perspective of a single character. Most stories which I considered of interest to me involved at least two characters, acting either in competition or in co-operation with each other. The next few years of my involvement with ROALD consisted of an ongoing series of modifications similar to those of Meehan's due to MIS-SPUN tales. Although I was successful in writing a Jack and Jill story, I found it difficult to get to where I intended to go from my TALE-SPIN starting-point. Any small change to the story world involved a series of modifications to part of the system which executed the routines corresponding to the actions of the characters. Partly due to the fact that the system was implemented in PROLOG, when the program went wrong it did really wild things. This is because PROLOG (Clocksin and Mellish, 1984) searches all possible combinations unless it has been explicitly advised otherwise by a special operator called 'cut'.

It was through looking at the wild outputs of my program that I developed a commitment to the model of creativity described here. I have come to believe that 'almost random' searches of a space of possibilities combined with a strict validation process for the usefulness of the outcome is a good way of looking at creativity in a variety of domains. My readings of the almost random outputs of my program strengthened my belief in this idea. There were surely many occasions when the unwanted outputs were more interesting (as I have pointed out in the case of MIS-SPUN tales) than the expected ones. I say 'almost random' because these explorations of the space of possibilities were usually results of a small change in a world which had already generated an acceptable result. In other words, we were only slightly twiddling a knob with which we already had familiarity of observing the results. However, the early version of ROALD (and I believe also TALE-SPIN) was in no way useful even as a test bed for this new model of creativity which had emerged. All the intermediate deliberations of ROALD were lost after the program had generated its output. What was needed was a computer program which could plan a story without actually generating it. The program could then look at its creation, reason about it, change it and, when satisfied, produce the final output. I have described my second attempt with ROALD, which goes some way towards doing this, elsewhere (Yazdani, forthcoming).

9.5 BACKGROUND

In last two sections we presented a number of scenarios for story-writing. Each was presented as a set of rules. As we moved from simpler scenarios to Klein *et al.*'s (1973) and Klein's (1975) structuralist system, and then to Meehan's (1976) simulation program, the variety of stories which could possibly be generated by each system increased. With ROALD we have argued that a further level of variety is added to Meehan's program. However, each of these scenarios in themselves only reflect a model of story production. They do not model the act of creativity. The creative act of discovering new extensions to each set of rules is performed by researchers who have proposed the later systems. A distinction is therefore necessary between 'production' of new stories and discovery or invention of new classes of stories.

It is this distinction between 'productivity' and 'creativity' which is also reflected in other domains such as picture-making and scientific discovery. Not all new ideas are the same in nature and therefore may not arise from the same basic source. This is the central point of the computational framework for creativity proposed by Boden (1977, 1981, 1982).

Boden (1982) points out that there are at least two kinds of new ideas: '. . . a thought which is new because it just had not been thought before and a thought which is new because it strikes us that it could not have been thought before'.

9.6   MULTI-LEVEL CREATIVITY

The most explicit exposition of creativity has been presented by Chomsky (1966) within the linguistic domain. Theoretically, the set of possible utterances in a language is infinite. The search for a finite basis underlying a potentially infinite number of manifestations has been the main incentive of modern linguistics in which Chomsky enjoys a major standing.

Creativity, as defined by Chomsky for language, is based on a system of rules (the generative grammar) which enables the construction of an infinite variety of sentences using a finite set of rules. The possibility of using Chomsky's definition of creativity in language as a 'general theory of creativity' has been proposed in several places (see for example de Beaugrande, 1979).

However, such a rule-based notion of creativity has many defects when taken in the context of a variety of tasks. Many, including de Beaugrande (1979), accept that violation of standard rules plays as important (if not more important) role in creativity than following the rules. Boden (1981) considers the effects of exploring the consequences of modifying or extending parts of the grammar as a major source of creativity.

While a framework based on a single level of rules for creativity has obvious shortcomings, there is a further possibility of a rule-based framework which needs to be considered seriously. This new approach considers a number of levels of rules for producing objects:

0. objects
1. rules for parsing/generating objects of domain 0
2. meta-rules for parsing/generating rules of domain 1

A multi-level system of rules either as shown above or as a series of rules about rules about rules . . . (in the same form as Minsky's 1966 models) poses an attractive solution to some of the defects of a Chomskyan rule-based approach to creativity.

Bundy (1984) has argued in favour of the general usefulness of meta-rules and meta-level reasoning. Lenat (1977) has shown how they can be used to produce an automatic mathematician. Lenat's computer program uses heuristics to explore the space of mathematical rules in search of new theorems with moderate success in finding new ones.

Hofstadter (1979), admittedly in a different context, seems to argue that for any intelligent being 'such multi-level architecture of concept handling' is necessary and that 'it is precisely at this same point that creativity starts to emerge'.

9.7 SEARCHING FOR NOVELTIES

If it is through tinkering with the rules that we achieve creative breakthroughs, then how does one go about doing this? As Forsyth (1986) points out in the context of machine learning, success is greatly enhanced if the system has a good grasp of what it already knows. Further, Forsyth points out that simplification of stored knowledge is related to the discovery of new knowledge at a later stage. It is probably for these reasons that Polya (1945) argues that 'finding a solution to a problem should mark not the end but the beginning of a mathematical enquiry: it should be followed by attempts to find simpler solutions, other kinds of solutions, and generalisations of the problem'. Lenat's (1983) EURISKO program seems to put this advice to work by wandering around its conceptual space making small alterations to its concepts and rules, seeing how well this would help the overall performance. Forsyth's (1986) own program, BEAGLE, uses a 'neo-Darwinian' approach where a rule is replaced by a new and superior one, usually constructed from a mutated combination of two other rules. This process takes two randomly chosen rules and combines portions of them.

9.8 RANDOMNESS BY DESIGN

In machine learning, scientific discovery, creative writing and many other areas, a playful exploration of the possibility offered by previously learnt rules could lead to new breakthroughs. However, the problem is that pure chance would take too long to provide any exciting results and if it does, they would be buried in the pile of useless results. As Boden (1983) points out, 'it would be a rare monkey that could type Hamlet'. And, as Cohen (1977) points out, what randomness provides for an artist or scientist is a starting-point for a proliferation of the decision space: '. . . "Let's try X" is a very powerful rule indeed in art-making, and more generally in what we call creative behaviour, provided that X is a member of a rigorously constrained set'.

AARON (Cohen, 1979) is a computer program which produces drawings which its programmer has never seen. It has a knowledge of image making in the form of a set of rules. However, it does not have a lexicon of shapes or parts of shapes to be put together into a complete drawing. Instead AARON uses a randomness by design strategy through a number of meta-rules which precisely define a space within which any choice will do exactly as well as any other choice.

AARON is not an interactive program accepting data from a user. It sets out to produce its own drawings which, by the virtue of their inclusion in major art galleries, are of high standards. Boden (1983) compares the success of AARON to that of a successful jazz drummer who, due to a neurological disease, suffers from involuntary muscular tics while playing his instrument. However, this jazz player uses these musically random sounds as seeds for exciting improvisations. As Boden (1983) points out, 'if the whole process were random, the result would only on chance occasions be judged "exciting" '.

9.9   EVALUATING CREATIVITY

Hofstadter (1979) argues that the reason behind the need for a randomness-by-design in creativity is that the world outside, which we perceive and to which we relate, is itself nothing but 'a giant heap of randomness'.

'Randomness is an intrinsic feature of thought, not something which has to be artificially inseminated, whether through dice, decaying nuclei, random number tables, or what-have-you' (Hofstadter, 1979).

Therefore the result of playful explorations should lead to the system improving its overall behaviour in the world outside in the case of machine learning, produce pleasing artefacts in the case of art, useful explanations in the case of science, and so on.

As long as the results of creativity are useful to us in one way or another, it should not really matter how they were arrived at. This point is captured by Boden (1981) by the constraints on the overall framework that 'the generation of new forms needs a consequent evaluation within a certain structural constraint in order to recognise something as useful'. Narayanan (1984) touches on the same issues when he subjects his 'type minus' grammar to 'certification and integrity checking procedures which check the correctness of the [new] rule'.

9.10   TEACHING CREATIVITY

If creativity is not as mysterious as it is believed by many, can the computational view of creativity lead to helping people become more creative? A sense of hope is emerging from many directions. For example, Edwards (1986) has succeeded in showing that picture-making is a matter of learning basic skills (realistic drawing of things seen 'out there') and analogue drawing (manipulation of visually structured verbal and visual data). Edwards (1986), in her best-selling books and classes, goes on to teach these skills to any interested person. Her instructions for improvement of realistic drawings consider issues such as placement within the format, heavy or light lines, sagged or curving shapes and expressive structural forms. For realistic drawings she teaches about edges, negative spaces, relationships and proportions, light and shadow.

For Edwards (1986), visual and perceptual skills are similar to verbal, analytic skills which benefit by education. She reports her experiences of a course designed for persons who feel they have no talent for drawing where 'the students who claimed to have no talent are happily drawing away on the same high level of accomplishment as the rest of the class'. The model of creativity used by Edwards (1986) surprisingly has many similarities to that of ROALD. She considers five stages to creativity: first insight (seeking problems), saturation (storing impressions), incubation (mulling over), illumination ('I found it') and verification (checking for errors and usefulness). While these five stages are similar to plot-making, world-making, simulation, narration and text generation of

ROALD, Edwards views them as stages of progression over a period 'from one stage to the next' and not interactions as in ROALD.

Edwards's (1986) model of creativity can be summarized as:

1. Creative individuals often actively search out and discover problems that no one else has perceived;
2. The creative mind has stored impressions, is caught up with an idea, a problem that defies solution despite prolonged study;
3. The creative process begins with conscious efforts at creation or problem-solving;
4. A flash of light is thrown on the subject: Ah, ha, I found it ('Eureka'), complete and dazzling perception of the answer is achieved;
5. Putting the solution into concrete form while checking it for error and usefulness ('a healthy ego requires its creation to be both communicated and accepted').

9.11   COMPUTER PROGRAMMING AS A MEDIUM FOR CREATIVITY

While Edwards (1986) encourages development of people's creativity via more traditional means, computer programming could also act as a new medium for creativity. However, the majority of programming languages use such abstract notions that the creative achievements of programmers are obscured from most observers. A good counter-example to this is the programming language LOGO which, due to Papert's (1980) educational philosophy, is accompanied by the turtle graphics micro world. The turtle is a mechanical device (also offered as a mark on the computer's visual display unit in some implementations) which will take simple commands from children. These commands are very basic picture-making primitives corresponding to movement for a number of steps or turning at an angle. Therefore a child can draw a hexagon by repeating the two commands FORWARD 5 and LEFT 60 six times (Fig. 9.1). The language offers standard programming constructs for iteration and for combining a set of commands into a procedure.

The LOGO folklore's most popular example is that of the house-drawing procedure in Fig. 9.2, taken from Howe *et al.* (1984). A child is shown how to

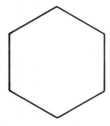

Fig. 9.1. A LOGO hexagon.

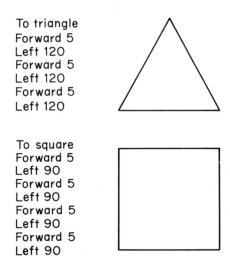

```
To triangle
Forward 5
Left 120
Forward 5
Left 120
Forward 5
Left 120
```

```
To square
Forward 5
Left 90
Forward 5
Left 90
Forward 5
Left 90
Forward 5
Left 90
```

Fig. 9.2. A LOGO triangle and a LOGO square.

draw a triangle and a square. He is then left to experiment on how to combine these two to produce a house.

The first attempts of the child are usually unsuccessful. However, most children learn the procedure for drawing the house either by reasoning about the behaviour of the turtle or by trial and error (Fig. 9.3).

This example, as Burnett (1984) reports, has become somewhat boring for people with day-to-day experience of LOGO. Burnett (1984) reports a colleague as saying, 'If I see another house, I think I'll scream!' However, one of Burnett's grade 3 students produced the pleasing picture in Fig. 9.4 which did not lead to any screams as it should have done!

Here the student had combined the two already learnt ideas of iteration and house-drawing to come up with a totally unexpected new picture. Lawler *et al.* (1986) reported a similar, yet visually different experience of Figs 9.5 and 9.6.

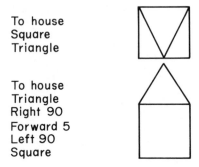

```
To house
Square
Triangle
```

```
To house
Triangle
Right 90
Forward 5
Left 90
Square
```

Fig. 9.3. The LOGO house.

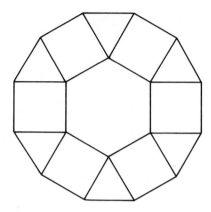

Fig. 9.4. Hexagon of houses.

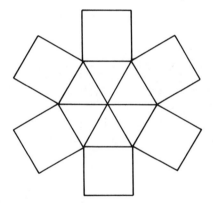

Fig. 9.5. Rotated house.

These are three of many possible pleasing patterns using a house, some of which might have more obvious counterparts in the child's everyday life (Fig. 9.7).

9.12 CONCLUSION

Elsewhere (Yazdani, 1987) we have argued that in creative writing we can afford to be sloppy as long as we evaluate our work at a later stage. In this chapter, we argue that a playful attitude towards the rules governing other domains, such as picture-making and scientific discovery, is behind creative breakthrough. A dutiful following of the rules which specify the set of valid forms in a domain (such as Chomsky's 1966 notion of creativity in language) is better viewed as

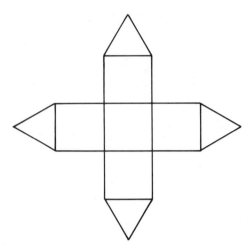

Fig. 9.6. Four houses.

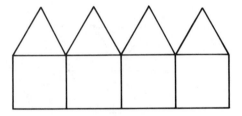

Fig. 9.7. Street.

'productivity'. While 'creativity' could be viewed as the discovery of new rules which specify new sets of valid forms.

The knowledge for manipulation and later validation of a rule set is captured in what we call meta-rules. Similarly to our proposal for creative writing, it is the *post hoc* checking of the results for error and usefulness which produces a gem from a potentially chaotic outcome.

We finally would like to point out that ROALD could possibly be used as an experiment for teaching creative writing. The users of the system would be able to change a small set of facts relating to a world and see the outcome. This potential of a counterpart to LOGO's pictorial educational success demands a good deal of worthwhile effort in the future.

9.13 REFERENCES

Boden, M. A. (1977) *Artificial Intelligence and Natural Man*, Basic Books, New York.
Boden, M. A. (1981) Failure is not the spur, Paper for NATO Workshop on Adaptive Control in Ill-defined Systems.

Boden, M. A. (1982) Mechanisms of creativity, Inaugural lecture, University of Sussex.

Boden, M. A. (1983) Creativity and computers, in *Harold Cohen*, The Tate Gallery, London.

Bundy, A. (1984) Meta-level inference and consciousness, in *Mind and the Machine* (ed. S. Torrance), Ellis Horwood, Chichester, pp. 156–67.

Burnett, D. (1984) LOGO for teacher education, in *New Horizons in Educational Computing* (ed. M. Yazdani), Ellis Horwood, Chichester, pp. 72–83.

Chomsky, N. (1966) *Current Issues in Linguistic Theory*, Mouton and Co., The Hague.

Clocksin, W. F. and Mellish, C. S. (1984) *Programming in PROLOG*, Springer-Verlag, Berlin.

Cohen, H. (1979) What is an image? *Proc. IJCAI-79*, pp. 1028–57.

De Beaugrande, R. (1979) Towards a general theory of creativity. *Poetics*, **8**, 269–306.

Edwards, B. (1986) *Drawing on the Artist Within*, Simon and Schuster Inc., New York.

Forsyth, R. (1986) Machine learning, in *Artificial Intelligence: Principles and Applications* (ed. M. Yazdani), Chapman and Hall, London, pp. 199–205.

Hofstadter, D. R. (1979) *Godel, Escher, Bach: An Eternal Golden Braid*, Penguin Book, London.

Howe, J. A. M., Ross, P. M., Johnson, K. R. and Inglis, R. (1984) Model building, mathematics and LOGO, in *New Horizons in Educational Computing* (ed. M. Yazdani), Ellis Horwood, Chichester, pp. 54–71.

Klein, S. (1975) Meta-compiling text grammars as model for human behaviour. *TINLP*, **1**, 94–8.

Klein, S. and Meehan, J. R. (1977) AI forum. *SIGART Newsletter*, no. 62, 2–4.

Klein, S. *et al.* (1973) *Automatic Novel Writing: A Status Report*, Wisconsin University.

Lawler, R. W., du Boulay, B., Hughes, M. and Macleod, H. (1986) *Cognition and Computers: Studies in Learning*, Ellis Horwood, Chichester.

Lenat, D. B. (1977) Automated theory formation in mathematics. *Proc. IJCAI-77*, pp. 833–42.

Lenat, D. B. (1983) EURISKO: a program that learns new heuristics and domain concepts. *Artificial Intelligence*, **21**, 61–98.

Meehan, J. R. (1976) The metanovel: writing stories by computer, Research Report 74, Department of Computer Science, Yale University.

Minsky, M. (1966) Matter, mind and models, in *Semantic Information Processing* (ed. M. Minsky), MIT Press, Boston, pp. 425–32.

Narayanan, A. (1983) What is it like to be a machine? in *Mind and the Machine* (ed. S. Torrance), Ellis Horwood, Chichester.

Papert, S. (1980) *Mindstorms: Children, Computers and Powerful Ideas*, Basic Books, New York.

Polya, G. (1975) (2nd edn 1957) *How to Solve it: A New Aspect of Mathematical Method*, Princeton University Press.

Propp, V. (1968) *Morphology of the Folk Tale*, University of Texas Press, Austin.

Yazdani, M. (1987) Reviewing as a component of the text generation process, in *Natural Language Generation: Recent Advances in Artificial Intelligence, Psychology and Linguistics* (ed. G. Kempen), Martinus Nijhoff, Dordrecht, pp. 183–90.

Yazdani, M. (forthcoming) A computational perspective on creative writing, DPhil Thesis, Sussex University.

Part four

Long-term perspectives

10

The road to knowledge-rich learning

ROY RADA

10.1 BASIC ISSUES

The development of intelligent computer systems requires that computers flexibly respond to people. One approach to building adaptive machines is to prime them with very little specific knowledge but to give them a rich set of examples from which to learn. The hope in such approaches is that the maximum flexibility will have been thus invested in the computer. An alternative approach is carefully to fill the computer with vast amounts of tailored knowledge and simultaneously to prepare it to integrate new incoming information. The problem addressed by this paper is how knowledge which has been developed for other than machine learning purposes can be semi-automatically incorporated into the computer.

The standard criterion for success of an artificial intelligence (AI) program is that the program behaves like people. What are necessary and sufficient conditions for intelligence? An organism's intelligence depends on its performance relative to other organisms. The organism generates trials; the trials are evaluated by the environment; and the organism adjusts its next trial. We assume that a generate-and-test mechanism is necessary in an intelligent system.

Generate + test are clearly not sufficient conditions for intelligence. In a system with noisy regularity, an organism that is to succeed must be able to make low-risk trials. A small change in the code should lead to a small change in the input–output behaviour manifested by the code. Gradualness also means that the range of behaviours searched by the small changes in structure well covers the small changes in function that are possible.

Conrad gives a biological argument for gradualness. The argument applies directly to the evolution of proteins but can be readily extended to the development of organisms. Quoting from Conrad (1979):

> Suppose that a population carries protein S_0, that S_m is the genetically closest protein of higher fitness, that M independent genetic changes are required to jump from S_0 to S_m, and that all intermediate protein forms are unfit. Then the average number of generations required for the appearance of S_m is given by

$$\tau_{0,m}^m = \frac{20^m}{N_0 p^m (1-p)^{(n-m)}}$$

where m indicates the number of required simultaneous genetic events, N_0 is the initial population size, n is the length of the protein, p is the mutation probability; the factor 20 enters because the $n-m$ remaining amino acids must not change. ... Alternatively, suppose that of the $m!$ possible ways in which S_0 can change into S_m by single changes in amino acid sequence, there is at least one for which every protein species in the sequence has at least slightly increased fitness. The average required number of generations is now given by

$$\tau_{0,m}^1 = \frac{20^m}{N_0 p (1-p)^{(n-1)}} + (m-1)D$$

where the delay time D is the number of generations which it requires for the population to grow to the same size as the old population.

For a protein of length 300, a mutation rate of $p = 10^{-8}$ and a step length of $m = 3$, the advantage is of the order of 10^{18} (assuming $D = 1000$ and $N_0 = 10^6$).

The AI literature addresses the role of gradualness in intelligence. When a program successfully learns, the predictability or regularity in the problem space has been captured. Carbonell (1983) argues that the key to learning by analogy is a similarity metric that retrieves solutions of previously solved problems that closely resemble the present problem. Philosophy also provides evidence of the role of gradualness in problem-solving. New theories of science evidently arise from combinations of good parts of earlier theories (Darden, 1982).

Ernst and Newell's (1969) General Problem Solver (GPS) solved problems by creating subgoals when the step from initial state to goal state was too big. Subgoaling is a way to achieve gradualness in a search space. Rosenbloom *et al.* (1984) have emphasized the role that knowledge can play in guiding the choice of subgoals. Pearl (1983) argues that problems are solved by consulting simplified models of the problem. The key to the applicability of these simplified models is the decomposability of the problem. Decomposability means in part that all subgoals can be solved independently. Pearl tries to discover the decomposability or gradualness of a problem by constructing models of the problem and manipulating parameters or constraints.

10.2   RANGE OF APPROACHES

10.2.1   Knowledge-sparse

(a) Knowledge-sparse basics

The perceptron (Minsky and Papert, 1969) is a famous example of a knowledge-sparse learning scheme. A weighted polynomial is used to classify patterns. Based on experience the weights are adjusted. For simple problem spaces the learning algorithm moves gracefully to the goal state.

The latest development in knowledge-sparse learning is Connectionism (Feldman and Ballard, 1982). This represents a revival of the old neural network experiments, but now the hardware is available to make the experiments several orders of magnitude more broad. Also cognitive scientists are renewing their efforts to explain how the parallel adjusting of weights on neural connections relates to cognition.

In another type of knowledge-sparse learning, numeric data is interpreted. Computer programs can look at databases about medical patients and use statistical decision theory to find patterns in the data which contribute to man's understanding of disease (Blum, 1982). To probe the process of scientific discovery computer scientists have developed programs which take numeric data about the planets' trajectories and discover the equations of planetary motion (Langley *et al.*, 1986).

There has also been a wealth of recent research that is related to adjusting weights on polynomials. In particular, the work with learning for weighted, rule-based expert systems has shown the ease with which adjustments to numeric weights can be made. A detailed example is given here of adjusting weights on a rule-based radiology expert system.

(b) An example

The radiology expert system had rules of the form: 'if location intracerebral and location vascular distribution and size moderate, then 0.5 diagnosis infarct'. The antecedents or 'if' parts of the rules are 'anded' together. Weights are part of each rule because a conclusion is typically reached with less than complete certainty. The above rule had weight of 0.5 on the 'then' part. The syntax and semantics of these rules are similar to that of EMYCIN (Van Melle, 1979).

Two basic strategies in knowledge refinement research are:

1. Start with almost no information (the bottom-up approach) and test what can be discovered; or
2. Take an almost perfectly working system, remove some small part of it, and investigate ways automatically to replace that lost information (the top-down approach).

If we take the top-down approach to a weighted, rule-based expert system, then a natural part partially to destroy is the number or weight part. These numbers have two attractive properties. First, numbers have an ordering – 0.1 is less than 0.2, 0.2 is less than 0.3, etc. This ordering is well understood and corresponds to the role or meaning that these numbers serve. Second, if the interaction among rules is not too great, as experience suggests (Lenat, 1983) then a change in the number on one rule should not radically alter the performance of the expert system. This second factor relates to the 'linear-like' relationship that exists among numbers in the rule base. Because of the first property, a small change in the structure or state of the numbers is easy to make. The second 'linear-like' property allows us to expect that a small change in structure corresponds to a small change in function.

The problem of finding the correct weights for the rules can be viewed as a search through a search space. A control strategy must choose which weight change operators to apply. The strategy may involve testing rules against a learning set and adjusting weights that are responsible for mistakes. The weighted, rule-based system resembles the perceptron (Minsky and Papert, 1969) but a set of rules is more powerful than a single perceptron.

Greedy search (Aho *et al.*, 1983) fails for weight adjustment. Consider the simple case where weights are either 0.5 or 1.0 and the initial state and learning set are as depicted in Fig. 10.1. A greedy search would notice that by changing the weight on $a \to 0.5 \to b$ from 0.5 to 1.0 that three diagnoses, d, e and f, would be correctly concluded and a score of $+3$ attained. On the other hand, only by keeping $a \to 0.5 \to b$ and increasing weights with $b \to 1 \to d$, $b \to 1 \to e$, and $b \to 1 \to f$ can all four diagnoses be correctly reached. A greedy search would not be willing to postpone the achievement of the $+3$ score and would thus make a mistake.

An algorithm, called LEARNER, for the systematic correction of the weights was elaborated. The strategy included raising the attenuations when a proposition was concluded without enough certainty and lowering the attenuations when a proposition was concluded with too much certainty. The amount by which a rule's weight was to be changed would depend on the past performance of that rule.

LEARNER has a credit assignment (CA) and weight adjustment (WA) phase. Each phase reads an element *ls* from the learning set. Each rule has a property list with the following identifiers: (i) Perfect, (ii) TooMuch and (iii) TooLittle. For a given *ls*, CA determines the sequences of rules that lead to each conclusion. For cases (i), (ii) and (iii) each of those rules has its Perfect, TooMuch, or TooLittle property, respectively, augmented with *ls*. WA changes the weights to improve the performance of the rules on the learning set. For case (i) no adjustments are necessary. For case (ii) the attenuations of the rules are lowered, if the number of *ls* on TooMuch–TooLittle–Perfect is greater than 0. Case (iii) is handled similarly to case (ii). LEARNER, with a number of embellishments, was implemented in a 500-line LISP program and performed well in several practical cases (Ackerman, 1984). The gradual changes that are invoked by LEARNER suit the smooth search space of weight refinement.

Initial State		Learning Set	
		Givens	Diagnoses
	$b \to .5 \to c$	(a,1)	(c,.25)
$a \to .5 \to b$	$b \to .5 \to d$		(d,.5)
	$b \to .5 \to e$		(e,.5)
	$b \to .5 \to f$		(f,.5)

Fig. 10.1. Greedy search fails on this case.

10.2.2 Knowledge-rich

Several fundamental paradigms for knowledge-rich machine learning can be delineated. Learning by example and inductive inference (Michalski, 1983) builds rules about classification. In learning by watching or apprentice learning interactive dialogue leads to amendments to a knowledge base (KB) (Davis, 1982). Apprentice learning may include sophisticated models of the user and the domain (Wilkins, 1987). Explanation-based learning often takes the difficult task of processing natural language and 'explaining' failures in the parsing in such a way as to learn how to improve the KB which supports the parsing (Pazzani, 1987).

(a) Interactively adjusting rules

The development of rules for an expert system is a complex task which requires experts diligently to transform their expertise into rule form. Often experts find it difficult to codify their knowledge. Accordingly, computer programs have been developed to interact with experts to help them refine rules. TEIRESIAS can guide an expert through the operation of a system like MYCIN and allow the expert easily to modify the rules which lead to erroneous conclusions (Davis, 1982).

One strategy for intelligent information retrieval is to have users create knowledge bases which describe their special interests. RUBRIC, for RUle-Based Retrieval of Information by Computer (Tong *et al.*, 1984), is an example of a production system that performs evidential reasoning (Buchanan, 1984). The text of a document provides the evidence on which the rules operate. The rules define a hierarchy of topics. By naming a topic, the user invokes a goal-oriented search of the tree beneath the topic. The lowest-level topics are defined in terms of patterns in the text itself. Thus the system ultimately depends on a string search of text. A small example of the operation of these rules takes a query for documents about machine learning. Start with the set of rules:

(a) IF machine AND learning THEN 1.0 machine learning
(b) IF computer OR machine THEN 0.8 machine
(c) IF learning OR adaptation OR acquisition THEN 0.5 learning

A document with the three terms computer, knowledge and acquisition would activate first rules (b) and (c) and then rule (a). According to the default uncertainty criteria (Tong *et al.*, 1983), the document would be rated as about machine learning at the 0.5 level.

RUBRIC has been implemented in several institutions which are responsible for sifting through large numbers of documents. These institutions have individuals who must scan certain types of documents. Each individual can create his own set of rules that describe the documents which he wants to see. If another individual has similar interest, the two can share their rules. Documents which come to the institutions are filtered through the rules, and each individual is given those documents which are particular to his interest. When a document is stopped by the filter but does not seem germane to the individual that created the filter, the program can explain how the decision was made and the individual can adjust the rules. This is an interactive form of knowledge acquisition or machine learning.

(b) Learning from natural language

(i) Learning from statements. If statements come into a system from a user, which the system does not recognize, then it could look for the nearest match in its set of statements and check with the user to determine whether that match is correct. Once a correct match has been found, various strategies can be employed to change the system so that next time it immediately recognizes the statement. This is a kind of syntax learning (Reeker, 1971).

For example, start with the utterance 'wings are clear'. Assume that the closest assertion to 'wings are clear' in the computer system is 'the insect has clear wings' and that the user agrees that 'the insect has clear wings' captures the correct meaning of the utterance 'wings are clear'. At its simplest, the system would say that 'wings are clear' should be transformed into 'the insect has clear wings'. More generally, given the syntactic parses of the two phrases, one might want to say that the structure S[NP[N]VP[COP ADJ]] goes into the structure S[NP[ADJ N]], where the subject 'insect' and verb 'has' are dropped. In this particular example, 'wings are clear' transforms to 'clear wings'. The program might now speculate based on the context, as to whether the NP 'clear wings' is the object of 'insect has'. Having made these grammatical conclusions based on the example, one could now try these on other examples, such as 'wings are opaque' or 'legs are long'. Something has been learned about all utterances of the form S[NP[N]VP[COP ADJ]] and S[NP[ADJ N]] and not just their superficial manifestations (Reeker, 1976).

The system NanoKLAUS, which is short for small Knowledge-Learning and Using Systems, has a basic knowledge of English and is capable of learning the concepts and vocabulary of new subject domains (Haas and Hendrix, 1980). NanoKLAUS comes preprogrammed with a seed vocabulary, a set of seed concepts, and a set of syntactic and semantic rules covering a small subset of English. These allow the system to engage in conversations such as:

User: A length is a measure.
System: You're saying that anything that is a LENGTH is also a MEASURE. Ok, now I have assimilated LENGTH.

Most of the linguistic processing performed by NanoKLAUS is done with a standard pragmatic grammar (Hendrix *et al.*, 1978), but there are specific syntactic structures that define new concepts. For instance, there is a construct which basically says

$$\langle \text{sentence} \rangle \rightarrow \langle \text{new-word} \rangle \; \langle \text{is-a} \rangle \; \langle \text{known-word} \rangle.$$

When a sentence satisfies this pattern, an acquisition procedure is invoked. This procedure may generate new entries for ⟨new-word⟩ in the system's lexicon and new well-formed formulae in the KB.

(ii) Learning from documents. Compare the way an expert stores knowledge about books to the way a library handles the same information. The library creates a classification structure which is hard to change and into which all new material must fit (Schank, 1982). An expert, on the other hand, can make observations about what is known and can alter the memory structures that catalogue what is known.

In order to account for dynamic memory – the ability to generalize and learn from past experience – information about how memory structures are linked in frequently occurring combinations is held in memory organization packets (MOPs). A MOP is both a structure and a processor. According to Schank (1982): 'A MOP consists of a set of scenes directed towards the achievement of a goal. A MOP always has one major scene whose goal is the essence or purpose of the events organized by the MOP.' A MOP processes new inputs by taking the aspects of those inputs that relate to that MOP and interpreting those aspects in terms of the memory in the MOP. Many different MOPs may be active at one time in response to one event. This view of memory is an embellishment of object-oriented programming (Filman and Friedman, 1984). The key to reminding and learning is the ability to create new structures that emphasize the abstract significance of a combination of MOPs.

Kolodner (1984) has developed a computer system called CYRUS which tests some of the ideas that Schank has advanced about dynamic memory. She argues that memory is organized and searched in accordance with the properties of a reconstructive memory. This means that information is retrieved by reconstructing what must have happened rather than by directly remembering what did happen.

Memory is automatically changed through time in CYRUS. As documents are indexed, they precipitate the modification of MOPs. The differences between the appropriate indexing for the new document and the previous indexing are assessed. Either the new document can be handled by amending existing MOPs or new MOPs are created. The memory organization that is built is a hierarchical organization of categories and their subcategories. As new events are indexed, new subcategories are created. To avoid the astronomical growth of the memory, generalizations are performed.

Lebowitz (1983) has also been investigating techniques of implementing dynamic memories. He argues that changes to a KB should be based on large amounts of textual information and generalization strategies. Generalization-based memory (GBM) has the following properties:

1. It is inherently incremental. As instances are added to the memory, the best available generalizations are made;
2. It handles large amounts of information. The use of a hierarchy of concepts

that organizes specific instances facilitates storage and retrieval of information;
3. Generalizations are pragmatic. No concept is removed by a single counterexample.

When GBM finds several instances that disconfirm a generalization, it tries to throw away the bad parts and keep the good parts of the generalization. To remove the overly specific parts of a generalization, GBM keeps track of the value of the generalization's components. A confidence level is maintained that indicates how many times each component was confirmed and how many times it was contradicted.

Schank's work on dynamic memory emphasizes several intuitively appealing principles, while work with cognitive graphs addresses the same problems in a different, more mathematical way. The method of cognitive graphing is based on the theory of directed graphs and is motivated by the belief that knowledge of the mathematics of abstract structures is of value in cognitive simulation. A KB can be automatically developed by reading documents and translating them through a sequence of cognitive graphs (Bonham, 1985).

If knowledge-based systems, of which the cognitive graph is an example, are to be economically profitable to the public at large, they will need a procedure for the incorporation of the textual knowledge now represented in scientific and technical journals, handbooks and libraries. In one experiment, a document is manually translated into its cognitive graph (Bonham, 1985). Then graph reasoning algorithms are applied to the task of integrating the graph of a particular document with the global KB (also represented as a cognitive graph).

10.3   INTERMEDIATE APPROACH

10.3.1   The problem of connecting knowledge bases

There are progressively more systems that provide access to information. Often these systems heavily rely on some KB to facilitate classification and retrieval. Connecting these KBs thus becomes a major problem in trying to facilitate information access.

The approach next examined in this chapter looks at existing KBs – less complex than natural language but more robust than unstructured examples – and asks how they can be put together. Building, updating and connecting KBs for information systems is currently a knowledge-intensive task and is part of the knowledge bottleneck in the development of more intelligent information systems. The parsing and matching of queries and documents (see Fig. 10.2) create a reservoir of data for experimentation on the value of the KB which supports the parsing and matching.

Given the ability to detect similarities and differences in structure and function of two KBs, it should be possible to do analogical merges of the two KBs. Based on the similarities in the two KBs, the salient differences are detected. Then these differences are brought together to produce one superior KB. In the course of such experiments, the failure to merge successfully with seemingly valid merge techniques may shed light on inadequacies in the evaluation methods.

10.3.2   Background information

There are information systems which store bibliographic data, such as MEDLINE. MEDLINE gives the author, journal, title, pages, date and keywords for 6 million biomedical articles (McCarn, 1980). There are also information retrieval services, such as DIALOG, which provide a uniform interface to many other databases. DIALOG provides indirect access to over 120 million records that include such diverse information as in-depth financial statements for particular companies, biographies of famous people, and MEDLINE (DIALOG Information Services, 1987).

A thesaurus may be viewed as a set of concepts. Each concept is represented as a frame, where each frame contains slots for hierarchical terms, associative terms, synonyms, definitions and more (National Library and Information

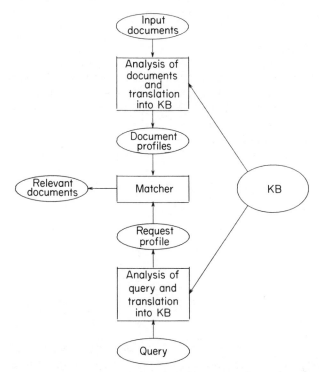

Fig. 10.2. Diagram of part of information retrieval system with emphasis on KB-encoding (KB means knowledge base) of documents and queries.

Associations Council, 1980). The hierarchical relationship includes such relationships as is-a (Brachman, 1983) and part-of (Smith and Mulligan, 1982). The associative relation includes the causal relation, the side-effect relation, the carried-by relation and more. The characteristics of a thesaurus allow it to be called a KB, a semantic net, a classification language or an ordering system (Dahlberg, 1983).

Thesauri are integral parts of many information systems. Documents are represented as sets of concepts from the thesaurus. Queries are represented as Boolean combinations of concepts from the thesaurus. This can be viewed as a parsing of documents and queries into the KB. The information system then matches the query to documents based on the parsed representations (see Fig. 10.2).

There are many thesauri. The Medical Subject Headings (MeSH) is a thesaurus used to classify medical literature. MeSH contains about 100 000 concepts in a large hierarchy that goes 11 levels deep (see Fig. 10.3) (Backus *et al.*, 1987). This hierarchy is a tangled one, as a concept may have more than one broader-than concept. The Computing Reviews Classification Structure (CRCS) is used to classify the literature of the Association of Computing Machinery. CRCS has about 1000 concepts in a 4-level tree. Its sub-trees cover such topics as software, hardware and theory of computation (Sammet, 1982).

10.3.3   Experiments

A series of experiments will be presented. First hierarchical KBs will be united with one another as concepts from one KB will be added via hierarchical relations to concepts in another KB. Then the addition of associative relations from one KB into another will be explored. Finally, the effect of adding simultaneously hierarchical and associative relations from one KB to another will be considered with the argument that while more complex it also lends itself to more powerful uniting.

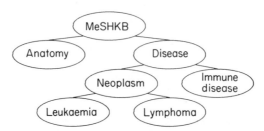

Fig. 10.3. Small portion of MeSH hierarchy that begins with the top of the knowledge base called MeSHKB. Overall the hierarchy is 11 levels deep and includes over 100 000 concepts.

(a) Hierarchical

Transitive hierarchical learning means that when x is narrower than y and y is narrower than z, then x is narrower than z. Such learning can be applied to hierarchical KBs. First two concepts a_2 in KB A and b_1 in KB B must be determined to be similar. Then the children of one node are copied to the other KB at the common node (see Fig. 10.4).

The hierarchical learning will involve the addition of concepts from CRCS to MeSH. The hypothesis is that the addition of these concepts to MeSH makes for a better thesaurus. To test this claim a measure of 'better' is needed. Here the measure is the extent to which MeSH versus augmented-MeSH supports automated indexing or parsing.

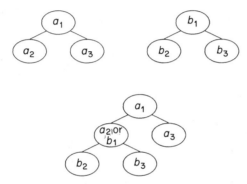

Fig. 10.4. Above: thesauri A and B; below: merged thesaurus formed by joining A and B at the common nodes a_2 and b_1.

The National Library of Medicine supports about a hundred full-time indexers whose job is to scan articles in the biomedical literature and to assign a handful of MeSH concepts to each article. The product of this indexing is stored on the computer and thus becomes available not only for searchers around the world but also for anyone wishing to do experiments. With the indexing is also stored other basic information about each article such as its title. There is reason to expect that there should be a significant correlation between the title of a paper and some of the MeSH concepts assigned to the paper.

After MeSH was augmented with a concept x from another thesaurus, the automatic indexer (INDEXER) might find a match between a title and x. By taking the step from x to the hierarchically nearest MeSH concept, INDEXER might succeed in duplicating the indexing that the human indexers had achieved with MeSH. In this way, the augmented thesaurus might support automatic indexing that was better than automatic indexing with MeSH alone.

For various reasons knowledge from different contexts may conflict. For instance, at one time 'artificial intelligence' was considered a subset of 'pattern recognition' whereas at another time 'pattern recognition' was considered a subset of 'artificial intelligence'. Two thesauri manifesting these conflicting views of the broader-than relation between 'artificial intelligence' and 'pattern recognition' would cause a united thesaurus to represent a conflict or else would require that the uniting procedure somehow resolve the conflict.

A conflict resolution strategy was developed (Mili and Rada, 1988) which gives preference to the placement of a concept which comes from the deepest hierarchical structure. For the case of directly contradicting broader-than against narrower-than relationships, the heuristic is to make the two conflicting concepts siblings. Figure 10.5 shows a case where concept c and concept a have opposite relations to one another in two thesauri and the resultant merge.

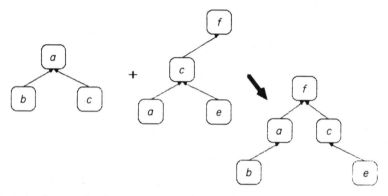

Fig. 10.5. Conflict resolution.

If one were to make a neat definition of the broader-than relation as one of set inclusion, of course, the preceding conflict resolution strategies would be inappropriate. For instance, if c is a subset of a and a is a subset of c, then there are only two possibilities: either $c = a$ or there is an error. The proper resolution in this case may not be to say that c and a are siblings. But in the world of KBs the broader-than relation is not defined as a subset relation. In the case of a system such as KL-ONE the broader-than relation implies inheritance of properties from parent to child but exceptions must be allowed (Brachman and Schmolze, 1985).

MeSH and CRCS were united with the conflict resolution strategy. Automatic indexing was then done on thirty-three titles from MEDLINE about computers and medicine. The notion of a distance between two concepts in the KB was introduced and applied to the evaluation. When INDEXER produced no output it was considered to be arbitrarily far from the human indexing. If INDEXER produced a concept that was narrower-than the concept generated by the human indexer, then the automatic indexer was considered to be close to correct. A formal elaboration of this strategy was devised and applied to the performance of INDEXER on MeSH and MeSH + CRCS. The augmented MeSH proved to support indexing significantly better than the unaugmented MeSH. The results of this merging of thesauri also led to many practical benefits to the National Library of Medicine (Rada *et al.*, 1987).

(b) Associative

The concepts in a KB should have more than hierarchical relations among them. Uniting associative relations from one KB with hierarchical relations from another KB should provide for a better KB. This section advances a method for doing and evaluating such uniting. The results of the experiments show a surprising aspect of spreading activation.

Associative relations may often be interpreted in a structure–function way. This is a different sense of function from that which refers to the function of the entire KB, for this refers to the function that a concept has in relation to other concepts within the KB. But, in fact, both of these kinds of structure–function are important in dealing with KBs.

The main KB to be used as the source of associative relations in the experiments to be discussed here is CMIT. CMIT is produced by the American Medical Association and contains about 4000 disease descriptions (Finkel *et al.*, 1981). Each disease has eleven slots where the slots include etiology, symptoms, signs and prognosis. The values of these attributes are represented in a noun phrase type format (see Fig. 10.6).

The strategy was to map a CMIT disease name to a MeSH concept and to map a CMIT attribute to a MeSH concept. Then the relation which connected the CMIT attribute to the CMIT disease was added to MeSH. This is a kind of simple analogical or similarity learning.

We have combined the notion of spreading activation with that of conceptual distance. If one concept is related to another concept, then the two are close. If instead many relations separate two concepts, they are not close. This

AYERZA SYNDROME
    See also Polycythemia, secondary;
    Hypertension, pulmonary, secondary.
at Arrillaga-Ayerza syndrome; Black cardiac
    disease; Pulmonary arteriosclerosis syndrome.
et Primary disease of pulmonary artery and
    branches; arterial, arteriolar sclerosis; syphilis;
    congenital hypoplasia of pulmonary artery.
ag Onset at about age 40; persistent cyanosis;
    dyspnea; enlargement of liver, spleen.
lb Blood; RBC increase.
cr Prognosis; unfavorable; right-sided heart
    failure.

Fig. 10.6. An example of a CMIT disease, as it appears in the CMIT publication.

observation has been generalized to sets of concepts so that a metric (called DISTANCE) on sets has been defined.

To our surprise, MeSH supported the ranking of documents in a way that significantly agreed with the ranking of experts. And yet more surprising, MeSH augmented with CMIT associative relations led to rankings by DISTANCE that did not significantly correlate with the rankings of experts.

Our algorithm for reasoning by analogy from CMIT to MeSH inserted relationships such as 'Rheumatoid arthritis has a pathological finding of granuloma'. DISTANCE treated the special relationships no differently than it would handle the 'is-a' relationships. The 'is-a' relationships are transitive: the fact that juvenile rheumatoid arthritis 'is-a' rheumatoid arthritis 'is-a' arthritis also means that juvenile rheumatoid arthritis 'is-a' arthritis. Some work in cognitive psychology has suggested that spreading activation proceeds across exactly one relationship and then stops (de Groot, 1983). For instance, people think 'cow' is close to 'milk' and 'cow' is close to 'bull' but 'milk' is not close to 'bull'. Our work suggests that for measures of conceptual similarity the spreading activation should emphasize traversal of transitive relations. One could go in that way from 'cow' to 'mammal' to 'animal' but not from 'mammal' to 'milk'.

We revised DISTANCE to take advantage of some of the different kinds of relationships that exist in augmented MeSH. This new DISTANCE or neo-DISTANCE can only follow an associative relationship when the query which is being processed specifies that relationship. The application of neo-DISTANCE to augmented-MeSH produced good rankings of documents to queries.

In the context of knowledge acquisition and gradualness these experiments show the need for structure–function linkage. An additional structural unit (such as an edge connecting granuloma and rheumatoid arthritis) does not help unless its corresponding functional significance is appreciated. When the reasoning or DISTANCE algorithm was modified to account for the difference between the original 'is-a' edges in MeSH and the variety of added edges, then the knowledge acquisition effort proved more effective.

(c) Inheritance

Having studied the addition of concepts into hierarchical relations and the addition of associative relations into hierarchies, we now want to consider the role of inheritance when hierarchical and associative relations are simultan-eously considered. Given the cognitive nature of the decisions which need at times to be made concerning the augmenting of KBs, an interactive system may be valuable.

People recognize the need to store large document spaces in special database management systems (Stonebraker *et al.*, 1983). That working with thesauri alone might require database management systems is less often appreciated. An attempt to store MeSH in a frame-based language called FRAMEKIT (Carbonell and Joseph, 1985) failed due to memory overflow problems. Likewise, attempts to store MeSH in KEE (Knowledge Engineering Environment) also failed due to memory overflow problems. Database management systems are one way to overcome the memory management problem.

A relational database was developed to reflect the entities and relationships within MeSH and CMIT. The relational schemes are presented in a form such as

DISEASE (Disease Name, Etiology, Symptom, Sign)

which states that the DISEASE relation has as its attributes Disease Name, Etiology, Symptom and Sign. For the purposes of the current experiment the focus is on disease descriptions. This is consistent with the way that medicine is often approached and with the knowledge in CMIT.

We have a procedure for inserting the CMIT disease names into the MeSH hierarchy. To connect CMIT disease names with MeSH, terms of one thesaurus are mapped to terms of another. First, all lexical matches between CMIT and MeSH disease names are determined. All synonyms for a disease name are also used in this matching. Whenever a match is found, the CMIT disease code is chosen to replace the MeSH disease code, not only in the DISEASE relation but also in the other relations that use the disease code.

Next, inheritance properties are used to find additional points of connection among the thesauri. The properties of each node are deduced from CMIT, once the disease name in CMIT is equivalent to or synonymous with the disease name of the node in MeSH. The relational databases facilitated the merging of the thesauri and also allowed efficient storage and retrieval.

(d) Analogical inheritance

To say that a concept inherits the attributes of its broader-than concept is only to characterize the attributes which the two concepts have in common and says nothing about why the relationship is unidirectional. We argue that there is a structure–function relationship in KBs which allows a special kind of inheritance that we call analogical inheritance.

We will present a simplified view of analogical inheritance in these preliminary explorations. Assume that every concept has both hierarchical and associative relations. In an ideal KB – one built according to the principle of analogical inheritance – each concept x would for each attribute $f(x)$ either

1. Inherit the value which its broader-than concept y had for that attribute $f(y)$; or
2. Have the value b which was narrower-than $f(y)$

This could also be viewed as maintaining an isomorphism in the KB. Given

$$f(x) = a$$

$$f(y) = b$$

$$\text{broader-than}(x) = y$$

and

$$\text{broader-than}(a) = b$$

then the isomorphism is broader-than$(f(x)) = f(\text{broader-than}(x))$.

The principle could be used to guide the development of KBs. Clearly, in reality the isomorphism property does not strictly apply. Among other things the KB is rich with relations and not functions. For another thing, human knowledge is fuzzy and subject to different views in different contexts. Nevertheless, this basic idea may lead to rich theory as it is explored and extended.

It could be evaluated by testing the extent to which KBs in the real world maintain the property of analogical isomorphism. It could also be a guideline for inserting concepts into a hierarchy. An example of how this might occur is in the placement of the Chairman of the Mathematics Department into the hierarchy of knowledge about the administration of the university (Fig. 10.7). If we know that the Chairman of Mathematics has an office in the School of Natural Sciences, then we might expect that the Chairman reports to the Dean of the School of Natural Sciences.

Hypertext has three key features: (1) a database for storing large amounts of document-like information; (2) a semantic net to connect components of the

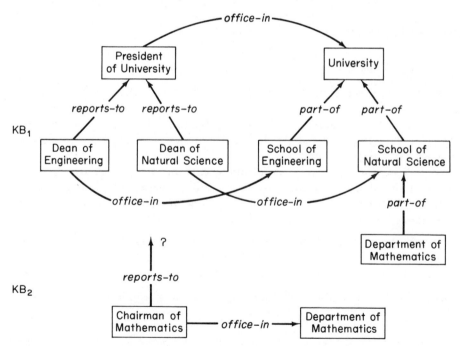

Fig. 10.7. Where to insert the Chairperson of Mathematics in the administrative hierarchy: a case for analogical inheritance.

document; and (3) a browsing facility (Conklin, 1987). In hypertext the goal is to make available to the reader in a readily understandable way rich relationships. In this way the semantic net or KB of hypertext may be a suitable ground for building KBs that follow the principle of analogical inheritance.

We have undertaken a number of experiments in the area of building semantic nets for hypertext. One unresolved question with hypertext concerns the relation between the outline of a document and the semantic net. The outline prescribes a sequential structure to the document, whereas the semantic net is traditionally a cognitive map. In existing hypertext systems these two structures, namely the outline and the semantic net, are treated separately (Trigg and Weiser, 1986; Price, 1982). We wonder to what extent an outline can be built which constitutes a KB as well as a guide to the sequential structure of the document. We have evidence that robust outlines manifest analogical inheritance.

10.4 DISCUSSION

This chapter does not attempt an exhaustive survey of work in machine learning. Rather the attempt here is to bring together in a novel way a number of interesting developments that point to the importance of knowledge-rich learning. The paper has been divided into a part on knowledge-sparse and a part on knowledge-rich learning. Some of the author's own work on refining expert systems and on merging thesauri is presented.

Knowledge-sparse learning depends mainly on a unidimensional, reward–punishment type of feedback. This is in contrast to knowledge-rich learning which might, for instance, depend on finding similarities between KBs and augmenting them so as to take advantage of the long history that has been distilled in the structures. All learning may be seen as having its roots in adaptation to yes–no feedback (knowledge-sparse learning), but it seems characteristic of intelligent systems that they also take advantage of existing knowledge and employ feedback in subtle ways; in other words, they also employ knowledge-rich learning.

Machine learning experiments often focus on the adjustment of numeric weights. If a program were to read directly from text and disambiguate the important meanings from the myriad of possibilities, it would have a natural language processing ability beyond that of existing programs. There are exciting projects that deal not with numbers or text but with intermediate structures – namely, KBs. As the accomplishments of machine learning broaden, they can be expected to produce interactive systems for merging existing KBs. This progress with building knowledge bases is an important step towards natural language processing and, ultimately, question-answering systems.

10.5 ACKNOWLEDGEMENTS

Hafedh Mili and Brian Martin did much of the experimentation with KB merging.

10.6 REFERENCES

Ackerman, L., Burke, M. and Rada, R. (1984) Knowledge representation of CT scan of the head. *Proceedings SPIE, Vol. 454: Applications of Optical Instruments in Medicine XII,* pp. 443–7.

Aho, A., Hopcroft, J. and Ullman, J. (1983) *Data Structures and Algorithms,* Addison-Wesley, Reading, Mass.

Backus, J., Davidson, S. and Rada, R. (1987) Searching for patterns in the MeSH vocabulary. *Bulletin of the Medical Library Association,* **75** (3), 221–7.

Blum, R. L. (1982) Discovery and representation of causal relationships from a large time-oriented clinical database: the RX project, PhD Dissertation, Palo Alto, California. (Also appeared in *Computers and Biomedical Research,* **15,** 164–87.)

Bonham, G. M., Nozicka, G. J. and Stokman, F. N. (1985) Cognitive graphing and the representation of biomedical knowledge. *Proceedings Expert Systems in Government Conference,* IEEE Computer Society Press, pp. 397–403.

Brachman, R. (1983) What IS-A is and isn't: an analysis of taxonomic links in semantic networks. *Computer,* **16** (10), 30–6.

Brachman, R. J. and Schmolze, J. G. (1985) An overview of the KL-ONE knowledge representation system. *Cognitive Science,* **9,** 171–216.

Buchanan, B. and Shortliffe, E. (1984) Major lessons from this work, in *Rule-Based Expert Systems: The MYCIN Experiments of the Stanford Heuristic Programming Project* (ed. E. Shortliffe), Addison-Wesley, Reading, Mass., pp. 669–702.

Carbonell, J. (1983) Learning by analogy, in *Machine Learning* (ed. T. Mitchell), Tioga Publishing, Palo Alto, Calif., pp. 137–61.

Carbonell, J. and Joseph, R. (1985) *FRAMEKIT+: A Knowledge Representation System,* Department of Computer Science, Carnegie-Mellon University, Pittsburgh, Pa.

Conklin, J. (1987) Hypertext: an introduction and survey. *Computer,* **20** (9), 17–41 (September).

Conrad, M. (1979) Bootstrapping on the adaptive landscape. *BioSystems,* **11,** 167–82.

Dahlberg, I. (1983) Conceptual compatibility of ordering systems. *International Classification,* **10** (1), 5–8.

Darden, L. (1982) Artificial intelligence and philosophy of science: reasoning by analogy in theory construction. *PSA 1982,* **2,** 147–65, Philosophy of Science Association, East Lansing, Mich.

Davis, R. (1982) TEIRESIAS: Applications of meta-level knowledge, in *Knowledge-Based Systems in Artificial Intelligence* (ed. D. Lenat), McGraw-Hill, New York, pp. 229–491.

DIALOG Information Services (1987) *DIALOG Database Catalog,* January.

Ernst, G. and Newell, A. (1969) *GPS: A Case Study in Generality and Problem Solving,* Academic Press, New York.

Feldman, J. and Ballard, D. (1982) Connectionist models and their properties. *Cognitive Science,* **6,** 205–54.

Filman, R. and Friedman, D. (1984) *Coordinated Computing: Tools and Techniques for Distributed Software,* McGraw-Hill, New York.

Finkel, A., Gordon, B., Baker, M. and Fanta, C. (1981) *Current Medical Information and Terminology,* American Medical Association, Chicago.

de Groot, A. M. B. (1983) The range of automatic spreading activation in word priming. *Journal of Verbal Learning and Verbal Behavior,* **22,** 417–36.

Haas, N. and Hendrix, G. (1980) An approach to acquiring and applying knowledge.

Proceedings National Conference Artificial Intelligence, American Association Artificial Intelligence, pp. 235–9.

Hendrix, G. G., Sacerdoti, E. D., Sagalowics, D. and Slocum, J. (1978) Developing a natural language interface to complex data. *ACM Transactions on Database Systems*, 3 (2), 17–32.

Kolodner, J. (1984) *Retrieval and Organizational Strategies in Conceptual Memory*, Lawrence Erlbaum, Hillsdale, N.J.

Langley, P., Zytkow, J. M., Simon, H. A. and Bradshaw, G. L. (1986) The search for regularity; four aspects of scientific discovery, in *Machine Learning*, Vol. 2 (ed. T. Mitchell), Morgan Kaufmann Publishers, Los Altos, Calif., 425–70.

Lebowitz, M. (1983) Concept learning in a rich input domain. *Proceedings International Machine Learning Workshop*, pp. 177–82.

Lenat, D. (1983) The role of heuristics in learning by discovery, in *Machine Learning* (ed. T. Mitchell), Tioga Publishing, Palo Alto, Calif., pp. 243–306.

McCarn, D. B. (1980) MEDLINE: an introduction to on-line searching. *Journal of the American Society for Information Science*, 31 (3), 181–92 (May).

Michalski, R. (1983) A theory and methodology of inductive learning, in *Machine Learning* (ed. T. Mitchell), Tioga Publishing, Palo Alto, Calif., pp. 83–134.

Mili, H. and Rada, R. (1988) Merging thesauri: principles and evaluation. *IEEE Transactions on Pattern Analysis and Machine Intelligence*, 10 (2), 204–20.

Minsky, M. and Papert, S. (1969) *Perceptrons*, MIT Press, Cambridge, Mass.

National Library and Information Associations Council (1980) *Guidelines for Thesaurus Structure, Construction, and Use*, American National Standards Institute, New York.

Pazzani, M. (1988) Creating high level knowledge structures from primitive elements. In *Lecture Notes on Knowledge Representation and Organization in Machine Learning* (ed. K. Morik), Springer Verlag, Berlin (in press).

Pearl, J. (1983) On the discovery and generation of certain heuristics. *AI Magazine*, 4 (1), 23–34.

Price, L. A. (1982) Thumb: An interactive tool for accessing and maintaining text. *IEEE Transactions on Systems, Man, and Cybernetics*, 12 (2), 155–61 (March/April).

Rada, R., Blum, B., Calhoun, E., Mili, H., Orthner, H. and Singer, S. (1987) A vocabulary for medical informatics. *Computers and Biomedical Research*, 20, 244–63.

Reeker, L. H. (1971) A problem solving theory of syntax acquisition. *Journal of Structural Learning*, 2 (4), 1–10.

Reeker, L. H. (1976) The computational study of language acquisition, in *Advances in Computers*, Vol. 15 (ed. J. Rubinoff) Academic Press, New York, pp. 181–237.

Rosenbloom, P., Laird, J., McDermott, J., Newell, A. and Orciuch, E. (1984) *R1-Soar: An Experiment in Knowledge-Intensive Programming in a Problem-Solving Architecture*, IEEE Computer Society Press, Silver Spring, Md., pp. 65–72.

Sammet, J. and Ralston, A. (1982) The new (1982) computing reviews classification system – final version. *Communications of the Association for Computing Machinery*, 25 (1), 13–25 (January).

Schank, R. (1982) *Dynamic Memory: A Theory of Reminding and Learning in Computers and People*, Cambridge University Press, Cambridge, UK.

Smith, B. and Mulligan, K. (1982) Pieces of a theory, in *Parts and Moments: Studies in Logic and Formal Ontology* (ed. B. Smith), Philosophia Verlag, Munich, Germany, pp. 15–109.

Stonebraker, M., Stettner, H., Lynn, N., Kalash, J. and Guttman, A. (1983) Document processing in a relational database system. *ACM Transactions on Office Information Systems*, **1** (2), 143–58.

Tong, R., Shapiro, D., Dean, J. and McCune, B. (1983) A comparison of uncertainty calculi in an expert system for information retrieval. *Proceedings International Joint Conference Artificial Intelligence*, pp. 194–7.

Tong, R., Askman, V. and Cunningham, J. (1984) RUBRIC: an artificial intelligence approach to information retrieval. *Proceedings 1st International Workshop on Expert Database Systems*, October.

Trigg, R. H. and Weiser, M. (1986) TEXTNET: a network-based approach to text handling. *ACM Transactions on Office Information Systems*, **4** (1), 1–23.

Van Melle, W. (1979) Domain-independent production-rule system for consultation programs. *Proceedings International Joint Conference Artificial Intelligence*, pp. 923–5.

Wilkins, D. (1988) Apprentice learning: ODYSSEUS. In *Lecture Notes on Knowledge Representation and Organization in Machine Learning* (ed. K. Morik), Springer-Verlag, Berlin (in press).

11

Databases that learn

DEREK PARTRIDGE

In this chapter we are concerned with collections of information that change and grow automatically as a result of interaction with some external world – in a nutshell: databases (DBs) that learn. The general idea is that external information is continuously assimilated into the DB thereby either improving its coverage of a static environment, or perhaps just maintaining its coverage of a dynamic external world.

The learning mechanisms employed form a continuum of possibilities, from relatively trivial rote learning – the simple addition of new information to the DB – to sophisticated integration of the 'essence' of the new information into the current body of knowledge. Systems at the rote-learning end are commonplace, and are typically not accorded the prestigious label of 'machine learning'. Systems at the other end of the spectrum are still very much research projects rather than practical software.

At first sight it might seem that my cursory introduction has omitted a broad class of possibilities, i.e. DBs that simply rearrange or restructure their current contents in order to perform more effectively. Inductive generalization, for example, might be usefully employed to replace a collection of specific rules by a single general rule. But, of course, if the DB does not change as a result of external information, then such restructuring is of benefit once only. A one-time automatic reorganization does not fall into the class of machine learning mechanisms for my current purpose. Hence my emphasis on externally driven DB reorganization.

11.1 TWO VERY GENERAL PARADIGMS

Two basic AI paradigms support the notion of machine learning in rather different ways. In the Connectionist Paradigm (CP) AI systems are networks composed of nodes connected by arcs whose sole function is to transfer 'activity' values from node to node as a function of the 'weight' associated with each arc. In a CP-based model, learning is implemented as the manipulation of these arc weights. Learning is thus a relatively slow, incremental process of arc-weight adjustment. Little or no work in the CP has been explicitly presented as DB learning, but in reality every CP-based model is a network DB and almost all models incorporate machine learning mechanisms. So I shall, from time to time in this chapter, make mention of relevant work in this new and exciting, but largely untested, class of models.

Within the Classical, or Symbolic Search Space, Paradigm (SSSP), which accounts for 99.9% of current AI systems, learning is implemented as a process of accretion: crudely put, symbolic structures, such as (COLOUR JOHN BLUE), are added to a DB. Thus the DB has learnt this new fact. Alternatively, a collection of such specific pieces of information may be replaced by a generalized piece of information. The major point of contrast with the CP is that learning involves the manipulation of bigger 'chunks' of information – semantically interpretable pieces as opposed to a set of arc-weight changes which have no 'meaningful' interpretation in isolation. Within the traditional SSSP-based AI systems complete propositions (or whatever) are typically added, generated or rearranged in the DB. In a CP-based system such one-step, large-scale changes to the DB are not possible. Learning as a result of arc-weight adjustment is necessarily a slow and incremental process.

11.2   MEMO FUNCTIONS

Many years ago, close to the dawn of AI, a machine learning mechanism called 'memo' functions was tried and tested within the context of the programming language POP-2 (see Michie, 1968). What is of interest in the current chapter is that the memo-function idea was implemented and tested as a component of a learning DB in the 1970s, and has recently resurfaced in suggestions for a knowledge base (KB) that learns – and KBs are after all only a (not very well defined) class of DBs.

The basic idea behind memo-function learning is that in a DB in which commonly accessed specific pieces of information are automatically made more quickly available than the infrequently accessed information the overall performance of the DB will be enhanced. Furthermore, it is not just a case of one-time reorganization to sort out the subset of commonly accessed items for preferential treatment. This important subset of items is expected both to vary with context (i.e. exactly how and where each copy of the DB is used) and with time (i.e. the commonly used subset this month may be different from that of next month). So the memo-function idea is meant both to tune the initial copy of the DB to the demands of individual usage environments, and maintain its efficiency over time in the face of continually changing usage patterns.

Thus we are considering a non-trivial machine learning mechanism. The DB must have some means of reorganizing itself to make some specific accesses highly efficient (a 'promotion' mechanism for frequently retrieved items), a means of 'demoting' specific items that have lost their earlier popularity, and finally a means of monitoring access usage to determine exactly which specific items are accessed frequently at each period of time – a usage profile must be kept and maintained. Two general implementation strategies hinge on the choice between continual or periodic reorganization. Under the former strategy little usage profile information need be kept but the DB is in danger of overreacting to minor usage fluctuations (and remember that reorganization takes time that must be offset by average access time speed-up if the mechanism is to be useful). Periodic reorganization demands maintenance of a more substantial usage profile, but allows both the filtering out of minor fluctuations and the minimization of reorganization time by exploiting the economies of scale, i.e. reorganization of *n* specific items at the same time can usually be achieved in less time than *n* reorganizations of single items.

Implementations of the memo-function idea have tended, in the interests of simplicity, to achieve the access-time speed-up on specific items by introducing a certain amount of redundancy into the DB. Specifically, frequently-accessed items are not removed from their general context within the DB, but are duplicated (not necessarily literally, but in a general sense) and the specific, redundant copies are placed in a position where they will be quickly retrievable.

One implicit requirement of the operating context upon which the possibility for success with memo function is predicated is that the DB access profile must be skewed, i.e. a few of the many possible accesses should dominate the actual accesses. Fortunately, such a skewed distribution (sometimes called the 90 : 10 law – 10% of the possibilities are used on 90% of occasions) is commonly encountered.

The original application of memo functions will serve as a first example. The memo-function idea was introduced, as the name suggests, to augment the implementation of the standard mathematical functions in the language POP-2. Typically a mathematical function, like say square root (SQRT), is added to a programming language as a block of code that will compute the square root of any positive number that it receives. When this block of code is augmented with a look-up table, which is always searched before invocation of the general procedure, we have a memo function. The table is filled with specific argument–result pairs, such as SQRT $(16) \rightarrow 4$, SQRT$(4) \rightarrow 2$ and so on. A specific result returned from a table look-up is faster than one returned as a result of computation with the stored code (and, of course, as the nature of the actual function becomes more computationally expensive, the relative time savings become greater).

The AI in this scheme then resides in the strategies used for maintaining the contents of the look-up table (size of the look-up table could be, but was not, another heuristically controlled feature). In general, the strategy implemented was to monitor usage of both the table's entries and the computational procedure and replace little-used table entries with the results of frequently invoked computations.

Mathematical functions are not what we would commonly term DBs, but there is a common basic functionality, in a highly simplified form, I would claim. Memo functions illustrate an implementation strategy, that of introducing redundancy into the DB, which can significantly simplify the problems of realizing robust and reliable DBs that learn. The cost of a redundant information is in terms of extra space needed to store the DB, but the gains are in terms of simplicity of maintenance – specific items can be deleted from the fast-response component of the DB without regard to the rest of the DB precisely because they are redundant items.

11.3   A GRAMMAR DATABASE THAT LEARNS

In the 1970s the memo-function idea together with several other strategies was employed in a grammar DB for a FORTRAN compiler that learned to adjust to the particular usage of the FORTRAN language within a range of different specific environments (Partridge, 1975).

Language usage, both natural language and programming language, exhibits a disparate frequency distribution – a few of the many possible constructs are used in most of the communications. Thus DBs to support language analysis tasks are appropriate candidates for memo-function-based learning mechanisms.

Within the FORTRAN DB a frequency-of-usage count was maintained for every grammatical feature in the DB. Then, periodically, usage of the DB was suspended while it reorganized itself to reflect more closely the structure of the usage profile accumulated since the last period of reorganization.

Two of the learning mechanisms implemented and tested were reordering of lists, and the memo-function idea. The list reordering simply restructured lists of alternative items so that the most frequently accessed items were nearer the top and would thus be retrieved fastest. The memo-function idea was implemented by copying frequently used but deeply embedded items to more superficial, and thus more quickly accessible, layers in the DB.

The total system was tested in a number of different environments, both commercial and academic. The simple frequency ordering of items consistently resulted in a 50% reduction in 'search length' (an internal measure that is expected to correlate quite closely with retrieval time) for the average retrieval of an item. When the memo-function idea was based on the strategy that 'promotion' of a specific item occurred when 25% or less of a set of alternative structures were accessed on 90% or more of occasions, the DB was typically increased in size by only a few per cent (1.5–3.0%), and retrieval times were 10–15% faster for these frequently accessed items.

Figure 11.1 illustrates the grammatical DB learning a specific pattern of item retrieval. It illustrates both the saving in search length (i.e. average actual search length as opposed to average search length if hierarchical subsets of items were to be randomly ordered) which soon settles to roughly 55% and the degree of DB reordering needed to reflect precisely the usage profile at each 100-statement (approximately 700 item retrievals) interval, which soon settles to the low value of a few per cent. The input data was a segment of the input stream to a university computer centre. It was primarily composed of student programs.

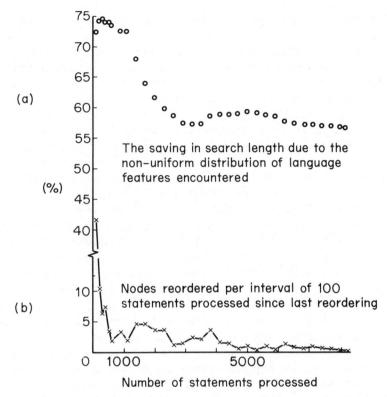

Fig. 11.1. The grammatical DB learning to exploit a disparate but stable pattern of item retrieval.

In addition, the grammatical DB supported a heuristically driven error-correcting function in the compiler. Learning the frequently used grammatical structures resulted in an overall improvement in the quality of error correction observed (Partridge, 1976). So, in this particular case, the learning mechanisms resulted in an improvement of the quality of DB performance as well as an increase in efficiency. Such results can usually be obtained only from empirical studies, and extended empirical studies are sadly absent in most research reports on machine learning (indeed, this unfortunate trend holds throughout most of AI).

11.4   MEMO FUNCTIONS AND KNOWLEDGE BASES

Now the 1980s are with us, bringing KBs in preference to mere DBs. Without getting deeply into the controversy as to what exactly a KB is as distinct from a mere DB, let me suggest that a KB is a collection of IF-THEN rules and facts from which information is retrieved by a mechanism of logical inference (hardly a definitive and thorough distinction, but one that will serve for our current purposes).

In applications software KBs are very common. In fact they are almost *de rigueur* for new software systems. The main application is to support 'intelligent' reasoning throughout the large and rapidly expanding domain of expert systems technology. But despite the fact that examples of this class of DB are being constructed and applied at a prodigious rate, no robust and reliable specimens actually involve a learning component, except in the most trivial sense of machine learning. Knowledge bases that learn are still very much in the research domain. However, it is my firm belief that if KBs and expert system technology are ever to reach the level of intelligence typically expected, then KBs that learn will have to become a practical reality (see Partridge, 1986).

Within the CP KBs do exhibit robust and reliable learning (see, for example, Smolensky's, 1986, model of electronic-circuit expertise), but all such demonstrations are as yet only small-scale models. Anything like a realistically large, CP-based expert system is yet to emerge from Connectionist strongholds.

Traditional, symbolic-rule-based KBs are, by way of contrast, often realistically large but, as I said above, lacking practically useful, non-trivial learning mechanisms. Nevertheless, it will be useful to examine briefly one example of the suggestions for KBs that learn, provided that we bear in mind that the ideas fall far short of practical applicability (as I have detailed elsewhere, Partridge, 1987).

As an example, Steels (1985) outlines a mechanism by means of which a KB would remember and store specific inference chains in the KB so that next time this inference was required it would be immediately available rather than generated by following the general sequence of inferences again – clearly a memo-function idea.

The information in the KB is structured as a causal network with rules such as: IF the headlights do not light up THEN the battery is flat. This causal knowledge is constructed to support diagnostic reasoning with car engines. Steels' system starts from an anomalous property (e.g., the engine does not start) and explores the possible causes of this property until some observable properties are arrived at. The user is then asked to report on these observables (e.g., is a battery terminal loose?). From the user response the system can determine if it has an explanation of the original anomalous property (i.e. the car engine does not start because the battery terminals are not tight), or if it must seek an alternative explanation (i.e. the battery terminals were tightly connected).

The learning mechanism proposed by Steels is that the cause-and-effect chains found during problem-solving (e.g., the engine does not start because the battery terminals are loose) can be added explicitly to the KB. Thus, next time the problem is that the engine does not start, the system will immediately suggest that the user check the tightness of the battery terminals. Clearly, this is a memo-function idea, but Steels does not address the necessary questions of how to accumulate and use the DB usage profile, nor how to control the number of specific cause-and-effect items added to the DB.

It should be obvious that much work remains to be done and many awkward problems need to be solved, to some degree, before such learning KBs will become practical software.

11.5   LEARNING GENERALITIES

So far I have explored some attempts to implement DBs that learn about and exploit particularities of their working environment. Unwanted generalization is automatically removed from the DB in order to increase efficiency. The opposite problem, that of automatically extracting generalities from a collection of specific instances, is the more popular, and perhaps harder, machine learning problem. In DB terms it is the problem of decreasing the size of the DB by condensing a collection of specific items into a general representation (e.g., one general rule instead of many different specific-case rules in a KB) – this is the age-old problem of inductive generalization and there are a host of machine learning projects which tackle it (e.g. Rendell, 1986). The basic problem is: how many black crows do you have to see before you can generate the useful notion that all crows are black? The answer is that you can never be sure that the next crow which you run into will not be white, or pink. Yet intelligent behaviour seems to be founded on the exploitation of such general notions. So inductive generalization appears to be an important component of learning, but it yields results which cannot be guaranteed.

An even harder version of this problem is incremental generalization learning: the generalized information in a DB is incrementally modified (hopefully, it is improved) as a result of one, or a few, new specific instances being encountered. The DB continually, or periodically, updates the rules or facts it contains as a result of new specific information which it receives. A large portion of the research in machine learning is attacking this general problem, sometimes termed generalization-based learning (GBL). Another popular term, which covers much the same area, is concept learning. But few projects are explicitly conceived of in terms of DBs that learn. Nevertheless, we can view many of these research projects, quite accurately, as attempts to implement DBs that learn.

11.6   UNIMEM: A GBL EXAMPLE

The UNIMEM system of Lebowitz (1986) provides us with a central example of a DB that employs generalization-based learning. UNIMEM is a general learning system that has been designed to build up a KB automatically from real-world information. It has been applied to a wide variety of real-world domains: information on universities, Congressional voting records, etc.

In UNIMEM generalizations are integrated with instances of the concepts to form a concept hierarchy. The internal structure of UNIMEM is then one or more hierarchies of generalizations which describe concepts of increasing specificity. Figure 11.2 (from Lebowitz, 1986) is given to illustrate the data representation

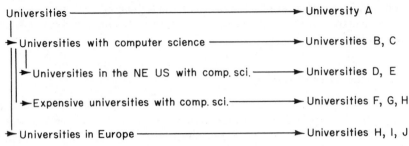

Fig. 11.2. A concept hierarchy in UNIMEM.

used. With each new input instance (i.e. a description of a specific university for the structure illustrated above) the concept hierarchy is searched until the most specific generalization that describes it is found. If the new instance has enough features in common with other instances stored at this point in the structure, a new concept is generalized, and the contributing instances are indexed with it.

Figure 11.3 is a schematic flowchart of the decision process used in UNIMEM when deciding where in GBM to place a new input instance.

This process of generalization on the basis of only a few instances always leads to over-generalization. Thus each learned concept is constantly re-evaluated in

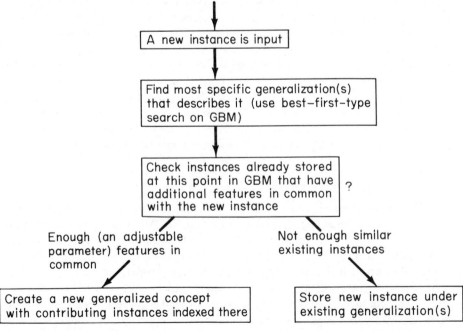

Fig. 11.3. A flowchart of the decision process for adding new instances to GBM.

the light of subsequent input. UNIMEM checks whether a relevant generalization is confirmed or contradicted by each new instance. But rather than abandoning poor generalizations, UNIMEM contains strategies for throwing away just the 'bad parts' and keeping the 'good' parts. 'The problem reduces to identifying the components of a generalization that are overly specific, so that they can be deleted, leaving intact a valid generalization.' (Lebowitz, 1986).

11.7   A BRIEF RETURN TO CP-BASED SYSTEMS

On reflection, it should be apparent that CP-based systems do not yield readily (if at all) to the structuring of DBs that I have described above. The terms 'general rule' and 'specific fact', etc. are by their very nature SSSP-based terms – they refer to symbolic entities. Thus a paradigm which eschews symbolic representations is unlikely to be readily divisible in terms of such concepts.

A major example of machine learning within the CP is that of NETtalk (Sejnowski and Rosenberg, 1986). This network learnt to pronounce English. More specifically, it learnt as a result of immediate feedback on its performance (the back propagation algorithm) to associate letters in the context of three characters to each side with a subset of twenty-six possible pronunciation features. No initial structuring is built in, i.e. the initial associations are random. Thus the output is a meaningless babble, but after link-weight adjustment dictated by feedback from the attempted pronunciation of the individual letters in several thousand words of text the pronunciation becomes quite good. Thus the network has learnt to pronounce English, but how does it do it? Classical work on pronunciation gives something like three hundred rules to account for this ability. Thus NETtalk must, in some sense, have learnt those rules, but they are not readily apparent in the network of hundreds of nodes and thousands of weighted links. Figure 11.4 sketches the structure of the NETtalk system.

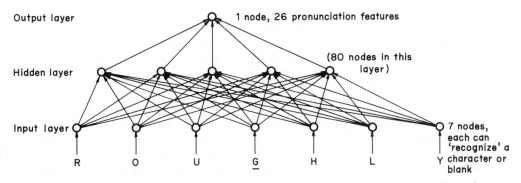

Fig. 11.4. A sketch of the NETtalk network about to generate a pronunciation of G in the context of ROUGHLY.

So in CP-based learning systems, roughly the domain of parallel-distributed processing or of Connectionism, we will not find a partitioning of projects in terms of learning to remove unwanted generalization as opposed to generalization learning. The terms that are used derive from the nature of the underlying mechanisms, e.g. Boltzmann machine or harmony model. This field of machine learning is still at the embryonic stage; if it does prove to be robust enough to survive and mature, it may generate a whole new set of terms for classifying DBs that learn.

11.8   THE PROBLEM OF BRITTLENESS

One feature that is often presented as a forceful reason why CP-based learning systems will indeed grow in importance and eventually challenge the classical SSSP-based ones in AI work is brittleness. SSSP-based systems tend to have the unfortunate characteristic of either working beautifully or else failing dismally – a bimodal functioning that is termed brittleness.

Intelligent systems are expected to degrade more gracefully. A KB, for example, should not be limited either to correct inferences on complete and consistent input, or nonsensical output when these quite stringent input requirements are not adhered to. Somewhat ill-formed queries, or queries outside the system's domain of expertise should elicit 'reasonable' responses rather than a stalled system, or worse, absurd (especially ones that are not obviously absurd) responses presented as if they are correct.

One of the selling points for CP-based systems is then that their performance degrades gracefully. Thus Smolensky's electronic-circuit KB will give the 'best' response (i.e. the response which conflicts with a minimum of the known information) when queried with incomplete or inconsistent information. In similar circumstances a symbolic-rule-based, logical. inference system breaks down completely.

The final point that I want to make is that brittleness may not be a necessary characteristic of SSSP-based systems. If this is true then the case for CP-based systems in AI is seriously weakened (quite independent of other concerns about the validity of the CP; see, for example, Fodor and Pylyshyn, 1988).

UNIMEM, for example, is built to avoid some of this brittleness problem. It does not rely on its generalizations being 'correct' in some absolute sense. It is built to accept noisy input data – many AI systems have yet to face these sorts of problems.

A last example, one that also illustrates an alternative strategy for generalization-based learning DBs, is provided by Quinlan's (1987) system for constructing decision trees as probabilistic classifiers. A decision-tree-based DB responds to queries by following a path through a decision-tree structure (effectively a sequence of choices among sets of alternative possibilities where the individual choices made are dependent upon the input query). Quinlan is explicitly concerned to combat the charge that SSSP-based systems are necessarily brittle. His system can support probabilistic rather than only categorical reasoning. It can accept information that is both incomplete or imprecise. In order to accommodate these necessary features of reality he employs 'soft thresholds' for choices by searching multiple paths whenever input parameter values fall close to the threshold points. The traditional brittleness is circumvented by introducing parallelism which avoids the necessity for the system to commit itself to a single line of reasoning when the quality and quantity of input data do not warrant it.

11.9 SUMMARY

DBs that learn in anything more than a trivial manner are still firmly in the domain of machine learning research. But DBs that learn are considered essential for the support of intelligent reasoning systems in the long term.

In addition to the problem that powerful, yet robust and reliable, learning mechanisms are still being sought by researchers, there is a more general problem of maintaining DBs containing such mechanisms. Large and static (or explicitly modified) DBs can be a challenge with respect to long-term maintenance. It is hard to imagine learning DBs as anything but an escalation of these maintenance problems. We may have not only to find the robust and reliable learning mechanisms but also to develop more powerful system maintenance techniques before learning DBs become a practical reality. Alternatively, we may decide that there is cut-off point in acceptable computer-system power and complexity, and that learning DBs lie on the far side, i.e. as much as we would like the power of a sophisticated learning DB the complexity and hence maintenance costs are unacceptably high.

11.10 REFERENCES

Fodor, J. A. and Pylyshyn, Z. W. (1988) Connectionism and cognitive architecture: a critical analysis. *Cognition*, **28** (1) 3–72.

Lebowitz, M. (1986) UNIMEM, a general learning system: an overview. *Proc. 7th ECAI*, 21–25 July, Brighton, UK, pp. 32–42.

Michie, D. (1968) Memo functions and machine learning. *Nature*, **218**, 19–22.

Partridge, D. (1975) A dynamic database which automatically removes unwanted generalisation. *Computer Journal*, **18**(1), 43–8.

Partridge, D. (1976) Tolerance to inaccuracy in computer programs. *Computer Journal*, **19**(3), 207–12.

Partridge, D. (1986) *AI: Applications in the Future of Software Engineering*, Ellis Horwood/Wiley, Chichester, UK.

Partridge, D. (1987) The scope and limitations of first generation expert systems technology. *Future Generation Computer Systems*, 3(1), pp. 160–9.

Quinlan, J. R. (1987) Decision trees as probabilistic classifiers. *Proc. 4th Internat. Workshop on Machine Learning*, Irvine, Calif., 22–25 June, pp. 31–7.

Rendell, L. (1986) A general framework for induction and a study of selective induction. *Machine Learning,* **1**(2), 177–226.

Sejnowski, T. J. and Rosenberg, C. R. (1986) NETtalk: a parallel network that learns to read aloud. *Tech. Rep. JHU/EECS-86/01,* Dept. E.E. and C.S., Johns Hopkins University, Baltimore, Md.

Smolensky, P. (1986) Formal modelling of subsymbolic processes: an introduction to harmony theory, in *Advances in Cognitive Science,* Vol. 1 (ed. N. Sharkey), Ellis Horwood/Wiley, Chichester, pp. 204–35.

Steels, L. (1985) Second generation expert systems. *Future Generation Computer Systems,* **1**(4), 213–21.

12

Cognitive architecture and Connectionism

AJIT NARAYANAN

12.1 INTRODUCTION

In this chapter, Fodor and Pylyshyn's recent critique of Connectionism will be examined in some detail. Their paper, or more strictly a 'Memorandum', is called 'Connectionism and cognitive architecture: a critical analysis', and appears as a *Cognitive Science Memorandum COGMEM 29*, available from the University of Western Ontario Centre for Cognitive Science. Their paper is currently in press and will appear in a 1988 volume of *Cognition*. All references in this chapter are taken from the original Memorandum.

It is worth considering their paper in some detail, since it represents the first comprehensive attack on Connectionism from within cognitive science. There is not enough space in this chapter to evaluate all their criticisms, so three major ones have been selected.

Fodor and Pylyshyn's paper contains ten major parts:

1. An introduction to Connectionism;
2. The claim that Connectionism is 'Representationalist';
3. A precise description of the disagreement between 'Classicists' and Connectionists;
4. An example of a weakness in Connectionist diagrams;
5. A re-evaluation of the claim that Connectionism is Representational;
6. An evaluation of how Connectionist graphs are to be interpreted;
7. An evaluation of the role of mental processes in Connectionist models;
8. An introduction to 'productivity' and 'systematicity';
9. An evaluation of why Connectionism has 'lured' many researchers;
10. A redefinition of Connectionism as simply an implementation theory.

Our concern, after presenting a comprehensive abstract of the paper, will be with points 3, 7 and 10 above. The argument will be that it is precisely because 'Classical' approaches have some conceptual inadequacies that Connectionism has crept in through the back door. The conclusion will be that Classicism and Connectionism are reconcilable along lines which:

1. Classicists must accept, since Connectionism can cover some holes in Classical theorizing; and
2. Connectionists must accept if their models are to have any psychological relevance.

The lines of reconciliation will be focused on the notion of 'movement between levels' in a cognitive architecture.

12.2   THE CRITICISMS

In their paper, Fodor and Psylyshyn make a number of points concerning Connectionism and its cognitive implications.

12.2.1   An introduction to Connectionism

Fodor and Pylyshyn point out that Connectionism appears to provide an alternative way of looking at cognitive architecture. Traditional cognitive science, or 'Classical cognitive science', as the authors call it (abbreviated hereafter to CCS), uses the notions of Turing machines and Von Neumann machines in so far as the idea of symbol manipulation is used for describing cognitive processes. For instance, natural language understanding can be described in CCS terms as a series of processes that take a string of symbols (the words of a sentence) as initial input, so that by means of various manipulations the structure and content (syntax and semantics) can be extracted as final output. The processes would typically involve pattern matching (looking for certain sequences or combinations of symbols/words), dictionary or lexicon search, and an internal representation of some sort that has some form of cognitive validity (e.g. logic, conceptual dependency). Connectionism, on the other hand, involves using a large number of interconnected units. Fodor and Pylyshyn (1987, pp. 2–3) summarize the basic Connectionist approach succinctly:

> Connectionist systems are networks consisting of very large numbers of simple but highly interconnected 'units'. Certain assumptions are generally made about the units and their connections. Each unit is assumed to receive a real-valued activity (either excitatory or inhibitory or both) along its input lines. Typically the units do little more than sum this activity and change their state as a function (usually a threshold function) of this sum. Each connection is allowed to modulate the activity it transmits as a function of an intrinsic (but modifiable) property called its 'weight'. Hence, the activity of an input line is typically some non-linear function of the state of activity of its sources. The behaviour of the network as a whole is a function of the initial state of activation of the units and of the weights on its connections, which serve as its only form of memory.

Fodor and Pylyshyn accept that their summary of Connectionism misses out on a lot of fine detail and variations, but their purpose is to evaluate, critically, Connectionism in general. They also accept that Connectionism has provided unexpected results and that many researchers are tempted by Connectionism, both for practical purposes (that is, the inherent and surprising power of a network of simple, interconnected units) and by the appearance of neural plausibility (that is, the human brain also appears to consist of a vast network of simple, interconnected units). Fodor and Pylyshyn's task in the paper is to evaluate the claim that Connectionism offers something new over and above the CCS approach, and the core of their argument that Connectionism does not offer anything new is based on a careful examination of mental processes and mental representations.

12.2.2 The claim that Connectionism is 'Representationalist'

Fodor and Pylyshyn (1987, p. 4) introduce the terms 'Representationalism' and 'Eliminativism' when discussing some preliminary methodological questions about levels of explanation:

> Representationalists hold that postulating representational (or 'intentional' or 'semantic') states is essential to a theory of cognition; according to Representationalists, there are states of the mind which function to encode states of the world. Eliminativists, by contrast, think that psychological theories can dispense with such semantic notions as representation. According to Eliminativists the appropriate vocabulary for psychological theorizing is neurological or, perhaps, behavioral, or perhaps syntactic; in any event, not a vocabulary that characterizes mental states in terms of what they represent.

Fodor and Pylyshyn (1987, p. 4) claim that 'Connectionists are on the Representationalist side of this issue' and refer to some Connectionist literature (written by Rumelhart and McClelland, and Feldman and Ballard) to justify this claim:

> As Rumelhart and McClelland [(Rumelhart and McClelland, 1986)] say, PDPs [Parallel Distributed Processing] 'are explicitly concerned with the problem of internal representation (p. 121)'. Correspondingly, the specification of what the states of a network *represent* is an essential part of a Connectionist model. Consider, for example, the well-known Connectionist account of the bistability of the Necker cube [(Feldman and Ballard, 1982)]. 'Simple units representing the visual features of the two alternatives are arranged in competing coalitions with inhibitory . . . links between rival features and positive links within each coalition . . . The result is a network that has two dominant stable states . . .' Notice that, in this as in all other connectionist models, the commitment to mental representation is explicit: the label of a node is taken to express the representational content of the state that the device is in when the node is excited, and there are nodes corresponding to monadic and relational properties of the reversible cube when it is seen in one way or another (stress supplied).

Hence, say Fodor and Pylyshyn (1987, p. 6), CCS and Connectionism are both Representational. That is, any level of a cognitive architecture '. . . at which states of the system are taken to encode properties of the world counts as a *cognitive level . . .*' (stress supplied). This means that if Connectionists wish to propose a Connectionist theory as a theory of cognitive architecture, '. . . [they] have to show that the processes which operate on *the representational states* of an organism are those which are specified by a Connectionist architecture' (Fodor and Pylyshyn, 1987, p. 6, stress supplied). That is, while accepting that Connectionism may well provide a suitable way of describing non-psychological (or non-cognitive) states of an organism, and may even provide an implementation model for CCS theories, that is of no use, as far as cognitive science is concerned. Instead, if Connectionists truly want their theories to be Representational, then the burden of proof is on them to show how the processes involved in their theory tie up with psychological, or cognitive, processes of an organism. If they could not, '. . . that would leave open the question whether the mind is [a Connectionist network] *at the psychological level*' (Fodor and Pylyshyn, 1987, p. 6, stress supplied).

Fodor and Pylyshyn believe that the main disagreement between researchers adopting a CCS approach and Connectionists centres around precisely the attempts made by Connectionists to tie up Connectionist processes with psychological ones.

12.2.3   A precise description of the disagreement between 'Classicists' and Connectionists

Fodor and Pylyshyn (1987, p. 7) then describe the disagreement between 'Classicists' and Connectionists. Since both are Representationalists, at some stage semantic content must be assigned to something: '. . . Classicists assign semantic content to *expressions* – i.e. to the sorts of things that get written on the tapes of Turing machines and stored at addresses in Von Neumann machines' (stress supplied) whereas Connectionists '. . . assign semantic content to "nodes" (that is, to units or aggregates of unit . . .) – i.e. to the sorts of things that are typically labelled in Connectionist diagrams'.

However, the main disagreement between the two sets of researchers centres around '. . . what primitive relations hold among these content-bearing entities' (Fodor and Pylyshyn, 1987, p. 7). Fodor and Pylyshyn state that 'causal connectedness' is the only primitive relation among nodes. That is, nodes in a network (i.e. the primitives) are linked (related) to each other by excitatory and inhibitory flows; one node can cause another node to go up or down in value, and that is the only primitive relation. Classicists, on the other hand, accept not only causal relations as primitives but also structural relations, '. . . of which constituency is paradigmatic' (Fodor and Pylyshyn, 1987, p. 7). Fodor and Pylyshyn (1987, p. 8) argue that this disagreement leads to two architectural differences between Connectionist and Classical cognitive theories:

1. Classicists postulate, and are committed to, symbolic structures, or complex mental representations (a 'language of thought') which have syntactic and semantic structure (i.e. a combinatorial syntax and semantics).
2. Classicists also accept that 'the principles by which mental states are transformed, or by which an input selects the corresponding output, are defined over structural properties of mental representations'. That is, because mental representations have structure (see (1) above), mental representations can be manipulated, or transformed, by rules or operations which are triggered by the form, and not the content, of those representations. Fodor and Pylyshyn use the phrase 'structure sensitivity of processes' to describe this notion.

For instance, the formula $[A$ and $B] \rightarrow C$ is syntactically well formed because it adheres to the syntactic principles of the propositional calculus, viz., three atomic symbols (A, B and C), connected by $\rightarrow$, with bracketing signifying that A and B are to be conjoined by and. The underlying form of this formula is $p \rightarrow q$. The operation, or rule, of *modus ponens* states that if $p \rightarrow q$ occurs, as does p all by itself, irrespective of how structurally simple or complex p happens to be, q all by itself can be derived. The application of this operation is determined by the form of the representation, and not the content, i.e. not on the basis of what A, B and C stand for.

Fodor and Pylyshyn (1987, pp. 8, 9) make two claims for Classicism. Firstly:

> We take [(1) and (2) above] as the claims that define Classical models, and we take these claims quite literally; they constrain the physical realizations of symbol structures. In particular, the symbol structures in a Classical model are assumed to correspond to real physical structures in the brain and the *combinatorial structure* of a representation is supposed to have a counterpart in structural relations among physical properties of the brain. For example, the relation 'part of', which holds between a relatively simple symbol and a more complex one, is assumed to correspond to some physical relation among brain states . . . (stress supplied).

Secondly,

> . . . Classical theory is committed not only to there being a system of physically instantiated symbols, but also to the claim that the physical properties onto which the structure of the symbols is mapped *are the very properties that cause the system to behave as it does*. In other words the physical counterparts of the symbols, and their structural properties, *cause* the system's behaviour (stress supplied).

12.2.4   An example of a weakness in Connectionist diagrams

Fodor and Pylyshyn then present a simple example to demonstrate a weakness, concerning the role of labels, in Connectionist theory. They use the diagram shown in Fig. 12.1. The Connectionist interpretation of Fig. 12.1 is that drawing an inference from A & B to A corresponds to an excitation at node 2 being caused

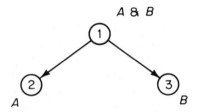

Fig. 12.1. Excited nodes.

by an excitation at node 1. A Classical interpretation is that whenever a formula with the form *p & q* appears, then *p* by itself can be derived. *A & B* conforms structurally to *p & q*, hence A can be derived.

Fodor and Pylyshyn point out that, if Fig. 12.1 represents a connection machine, the labels *A & B*, *A*, and *B* play no part: the operation of the machine is unaffected by changing the labels to, say, those shown in Fig. 12.2, since node 2 is still excited by activation at node 1. That is, '. . . the node labels in a Connection machine are not part of the causal structure of the machine' (Fodor and Pylyshyn, 1987, p. 11). Fodor and Pylyshyn (1987, p. 11) then go on to claim:

> Whereas, by contrast, the state transitions of Classical machines are causally determined *by the structure – including the constituent structure – of the symbol arrays that the machines transform:* change the symbols and the system behaves quite differently . . . So, although the Connectionist's labels and the Classicist's data structures both constitute languages, only the latter language constitutes a medium of computation . . . (stress supplied).

12.2.5   A re-evaluation of the claim that Connectionism is Representational

Fodor and Pylyshyn then examine the notion that a Connectionist representation does indeed have structure. Connectionists claim that mental representations are distributed, in that '. . . commonsense concepts (CHAIR, JOHN, CUP, etc.) are "distributed" over galaxies of lower level units which themselves have representational content' (Fodor and Pylyshyn, 1987, p. 12). For instance, the concept BACHELOR might be thought to correspond to a 'vector in space of features' that includes +**human**, +**male**, −**married**, +**adult**. It is then tempting

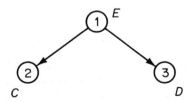

Fig. 12.2. Re-labelled nodes.

to think that, for example, +**human** is a constituent of BACHELOR. However, Fodor and Pylyshyn claim that this is very unlike 'Mary' being a constituent of the expression 'John loves Mary'. In the latter case, called 'real constituency', 'Mary' literally appears in the expression 'John loves Mary', whereas in the former case we are expressing a definition; that is, we are defining BACHELOR in terms of primitive expressions: 'It really is very important not to confuse the semantic distinction between primitive expressions and defined expressions with the syntactic distinction between atomic symbols and complex symbols' (Fodor and Pylyshyn, 1987, p. 14). That is, Connectionists cannot adequately describe the important relationship between atomic and complex symbols. If the Connectionist replies that 'John loves Mary' can be represented by a feature vector or set, such as {+John-subject; +loves; +Mary-object}, and that the Classical distinction between complex symbols and atomic symbols can be replaced by the distinction between feature sets and their subsets, then this too will not work since there are various subsets, such as {+John-subject; +Mary-object}, '... which do not, of course, correspond to constituents of the complex symbol "John loves Mary"' (Fodor and Pylyshyn, 1987, p. 15). That is, Fodor and Pylyshyn claim that 'real constituency', as they have described it, just cannot adequately be described in a Connectionist framework. Since real constituency embodies the basic, and important principle of a primitive syntactically belonging to a larger complex, Connectionism just cannot handle this important Representationalist feature. If that is the case, then semantic structure also cannot be catered for, since in Representational approaches semantic structure is dependent on the form of the expression, be it syntactic (e.g. logic) or graphic (e.g. conceptual dependency).

12.2.6   An evaluation of how Connectionist graphs are to be interpreted

Fodor and Pylyshyn claim that one of the reason why this lack of syntactic and semantic structure has been overlooked or ignored may be because '... Connectionist graphs look like general graphs'. But whereas graph notation can be used to describe or express the internal structure of a representation by means of arcs and nodes, e.g.

$$\text{John} \langle\!\xleftarrow{\text{actor}} \text{loves} \xrightarrow{\text{object}}\!\rangle \text{Mary}$$

'... this interpretation is inappropriate for graphs of Connectionist networks'. Fodor and Pylyshyn (1987, pp. 16–17) go on to say:

> Connectionist graphs are not structural descriptions of mental representations; they're specifications of causal relations. All that a Connectionist can mean by a graph of the form 'X→Y' is: *states of node X causally affect states of node Y*. In particular, the graph can't mean 'X *is a constituent of Y*' or 'X *is grammatically related to Y*' etc., since these sorts of relations are, in general, not defined for the kinds of mental representations that Connectionists recognize ... Another way to put this is that

links in Connectionist diagrams are not generalized pointers that can be made to take on different functional significance *by an independent interpreter*, but are confined to meaning something like 'sends activation to'. The intended interpretation of the links as causal connections is intrinsic to the theory. If you ignore this point, you are likely to take Connectionism to offer a much richer notion of mental representation than it actually does (stress supplied).

12.2.7   An evaluation of the role of mental processes in Connectionist models

Fodor and Pylyshyn also claim that the notion of mental process is accounted for differently by Classicists and Connectionists. Classicists postulate three distinct levels of organization: a physical level, a semantic level and a syntactic level. At the physical level, symbols are mapped on to physical states that cause the system to behave in a certain way. At the syntactic level, symbols are combined structurally to form more complex representations. At the semantic level, the meaning of a representation is a function of the meaning of its syntactic parts. Operations, such as inference, are structure-sensitive in that, given a representation such as $p \& q$, p can be derived syntactically. The inference is, of course, truth-preserving (i.e. semantically correct). Mental operations, according to Classicists, are structure-sensitive in that the logical, or syntactic, form of mental representations is used to define the starting-point and end-result (or input and output, or domain and range) of mental operations. 'This notion is, however, unavailable to orthodox Connectionists since it [i.e. the notion that the form of mental representations "... can be used to define the ranges and domains of mental operations"] presupposes that there are nonatomic mental representations' (Fodor and Pylyshyn, 1987, p. 17), which Connectionism cannot account for. Instead, Connectionism must account for, say, inference by using processes that are not structure-sensitive but frequency-sensitive (Fodor and Pylyshyn, 1987, pp. 19–20):

> If a Connectionist learning machine converges on a state where it is prepared to infer A from A&B (i.e., to a state in which when the 'A&B' node is excited, it tends to settle into a state in which the 'A' node is excited) the convergence will typically be caused by statistical properties of the machine's training experience: e.g. by correlation between firing of the 'A&B' node and firing of the 'A' node, or by correlations of the firing of both with some feedback signal. Like traditional Associationism, Connectionism treats learning as basically a sort of statistical modelling.

From this, Fodor and Pylyshyn (1987, p. 20) go on to conclude that Connectionist theories are Associationalist in that, for traditional Associationism, '... the probability that one Idea will elicit another is sensitive to the strength of the association between them ... And the strength of this association is in turn sensitive to the extent to which the Ideas have previously been correlated.'

12.2.8 An introduction to 'productivity' and 'systematicity'

Fodor and Pylyshyn then go on to examine the 'productivity argument' which essentially is based on the Chomskyan notion of generative capacity. That is, Fodor and Pylyshyn agree with Chomsky that, from a finite vocabulary of symbols and rules, an infinite number of linguistic expressions can, in principle, be generated because at least one of the rules is recursive. Fodor and Pylyshyn adopt this stance with respect to mental representations. One of the reasons why Classical theories can cater for the notion of productivity is that there is a distinction, on Von Neumann lines, between memory and program. The rules (program) are finite and fixed, and it is memory that is affected as the rules (some of which are recursive) are applied. Connectionist cognitive architectures '. . . cannot, by their very nature, support an expandable memory, so they cannot support productive cognitive capacities' (Fodor and Pylyshyn, 1987, p. 22). This leads to Connectionists being forced to deny that recursion is an important, cognitive capacity. Fodor and Pylyshyn (1987, p. 23) quote Rumelhart and McClelland (1986): 'We have not dwelt on PDP implementations of Turing machines and recursive processing engines because we do not agree with those who would argue that such capacities are of the essence of human computation' (p. 119).

Fodor and Pylyshyn point out that even for Rumelhart and McClelland any independent evidence that demonstrates that some cognitive capacities are recursive is sufficient for Connectionism to be rejected in favour of Classicism, as far as cognitive modelling is concerned. Rather than pursue this point in their paper, Fodor and Pylyshyn are content to argue for systematicity of cognitive representation. If systematicity is demonstrated, that '. . . provides as good a reason for postulating combinatorial structure in mental representation as the productivity of cognition does . . .' (Fodor and Pylyshyn, 1987, p. 24). Fodor and Pylyshyn (1987, p. 24) then describe what they mean by systematicity: 'What we mean when we say that linguistic capacities are *systematic* is that the ability to produce/understand some sentences is *intrinsically* connected to the ability to produce/understand certain others' (stress supplied).

After producing some example sentences which are claimed to demonstrate a systematic linguistic capacity, e.g. '. . . no speaker understands the form of words "John loves the girl" except as he also understands the form of words "the girl loves John" (Fodor and Pylyshyn 1987, p. 25), these authors (1987, pp. 25–6) claim that thought is systematic also:

> . . . just as you don't find people who can understand the sentence 'John loves the girl' but not the sentence 'the girl loves John', so too you don't find people who can *think the thought* that John loves the girl but can't think the thought that the girl loves John . . . But now if the ability to think that John loves the girl is intrinsically connected to the ability that the girl loves John, that fact will somehow have to be explained. For a Representationalist (which, as we have seen, Connectionists are), the explanation is obvious: . . . just as the systematicity of language shows that there must be some

structural relations between the sentence 'John loves the girl' and the sentence 'the girl loves John', so the systematicity of thought shows that there must be structural relations between the mental representation that corresponds to the thought that John loves the girl and the mental representation that corresponds to the thought that the girl loves John; namely, the two mental representations, like the two sentences, *must be made of the same parts.* But if this explanation is right (and there doesn't seem to be any other on offer), then mental representations have an internal structure and there is a language of thought. So the architecture of the mind is not a Connectionist network (stress supplied).

Fodor and Pylyshyn (1987, p. 28) adopt exactly the same line or argument to show that representations are compositional. The principle of compositionality is described thus:

> . . . insofar as a language is systematic, a lexical item must make approximately the same semantic contribution to each expression in which it occurs. It is, for example, only insofar as the 'the', 'girl', 'loves', and 'John' make the same semantic contribution to 'John loves the girl' that they make to 'the girl loves John' that understanding the one sentence implies understanding the other.

Hence, '. . . systematicity depends on compositionality, so to the extent that a natural language is systematic it must be compositional too'.

Having argued for compositionality of language, Fodor and Pylyshyn (1987, p. 29) extrapolate the argument to thought:

> . . . Sentences are used to express thoughts; so if the ability to use some sentences is connected with the ability to use certain other, semantically related sentences, then the ability to think some thoughts must be correspondingly connected with the ability to think certain other, semantically related thoughts.

The point that Fodor and Pylyshyn (1987, p. 30) wish to make here is that Connectionism has nothing to say on these matters:

> It's certainly true that compositionality is not generally a feature of Connectionist representations. Connectionists can't acknowledge the facts of compositionality because they are committed to mental representations that don't have combinatorial structure. But to give up on compositionality . . . [leads] . . . to the rejection of Connectionist networks as cognitive models.

Later, Fodor and Pylyshyn (1987, p. 33) are more explicit in their rejection of Connectionism:

> What's deeply wrong with Connectionist architecture is this: Because it acknowledges neither syntactic nor semantic structure in mental representations, it perforce treats them not as a generated set but as a list. But lists, qua lists, have no structure; any collection of (causally connected) representational states is a possible mind. So, as far as Connectionist architecture is concerned, there is nothing to prevent minds that are arbitrarily unsystematic. But that result is *preposterous* (stress supplied).

12.2.9   An evaluation of why Connectionism has 'lured' many researchers

Next, Fodor and Pylyshyn examine the various reasons why Connectionism has 'lured' researchers. First, there is the argument based on speed. In the time that it takes for a human to, say, recognize a word or picture, only a hundred or so instructions can be carried if one assumes a serial program and given the speed with which neurons fire. Connectionists argue that since simple cognitive tasks may require millions of instructions, the brain must operate differently from serial computers, i.e. the brain must be organized in a massively parallel way. Fodor and Pylyshyn (1987, p. 38) point out that this confuses architecture with implementation. A conventional computer, such as a VAX, runs many serial programs quite happily in parallel and at great speed:

> Operating on symbols can even involve 'massively parallel' organizations; they might indeed imply new architectures, but they are all *Classical* in our sense, since they all share the Classical conception of computation as symbol-processing . . . The point here is that an argument for a network of parallel computers is not in and of itself either an argument against a Classical architecture or an argument for a Connectionist architecture (stress supplied).

A second lure is that Classical approaches, by using rules, adopt an all-or-nothing approach to cognitive tasks: either a rule is applicable because, say, certain conditions are satisfied, or it is not. A Connectionist approach, by doing away with explicit rules, adopts a different line. First, there is continuous variation in the degree of applicability of different principles, where many '. . . different constraints are brought to bear on a problem simultaneously and the outcome is a combined effect of all the different factors' (Fodor and Pylyshyn, 1987, p. 36). Second, cognitive processes '. . . are never rigidly determined or precisely replicable', as would be implied by the Classicist's use of rigid, deterministic rules. And, third, cognition displays 'graceful degradation': a person will not give up just because a rule fails. Connectionists therefore propose, in opposition to Classicists, a system where graceful degradation is displayed by means of prototypes and match patterns, and not explicit rules.

Fodor and Pylyshyn (1987, p. 42) reply that the distinction between rule implicitness and rule explicitness is an empirical one and should not be confused with the Classicism versus Connectionism issue, since Classicists themselves disagree on the implicitness or otherwise of rules. In some cases, '. . . Classical machines can be *rule implicit* with respect to their programs, and the mechanism of their state transitions is entirely subcomputational (i.e. subsymbolic)' (stress supplied). However, Fodor and Pylyshyn (1987, p. 42) admit that although rules in Classical models can vary in their explicitness, data structures cannot: objects that are manipulated by rules, no matter what level of explicitness the rules take, must be explicitly represented:

> A [Universal Turing Machine] is 'rule explicit' about the machine it is simulating (in the sense that it has an explicit representation of that machine which is sufficient to

specify its behaviour uniquely). Yet the target machine can perfectly well be 'rule implicit' with respect to the rules that govern *its* behavior (stress supplied).

Fodor and Pylyshyn instead turn the argument around and say that, whereas Classicism cannot be attacked by showing that certain processes are rule implicit, Connectionism can be attacked by showing that a cognitive process is rule explicit: since, as we have seen, Connectionism rejects '. . . logico/syntactic capacities that are required to encode rules', any rule-explicit cognitive process would embarass Connectionists. Fodor and Pylyshyn point to empirical work in linguistics and mathematical learning theory to back up their point.

The final lure that Fodor and Pylyshyn discuss is the special relationship that Connectionism appears to have with neuroscience. Many Connectionists believe they are attempting to build brain models based on neural properties. Others, like Smolensky, believe they are providing mathematical models which can be given either a neural or psychological interpretation. Fodor and Pylyshyn ask whether anything is gained by providing models when the proposers fail to state exactly how the models are mapped on to the brain. That is, assuming that various biological facts are included in Connectionist models, such as neurological connections and threshold properties, in what way are these facts relevant to inferring the nature of a cognitive architecture? According to Fodor and Pylyshyn (1987, p. 44), very little is gained. For example, assuming that neural systems are networks that transmit activation which results in some state change, this does not mean that reasoning consists of the spread of activation among represen-tations:

> After all, a VAX is also correctly characterized as consisting of a network over which excitation is transmitted culminating in state changes of quasi-threshold elements. Yet at the level at which it processes representations, a VAX is *literally* organized as a Von Neumann architecture (stress supplied).

12.2.10   A redefinition of Connectionism as simply an implementation theory

Finally, Fodor and Pylyshyn (1987, p. 45) discuss Connectionism as a theory of implementation:

> A recurring theme in the previous discussion is that many of the arguments for Connectionism are best construed as claiming that cognitive architecture is *implemented* in a certain kind of network . . . Understood in this way, these arguments are neutral on the questions of what the cognitive architecture is (stress supplied).

That is, all the previous implementation properties associated with a particular realization of algorithms that Classical theorists happen to propose are irrelevant to the psychological theory; '. . . only the algorithm and the representations on which it operates are intended as a psychological hypothesis' (Fodor and Pylyshyn, 1987, p. 45). But this implies that Connectionism, as implementation theory, is neutral about the nature of cognitive processes: 'In fact, [Connectionist models] might be viewed as advancing the goals of Classical information processing psychology by attempting to explain how the brain . . . might realize the types of processes that conventional cognitive science has hypothesized' (Fodor and Pylyshyn, 1987, p. 46). It is worth quoting at length (1987, pp. 46–7) their concluding remarks on Connectionism as a theory of implementation:

> But once one admits that there really are cognitive-level principles distinct from the (putative) architectural principles that Connectionism articulates, there seems to be little left to argue about. Clearly it is pointless to ask whether one should or shouldn't do cognitive science by studying 'the interaction of lower levels' as opposed to studying processes at the cognitive level since we surely do *both* . . . We have, in short, no objection at all to networks as potential implementation models, nor do we suppose that any of the arguments we've given are incompatible with this proposal. The trouble is, however, that if Connectionists do want their models to be construed in this way, then they will have to radically alter their practice. For, it seems utterly clear that most of the Connectionist models that have actually been proposed must be construed as theories of cognition, not as theories of implementation. This follows from the fact that it is intrinsic to these theories to ascribe representational content to the units . . . that they postulate. And . . . a theory of the relations among representational states is *ipso facto* a theory at the level of cognition, not at the level of implementation. It has been the burden of our argument that when construed as a cognitive theory, rather than as an implementation theory, Connectionism appears to have fatal limitations. The problem with Connectionist models is that all the reasons for thinking that they might be true are reasons for thinking that they couldn't be *psychology* (stress supplied).

Summing up, Fodor and Pylyshyn claim that there are four ways that Connectionists can proceed. Firstly, they can argue that mental representations are indeed unstructured, in which case they must tackle productivity and systematicity. Secondly, they can adopt structured mental representations but insist upon an Associationist account of the nature of mental processes. This not only is a retreat to Hume's view of the mind (and the scepticism that results) but also rejects structure sensitivity of operations. Thirdly, they can accept that Connectionism is an implementation theory, in which case a lot of material must be rewritten. And, fourthly, they can give up the idea that networks offer '. . . a reasonable basis for modelling cognitive processes in general', i.e. they can weaken Connectionism to such an extent that Connectionist models are useful only for drawing statistical inferences, and nothing more. In this case, Connectionism retreats to the position of offering statistical models of learning that, since Chomsky in 1957, are widely acknowledged as extremely limited in their applicability.

12.3 DISCUSSION

On the face of it, Classicism and Connectionism appear irreconcilable, but the remainder of this chapter will adopt the strategy that, as usual, between two extremes the truth lies somewhere in the middle.

12.3.1   Primitives

Let us look first at the precise disagreement between Classicists and Representationalists. According to Fodor and Pylyshyn, Connectionism has 'causal connectedness' as the only primitive relation among nodes, i.e. only excitatory and inhibitory links between nodes are allowed. Classicists allow not just causal relations but also structural relations, of which constituency is paradigmatic. This in turn leads to two architectural differences. Firstly, Classicists are committed to symbolic structures that have syntactic and semantic structure and, secondly, Classical mental representations are manipulated by structure-sensitive processes.

However, these differences are not so apparent once we examine more carefully the notion of cause, which Fodor and Pylyshyn claim is the only primitive relation among nodes in a Connectionist model.

Let us adopt a simple propositional logic approach. If C1 is

> Node A is excited

and E1 is

> Node B is excited

what sort of relationship can there be between C1 and E1? We shall examine two sorts of relationships that can occur between the C1 and E1 above: causal and logical (Hospers, 1967, pp. 290–4).

If we say that C causes E, we usually mean more than C preceding E, since it is quite possible that at a certain moment in time a cat miaows and that at a following moment in time, on the other side of the world, a dog barks, but the first does not cause the second. Instead, let us look at the notions of 'necessary condition' and 'sufficient condition'.

If C is necessary for E, what we usually mean is that in our experience, in order for E to occur, C needs to occur, i.e. without C, E never occurs.

C is usually said to be *sufficient* for E if whenever C occurs, E occurs, i.e. if E does not occur, then nor does C.

The British philosopher, John Stuart Mill, defined 'cause' as a sufficient condition. That is, for an event to occur, there will be many conditions. When all the necessary conditions are fulfilled or present, the event occurs. In other words, 'cause' stands for a set of antecedents, or necessary conditions (see also Chapter 1).

In most cases, however, the list of necessary conditions will run to hundreds, if not thousands, but for Mill, despite the lengthy list of conditions that may need to be identified and to occur before a sufficient cause exists, this is the only scientific way to proceed. For instance, determining through experimentation that a proposed cause is not, in fact, a cause is still part of the scientific process.

The logical connection between C and E must not be confused with the scientific one described above. The notion of logical necessity is a relationship between statements or propositions, rather than events. Usually, this sort of relationship is brought out by the concept of inference and logical deduction: 'If p implies q and p is the case, then q must be the case.' That is, if the argument is valid and the premiss true, then the conclusion must be true.

Let us look closely at the causal interpretations first. Remember that C1 is 'Node A is excited' and E1 is 'Node B is excited'. What sort of causal relationship holds between C1 and E1?

1. The necessary condition interpretation, that C1 is necessary for E1, would be 'If not-C1 then not-E1', i.e.

> S1: If Node A is not excited then Node B is not excited

That is,

> S1': If Node B is excited, then Node A is excited

The sufficient condition interpretation, that Node A firing is sufficient for Node B firing, would be unpacked as follows:

> S2: If Node A is excited then Node B is excited

or

> S2': If Node B is not excited then Node A is not excited

There is a third way of looking at cause, this time as both a necessary and sufficient condition:

> S3: Node A being excited is both a necessary and sufficient condition for Node B being excited

or

> S3': Node A is excited if and only if Node B is excited

The logical interpretations, on the other hand, go like this:

> L1: If Node A is excited (C1) then Node B is excited (E1). Node A is excited (C1). Therefore Node B is excited (E1)

That is, we have the argument form: If C1 then E1; C1; therefore E1.
Another logical interpretation goes like this:

> L2: Only if Node A is excited (C1) is Node B excited (E2). Node A is not excited (not C1). Therefore Node B is not excited (not E1)

That is, we have: If E1, then C1; not-C1; therefore not-E1.

Notice that the introduction of the word 'only' before C1 in L2 changes the form of the argument.

Again, just as in the causal interpretations, both logical interpretations are possible, which then leads to a third logical interpretation:

L3: If and only if Node A is excited (C1) is Node B excited (E1)

That is: If C1 then E1 and if E1 then C1, which is valid if C1 and E1 can be shown to be the case.

As we have just seen, 'cause' can be unpacked in logical terms. That is, the concept of something causing another can be rephrased in the terms of the propositional calculus. Although Connectionists may not be explicit in their assumptions concerning causality, neither are Fodor and Pylyshyn. If causality can be unpacked in terms which Fodor and Pylyshyn accept as including a combinatorial syntax and semantics, as well as structure sensitivity, the main disagreement is not about the primitive relations but the depth of representation, i.e. how far back does one need to go before proposing a conceptual structure? Fodor and Pylyshyn may justifiably claim that Classical representations explicitly go deeper or further than Connectionist ones, but that is a different claim from the one they wish to make, namely, that Connectionist representations have fewer primitive relations than Classical ones, both at the surface level and at a deep level. It is then their task to demonstrate that Classical representations have primitive relations which cannot, in principle, be represented by Connectionist representations. Fodor and Pylyshyn may well be right, but further conceptual analysis is required on their part.

12.3.2   The semantics of mental representations

The next major point that Fodor and Pylyshyn make concerns the notion of mental processes. In Classical representations, Fodor and Pylyshyn claim, '. . . the syntax of a formula encodes its meaning . . .'. Namely, the meaning of a formula is somehow a function of the meaning of the individual syntactic elements. (By the way, it is interesting to note that Fodor and Pylyshyn claim that not only logic but also English has this property 'more or less', a somewhat startling claim that ignores much of post-1950 philosophy of language with its late-Wittgenstein leaning.) Fodor and Pylyshyn claim that languages having this property encode those aspects of the meaning of a formula that determine its role in inference, i.e. truth-preserving transformations. We now have the following circularity, a traditional one for Classicists: on the one hand, we are told that the syntax of a formula encodes those aspects of its meaning that determine its role in inference; on the other, we do not know which aspects of the meaning of a formula are important enough to encode until or unless we use inference; but inference (transformations) cannot operate unless they have formulae, which cannot be encoded unless we know what are the important semantic aspects . . .

This may not be a damaging criticism, since Fodor and Pylyshyn can claim that the process whereby a formula is constructed that adequately encodes those aspects of its meaning that determine its role in inference is a trial and error one: once we obtain an appropriately coded formula, everything snaps into place. But there is a far more damaging criticism that can be levelled at Classicism here, which is that it is quite possible to have a different view of semantics. For instances, in computer science, there is a view of semantics known as operational semantics, which can be described as follows (Allison, 1986, p. 2):

> Concentrating on the program as a function mapping inputs . . . into . . . results . . . leads to operational . . . semantics. Operational semantics imagines the program running on an abstract machine. This machine may be quite unlike any real computer, either low-level, simple and easy to analyse, or high-level with an easy translation from the programming language. The machine and translation must be specified. Such a definition is most useful to a compiler writer if the abstract machine is close to real hardware.

If Classicists argue that in the specification of an abstract machine and a translation the syntax at least of the formulae in the source language is used to map on to formulae in the target language, and that therefore the formulae in the target language are the semantic representations of formulae in the source language, exactly the same response can be proposed by Connectionists, i.e. that 'translating' Classical representations into Connectionist ones is to give some meaning to the Classical representations. Classical representations can then be imagined to run on abstract machines called Connection machines. Specifying the (abstract) behaviour of these (abstract) machines then provides the semantic interpretation of Classical representations. If Fodor and Pylyshyn want to rule out this possibility, it is up to them to come up with examples of Classical representations which in principle cannot be translated into Connectionist representations. Again, this is not to claim that such examples cannot be found, only that Fodor and Pylyshyn need to do some more work if they are to make their criticisms stick.

12.3.3 Implementation

This takes us on to the comment concerning implementation. Fodor and Pylyshyn claim that they have no objection to the view that Connectionist theories are implementation theories. Hence, they are happy to view Connectionism as a theory of how cognition is neurally implemented, since it, i.e. Connectionism, '. . . may constrain cognitive models no more than theories in biophysics, biochemistry, or, for that matter, quantum mechanics . . . The point is that 'implements' is transitive, and it goes all the way down' (Fodor and Pylyshyn, 1987, p. 48). This may well be true, but given our previous comments it is clear that a translation is not an implementation. That is, if Classical representations can be translated into Connectionist ones which are imagined to run on an abstract machine, it is the running (imagined or otherwise) which gives rise to the implementation (imagined or otherwise), not the translation itself. If Connectionists want to argue that their representations could in some sense be regarded as translations and not implementations of Classical representations, and that it is these translations that are cognitively valid, Fodor and Pylyshyn must adopt a different line. They could:

1. Deny that connectionist translations are possible by providing examples of Classical representations which are not in principle translatable (as previously described); or
2. Accept that Connectionist 'translations' are possible but argue that such translations are really implementations (in which case they deny any other semantic model apart from their own); or
3. Argue that Classical representations are at a higher level than Connectionist translations because the translation process can only be one way, i.e. it is not possible to translate from Connectionist representations to Classical ones and therefore 'translates' in this case is transitive, just like 'implements'.

It is not at all clear, after a thorough reading of their critique, which of these strategies Fodor and Pylyshyn would adopt. If they adopted (3), they would have to be careful that they did not come up with an inconsistent critique: for much of the paper they deny that Connectionist representations have any syntactic or semantic structure, yet (3) would involve them accepting Connectionist representations as somehow meaningful.

12.4 RECONCILIATION?

We stated at the beginning of the chapter that there is a scenario in which Classicism and Connectionism are reconcilable. The clue as to how the reconciliation can take place comes from Fodor himself! In 1982, when discussing the relationship between different levels of a cognitive architecture, he states (Pylyshyn and Demopoulos, 1986, p. 191):

> The condition that's wanted is not that for each symbol at one level there should be a corresponding symbol at the other, but simply that a necessary and sufficient condition for states described at one level is that they should be specifiable in the vocabulary of the other level. It's a much weaker condition.

Connectionism may help Fodor here. If he believes that causality is the only primitive relation in Connectionist theories, Connectionism should suit him very well as a way of moving up and down a (Classical) cognitive architecture, since causality has precisely the notions of necessary and sufficient conditions he is looking for. But for this to happen, Connectionism needs a language of some sort. (It has been suggested that the transputer language, occam, is precisely the sort of language that can happily deal with Connectionist concepts.) It is conceivable that, in future, the test of a Classical cognitive architecture, at all levels and between all levels, lies precisely in whether Fodor's criteria of states at one level being described or specifiable in the vocabulary of the other level are satisfied. If Connectionism obtains a decent vocabulary, perhaps Connectionism will provide the glue that will help a Classical cognitive architecture to be built. It may well be the case that Classicism is useful for describing what happens within a level but Connectionism is needed to describe what happens between levels.

Now, that's an interesting thought!

12.5   REFERENCES

Allison, L. (1986) *A Practical Introduction to Denotational Semantics*, Cambridge University Press, Cambridge, UK.

Feldman, J. A. and Ballard, D. H. (1982) Connectionist models and their properties. *Cognitive Science*, **6**, 205–54.

Fodor, J. A. and Pylyshyn, Z. W. (1987) Connectionism and cognitive architecture: a critical analysis, *Cognitive Science Memorandum COGMEM 29*, Centre for Cognitive Science, University of Western Ontario, London, Ontario, Canada.

Hospers, J. (1967) *An Introduction to Philosophical Analysis*, 2nd Edn, Routledge and Kegan Paul, London.

Pylyshyn, Z. W. and Demopoulos, W. (1986) (eds) *Meaning and Cognitive Structure*, Ablex Publishing, Norwood, N.J.

Rumelhart, D. E. and McClelland, J. L. (1986) PDP models and general issues in cognitive science, in *Parallel Distributed Processing*, Vol. 1 (eds D. E. Rumelhart, J. L. McClelland and the PDP Research Group), MIT Press, Cambridge, Mass., pp. 7–23.

13

Machine learning: the next ten years

DIMITRIS CHORAFAS

13.1 READING AND WRITING

In the intellectually conservative culture of the Middle Ages, more people learned the receptive skill of reading rather than the more active art of writing. Some authors have taken the view that 'It is tempting to think of writing as a process of making linguistic choices from one's repertoire of syntactic structures and lexical items. This would suggest that there is a meaning or something to be expressed, in the writer's mind.'*

But in religious seminaries focusing on an analytical culture, reading is taught as a form of independent inquiry, rather than passive acceptance of the written word. Such independent inquiry was originally practised through discourse. At its origin was Socrates and his school. This was the sense of verbal literacy in ancient Greece.

Like verbal literacy, computer literacy includes a wide range of skills, none of which can be taught in isolation. Students should learn how to work with multimedia, how to analyse an interactive video form, but also how to critique present and potential uses of computing. Through introspection, we should be just as critical about ourselves.

This is not so often done by *Homo sapiens*. In the majority, we still follow the medieval concept of reading rather than writing. Thus 99% of humanity lives well below its intellectual means, below the line of poverty in terms of skill and know-how. 'People think I am a genius, because I use my brains twice per week,' George Bernard Shaw once said.

Reading, by the way, is precisely what *Silico sapiens* does well – once a program, text, data or graph is input to them. But writing is a creative process. It employs a composing approach which involves recursive activities:

1. prewriting
2. writing
3. rewriting

*This quotation comes from a conference in Rome, for which I have lost the precise reference.

Recursion can be performed by men or machines disposing enough intelligence to undertake it. This is a subtle way of suggesting that *Homo sapiens* is not the only species to feature

1. memory
2. computing
3. learning ability

Silico sapiens can do just as well. Let us look at these three issues individually.

13.2   HOMO SAPIENS AND SILICO SAPIENS

We do not really know how big is the human brain in terms of storage and switching elements, though a prevailing hypothesis has been that it has about 10^{12} neurons. John von Neumann speculated that the human can store not only in the brain itself, but also in the rest of the body. He guestimated that the total information storage capability might be between 10^{16} and 10^{18} bits.

If we take as an example the Connection Machine (Hillis, 1985) with its 128 000 (ALUs) arithmetic/logical units and 4096 bytes of cache memory per ALU, we get less than 10^{10} bits in distributed central memory. The numbers change when we look at 'the rest of the body'.

Photonics being the foremost technology today, let us consider optical discs. FileNet, one of the juke-boxes in the market, has 64 discs of 2.6 gigabytes each. Four juke-boxes can be combined together to a total capacity of 6.6×10^{11} bytes – or more than 5×12^{12} bits.

A new version expected by the end of 1988 will feature 8.0 gigabytes per disc, 200 discs per unit and an aggregate of eight interlinked juke-boxes. As an order of magnitude, the resulting storage capacity will be about 10^{15} bits of storage. That is three orders of magnitude more than the brain bits – though in the average two orders of magnitude less than the von Neumann hypothesis on total *Homo sapiens* memory. Yet, 10^{15} bits of on-line storage is indeed an impressive number.

The memory gap is closing. Furthermore, since we do not know how we really use our 10^{16}–10^{18} bits of storage it is hard to say if 10^{12} is effectively more or less than what man disposes. Fortunately, we do know a little better how to count calculating ability in men and machines:

1. A conventional mainframe has 1 ($10°$) processor;
2. Multiprocessing solutions feature 3 or $4 \times 10°$ processors;
3. Coarse grain parallelism supports 10^{2}–10^{3} processors (for instance, the Teradata database computer);*
4. Fine grain parallelism has 10^{5}–10^{6} processors (that is the example of the Connection Machine) (Hillis, 1985);
5. The human brain, as we said, features 10^{12} processors. (The neurons serve both for storage and for switching.)

*Teradata Corporation, Los Angeles, Calif.

But each switch of the brain works slowly (10^{-2} sec), while computers operate at a cycle speed of 10^{-6}–10^{-7} sec, though the individual elements switch at 10^{-9} sec. So the difference is not as big as it seems if we consider the important measure of bits per second per system (BPSS).

Just because the switching of the neurons is very slow* in the human system, BPSS stands at 10^{14}. Precisely: $10^{12}/10^{-2}$.

What about *Silico sapiens?* We said that the processors of the Connection Machine work at 10^{-6}–10^{-7}. With 10^5–10^6 processors, it features a BPSS of 10^{11}–10^{12}. The difference from the human nervous system stands at less than 10^3 to the latter's favour. Given technology's advances, it will close prior to the year 2000.

In other terms, if computers continue to double in speed every two or three years, it will be possible to build a computer of equivalent power to the human brain prior to the end of the century. The question is how this machine will learn – and what may be its literacy level. That is the third basic element.

13.3   INTELLECT IN MEN AND MACHINES

As *Homo sapiens*, we have to learn how to speak, read and write a language, even if we are equipped at birth with the genetic code. We also have to learn skills: how to work, how to follow a methodology. Work is a level of intelligence well above the genetic code.

Learning is a lifelong process. People who progress in life are those who steadily learn. Even the oldest head among us is a brand new learner – if he really intends to stay alive in a professional and intellectual sense.

Our civilization has been characterized by the battle for intelligence. Pioneers fought against stupid regulatory hand-overs, out-of-date schools, depressive economic systems, because their experience taught them these are ineffective. Such moves required conceptual skills and imagination, which is the highest level of intelligence ever.

Silico sapiens may mimic the diversity of carbon life-forms and rival the powers of their human creator. As the preceding section demonstrated, very large-scale integration (VLSI) made the computer more powerful than specialists would have expected, and surprisingly familiar to the level of ordinary people. Even if present technology went no further, its impact would still be profound.

What about learning by *Silico sapiens?* Skill acquisition is the ability of a machine to improve its performance in selected problem areas. Such improvement is based on knowledge and previous experiences. This particularly characterizes a goal-directed system.

For *Silico sapiens* learning means enabling a program to improve its future behaviour. Such improvement is based on observing its own past performance on

---

*In reality neurons switch at 10^{-3} sec but because of synapses and fatigue 10^{-2} sec is taken as a realistic measure.

related tasks. This is one of the foremost contributions of artificial intelligence (AI), though it is not always recognized to be so.

Assume an AI system operating in a real environment and able to combine:

1. a problem-solving component and
2. a learning component

The learning component analyses the system's failure to solve some specified problem and refines the problem-solving knowledge. Gradually the AI construct solves more problems of a similar nature in an increasingly efficient way.

In a way, machine learning resembles the independent inquiry of religious seminaries, referred to in the first section. Introspective systems reason about themselves. They access representations of themselves and modify them in a causally connected manner. Introspection has much to do with metaknowledge and reflection. Subsystems of a reflective organism are:

1. the inference engine for reasoning
2. the knowledge bank as a depository of domain facts and states

They are linked through a causally connected representation. Knowledge impacts on the external domain and is influenced by it. This is quite similar to how *Homo sapiens* learns through interaction with the environment.

We know that channelling intelligence back into self-improvement is fundamental in biological systems. Biological creatures use their existing knowledge to learn more effectively and even to improve the intelligence of their species by reproductive preferences. That is why memory and calculating ability are so important.

It is therefore proper to take notice that, like biological creatures, new generation AI constructs can learn from experience to improve their performance, and also their potential. The criteria of machine intelligence are no more those Geoffrey Jefferson once suggested: * 'Not until a machine can write a sonnet or compose a concerto, because of thoughts or emotions felt, and not by the chance fall of symbols, could we agree that machine equals brain.'

To Jefferson's references could be added other expressions of art, such as painting. We do have today expert systems which do paintings and others which help in composing music. But we do not yet have machines with imagination – though computers are widely used in planning.

Employed in the sense of problem-solving, AI constructs can act as assistants to the human mind, expanding its capabilities. But are we ready to use such intelligent machines?

13.4 LIVING IN A TECHNOLOGY-INTENSE AGE

Those of us who live and work in a technology-intense environment do appreciate that sophisticated computer resources have begun to change our life-

*'The Mind of Mechanical Man', an address delivered at the Lister Oration, 9 June, 1949.

styles. It is now projected that *the AI revolution will rival the invention of writing and that of the printing press*; that it will usher changes as fundamental as the appearance of the wheel to the evolution of the internal combustion engine.

What we lack is the ability to calculate the effect of *Silico sapiens* on *Homo sapiens* in fifty or a hundred years. We do know, however, that the computers now familiar to most people are only a rudimentary beginning. They are the first encounter of *Homo sapiens* with *Silico sapiens*.

Factory robots of today and their autonomous descendants of tomorrow will deal with an increasing variety of objects and environments. Knowledge of the basic properties of these objects and environments will be their level of literacy. We will look at some examples.

For *Silico sapiens*, such knowledge will be constituted by the:

1. geometry of shapes and sizes
2. kinematics of forces and torques
3. dynamics of mechanisms in motion

Such fundamental knowledge does not come naturally to robots, neither for that matter to human production engineers. No robot, without being explicitly told, would know the basic notions of its work. Does it sound familiar to *Homo sapiens*?

Our own work in computer-aided design and computer-aided manufacturing (CAD/CAM), for instance, cannot develop effectively without an extensive knowledge foundation, without our knowledge bank to call upon. All of the materials and components involved in CAD must be taught to the designer (and to the system) before they can be used. They are taught by the designer to an apprentice designer, prior to inserting him in the production process.

Frederic Winslow Taylor, the man who in 1912 established time study through his Bethlehem Steel experiments, once tried to define a good foreman. He came up with eight qualifications so difficult to attain that he concluded: 'A man who possesses them should be the company president rather than just a foreman.'*

Naïve developers of machine learning skills are in Taylor's path with three-quarters of a century delay. Many projects try to develop machine learning as a universal skill. We have not been able to do it with humans. What makes us think we can make it with machines?

But there is scope in specialized machine learning. The new generation of CAD tools gives a good example. Manufacturing industries today are snowed under hundred of thousands of blueprints of the pre-CAD era, which lasted till the late 1970s. They are ending up with a split system: 10% automated and 90% on paper. What about putting *Silico sapiens* to do the necessary, currently manual, slow and costly conversion job?

Computers will have to be taught pattern recognition. There are major breakthroughs in artificial vision. Facilities are becoming available to scan existing drawings and store them in raster format; edit these drawings; convert in

*I quote from memory of a seminar given at UCLA by the late Prof. Ralph Barnes in 1953.

part or in whole, selected drawings; correct inaccuracies and create new CAD drawings employing parametric approaches to produce a family of parts.

Expert systems provide checking features to verify part design. The now developing electronic image management systems present impressive learning capabilities. Dimensions drive the geometry. By changing dimension values, intelligent machines can create completely new parts. They can also employ an intelligent database structure.

Within the next five to seven years, expert systems will check designs for dimensional completeness and consistency, displaying the results in a way meaningful to *Homo sapiens*. Thus designers could detect design errors early in the product development cycle, improving the quality of their work. That is a significant learning skill by *Silico sapiens*.

13.5 INTELLIGENT WALKING ROBOTS

Projected for the mid-1990s, autonomous intelligent vehicles are considered to be test beds of sixth-generation computers (6GC). One way of looking at computer generations is the topmost design and implementation aims we have attained. The years 1953–1968 have been characterized by designing machines which were:

1. faster and faster

During this period, the von Neumann concept dominated – even if two major changes took place in the meantime. First, in 1958 transistors replaced vacuum tubes. Second, in 1965 computer design became memory centred rather than ALU based.

The motto of the following decade (1968–78) has been:

2. smaller and smaller

The minis made this change possible with evident impact on applications: distributed data processing and distributed databases were the result. Another challenge started in 1978 with the PC. The new trend line became:

3. cheaper and cheaper

For about ten years following the 1978 milestone, the goal was one of making the same architectures, but cheaper. Now the goal is:

4. newer and newer

Practically every six months we have a major breakthrough in communications and in computers. Before the end of this century, the sign of excellence will be:

5. smarter and smarter

while at the same time these incredibly intelligent robots would have been taught to walk. To reach this goal, multifunctional capabilities should come into play:

vision, movement, positioning, senses, planning and reasoning. We cannot divorce planning and reasoning from the senses.

The seemingly simple act of walking is actually a complex blend of balance and co-ordination. *Homo sapiens* and other animals have developed their own way of walking. For years technicians studied it in an effort to create a robot that can walk.

Today robotics firms produce machines that can not only walk but climb. Eventually intelligent robots may be handling jobs ranging from sentry duty to herding and farming. After all, wheeled robots are already in general use for security, bomb disposal and other tasks.

The difference between the coming generation of autonomous intelligent vehicles and current walking machines is significant in the sense that the latter travel quickly over flat surfaces. They cannot move across rocky terrain, manage staircases, make their way through cluttered manufacturing plants. But a successful walking robot must be able constantly to change its way – and to shift its weight from one leg to another without toppling over.

With this, *Silico sapiens* will closely parallel *Homo sapiens*. As humans, we do what the preceding paragraph suggested by using complicated nerve and muscle networks to maintain balance while in motion.

Some living organisms like beetles avoid the balance problem on flat terrain by always having at least three legs on the ground. This alternating tripod approach may not be so elegant, but is simple and dependable. As such, it has been used in designing walking robots.

13.6 AUTONOMOUS NAVIGATION

A six-legged robot can adopt a relatively sedate alternating tripod gait, repositioning three legs while maintaining a stable tripod base. Other designs and gaits, such as Raibert's one-legged hopper, must compute and execute their actions literally on the fly.

Walking robots can cover terrain that is naturally inaccessible to standard vehicles. In military operations, walking reconnaissance and combat robots may in the beginning have human drivers. One method investigated with the Ohio State University hexapod,* accomplished this by pointing a laser spot on the ground at potential footholds. But eventually robots will have to learn to walk.

In retrospect we can say that some ideas on walking robots emanate from the nineteenth century: attaching a pick-up, and measuring speed, acceleration, distance. But most tools have come to light through research and AI; hence, the kernel of the new approach to how a man-made system balances. As an ICOT

---

*The Hexapod Project at Ohio State University is directed by Dr McGhee. It is sponsored by the Defense Advanced Research Projects Agency of the US Dept of Defense. It is interesting to note that a US Army study indicates that over 50% of the earth's terrain is inaccessible to current wheeled and tracked vehicles.

(Institute of Computing Technology) sponsored project* on artificial vision suggests, with *Silico sapiens*:

1. The sensors will be TV cameras and ultrasonics;
2. The matching paradigm: pattern kinetics; network algorithms; nearest echo connection; list matching; heuristics;
3. The involved knowledge will include object images, distance measurement, echo, image structures – but the foundation is learning.

Object image may, for instance, exhibit deformation uniquely determined by viewpoint shift. Distance to an object could demonstrate variation; echo will be reflected outside of objects; image structures specified by the type of objects and their status. Still the autonomous intelligent robot needs a learning process for cognition, perception and comprehension.

Environment status identification can be effectively done through learning and experience on the AI construct's behalf. This permits a structure to be analysed. For instance, take the image observed in front of the staircase. First, the feature point of the staircase is detected, then the area in which the door is expected to be located is specified. Detected vertical and horizontal segments are parametrized. The obtained parameter list is matched with the reference list and map, to identify the door status as open.

Cognition of objects, perception of errors, flexible mapping and spatial movement, require a host of capabilities to be supported through AI:

1. spatial reasoning (findpath, findspace)
2. pattern and object recognition
3. inductive learning of force trajectories
4. geometric reasoning
5. movement planning and execution
6. feedback and correction

Every step involves machine learning mechanisms, and that is one of the better examples of what we can expect during the next ten years.

This can be said in conclusion: a new concept for autonomous navigation is in development, and mobile robots using a priori knowledge of surroundings, AI-enriched observation channels, and learning capabilities are a key technology developed through AI implementation. This technology has been shown to be practical by leading-edge projects such as Alvey in England, GMD in Germany, ICOT in Japan and MCC (Microelectronics Computer Corporation) in the USA. Further advancements in machine learning techniques are expected to contribute to the development of a wide range of intelligent robots. Learning by *Silico sapiens* is not for tomorrow. It is being practised today.

---

*I obtained this information during meetings with ICOT and MITI (Ministry of International Trade and Industry) in September 1986.

13.7 MACHINE LEARNING IN A FINANCIAL ENVIRONMENT

Financial services range from the simplest short-term credit to the most complex leveraged buy-out or project financing. They also include:

1. all sorts of trading
2. origination and distribution functions
3. interest rate and currency swaps

Emphasis is on blending investment banking with commercial banking, and setting the various product and marketing areas to work together. In the financial markets where rates and values change almost every second, such blending requires a fast, flexible and accurate learning mechanism.

Foreign operations, stock trading and fund management are fertile but difficult areas of AI implementation. By contrast, loan advising is relatively simple and therefore it has been a favoured expert systems field. Not only is machine learning fundamental in foreign exchange and arbitrage, but we must also account for two dealer personalities:

1. The hunter type who will move like a killer beast when his counterpart hestitates and changes his mind;
2. The chartist and analytical type who will not move till statistics tell him the time has come.

Given experience and very fast computers, we can project an AI construct as the fastest covered interest arbitrageur. It will be trained to perform massive currency transactions (billions of dollars hourly) to take advantage of transient currency exchange rate inequalities.

It may be possible, for example, to change dollars to Deutschmarks, marks to pounds, pounds to yen, and yen to dollars again, and wind up with more dollars than we started, if we can detect the financial undercurrents and do transactions fast enough. Properly taught, *Silico sapiens* can do it.

By involving the AI construct in a process of machine learning, we can capitalize on financial market inequalities. Like a killer-type foreign exchange dealer, the expert system would:

1. Follow the wire traffic with attention;
2. Call correspondents to fill gaps in information;
3. Run this input against a database with known opportunities; and
4. Upon decision, ring up opponent dealers to make an offer using voice synthesis interface.

In terms of an inference engine and learning mechanism, there are two approaches to this problem. One is to use production rules: antecedent for examination of data; consequent for modification of data or to cause other actions.

A more generic approach is episodic memory. Supported through fifth-generation computers' memory-based reasoning (MBR), it is a method for making decisions through the examination of instances in a global database. It has been developed at Brandeis University by a team directed by Professor David Waltz. The database can be multimedia, containing information that represents situations along with outcomes or actions.

Memory-based reasoning involves three phases:

1. Hypotheses formation;

The AI system selects from a large database a number of past situations that are similar to the current one it wishes to understand. It is important that the database is fairly large.

2. The hypotheses suggested by the returned instances are examined – one at a time;
3. Support for each of the possible hypotheses is evaluated using Bayesian or possibility theory.

Through machine learning, the system would improve the quality level of its hypotheses. It will also make the search for similar instances tractable.

Memory-based systems can also reason from a small number of instances, which is what we often do in learning. If even one previous item in the database is very similar to the current item, it can serve as a basis for hypothesis formation. Another learning similarity between MBR and *Silico sapiens* is that the more items are similar, the better the system learns.

If no instances in the global database are similar to the current situation, the system can inform its user of this fact. In the general case, MBR with learning capabilities is much more robust than classical rule-based systems, since it is unlikely to make a misjudgement just because the domain expert missed something.

Furthermore, MBR-type solutions continuously adapt to the world around them. As new instances are encountered, they are added to the systems' knowledge bank as experiences – a learning characteristic *par excellence* – thus becoming immediately available to support all subsequent decisions.

While focus has been placed in financial implementation, such solutions are generally applicable in communications-intense environments. Telephone exchanges at large can greatly profit, particularly if enriched with real-time translation capabilities. The latter will soon be a top competitive tool in many fields, banking being once more an example.

There are large profits to be made in the financial business. Among well-to-do institutions are some with a good coverage of all markets, others with a specialist niche. But what distinguishes them all from less profitable banks is that they have a constantly growing, well-directed investment in technology.

Most recently, this investment focuses on AI. Financial institutions suffer if they do not continue to invest in brainpower or try to compete against increasingly integrated opponents – rich in expert systems support. While the form of future banking technology cannot be predicted with certainty, machine learning is the way to bet.

13.8   ENHANCING OR ENDANGERING THE HUMAN SPECIES?

The emerging AI species raises fundamental questions about the future of *Homo sapiens*. The intellectual and technological challenges of creating autonomous vehicles are attracting many of the best human minds in the world today. The same is true of financial models. Let us not forget that more than half the engineers and scientists who ever lived on earth are alive and productive at this time.

Intelligence building takes many forms. Learning allows an individual intelligent system to incorporate invaluable new knowledge and develop strategies. Evolution, of both ideas and structures, transforms intelligence in individual systems and transfers it to their successors.

If a chain reaction can be initiated and sustained for robots, it might provide for exponential growth going from today's rudimentary or adolescent AI systems to high-level ones.

Experience from a biological context tends to suggest that with AI constructs learning ability can be simultaneously

1. A yardstick of intelligence; and
2. The tool by which the latter grows from experience.

Learning is the basis of further development and so is the role of knowledge in a specific culture. Culture is the real learning mechanism which transforms *Homo sapiens*. Tomorrow, it will do the same with *Silico sapiens*.

For *Homo sapiens*, the culture transport engines have been philosophy, history, the humanities, arts, linguistics, psychology and mathematics. These arts and sciences have created our rich intellectual environment – and they keep enriching it with the passage of time.

Through culture, learning and intelligence, carbon life-forms achieved direct control of their own actions, and therefore, of their destiny. Without AI enrichment, the incredible shrinking computer chip remains unconscious and impotent, in spite its internal processing capabilities. Learning machines are the new frontier in AI.

It is precisely because of learning that AI will have a very deep impact in our society. It will be an impact similar to that of the radical proposals by Nicolaus Copernicus (1473–1543) and Galileo Galilei (1564–1642). Both men demoted the earth from its pivotal cosmic status. Quite similarly, the suggestion that a new species of autonomous intelligent beings is emerging clashes deeply with our cherished notions of self-importance.

The fact is that AI constructs seem capable of eventually acquiring many significant human traits – including thinking and learning capabilities. Based on the trends outlined in Section 2, I am correcting upon the dates Sir Clive Sinclair projected during the seventh European Conference on AI (1986):

1. By the year 2000, there will be available a machine of nearly human complexity: the android brain.

Then, by the year:

2. 2010, there may be circuitry equating to biological densities;
3. 2020, software adaptive to environmental stimuli will be perfected;
4. 2030, teachable computers with brain-type metalanguage may become available;
5. 2040, automated intuition and imagination might see the light; and
6. 2050, there might exist intelligent man-made systems more powerful in intellect than humans, by one or two orders of magnitude.

In essence, does it really matter? The idea of test-tube babies does not upset us. What difference does it make that intelligent computers are man-made?

13.9 REFERENCES

Hillis, D. (1985) *The Connection Machine*, MIT Press, Cambridge, Mass.
Sinclair, C. (1986) Keynote Address, *Proc. 7th ECAI*, Brighton, Sussex.

Select bibliography

Aleksander, I. and Burnett, P. (1984) *Re-inventing Man*, Penguin Books, Harmondsworth, Middx.

Arciszewski, T., Mustafa, M. and Ziarko, W. (1987) A methodology of design knowledge acquisition for use in learning expert systems. *Internat. J. Man-Machine Studies*, **27**, 23–32.

Biswas, P. and Majumdar, A. (1981) A multistage fuzzy classifier for recognition of handprinted characters. *IEEE Trans. on Systems, Man and Cybernetics*, **SMC-11**(12), 834–8.

Bratko, I. and Lavrac, N. (eds) (1987) *Progress in Machine Learning*, Sigma Press, Wilmslow, UK.

Breiman, L., Friedman, J., Olshen, R. and Stone, C. (1984) *Classification and Regression Trees*, Wadsworth and Brooks, Monterey, Calif.

Carbonell, J., Michalski, R. and Mitchell, T. (1983) Machine learning: a historical and methodological analysis. *AI Magazine*, **4**(3), 69–79.

Cognitive Science, Special Issue (1985) Connectionist models and their applications. *Cognitive Science*, **1**(9) (March).

Cohen, P. and Feigenbaum, E. (1982) *The Handbook of Artificial Intelligence*, Vol. 3, Pitman Books, London.

Dieterich, T. and Michalski, R. (1981) Inductive learning of structural descriptions. *Artificial Intelligence*, **16**(3) 257–94.

Fodor, J. and Pylyshyn, Z. W. (1988) Connectionism and cognitive architecture: a critical analysis. *Cognition*, **28** (1), 3–72.

Forsyth, R. and Rada, R. (1986) *Machine Learning: Applications in Expert Systems and Information Retrieval*, Ellis Horwood, Chichester.

Hart, A. (1986) *Knowledge Acquisition for Expert Systems*, Kogan Page, London.

Hilgard, E. R. and Bower, G. H. (1966) *Theories of Learning*, Appleton-Century-Crofts, New York.

Hinton, G. E. and Anderson, J. (eds) (1981) *Parallel Models of Associative Memory*, Lawrence Erlbaum, Hillsdale, N.J.

Hofstadter, D. (1985) *Metamagical Themas*, Basic Books Inc., New York.

Holland, J. (1975) *Adaptation in Natural and Artificial Systems*, University of Michigan Press, Ann Arbor.

Holland, J. H., Holyoak, K. J., Nisbett, R. E. and Thagard, P. R. (1986) *Induction: Processes of Inference, Learning and Discovery*: MIT Press, Cambridge, Mass.

James, M. (1985) *Classification Algorithms*, Collins Tech. Books, London.

Lakatos, I. (1976) *Proofs and Refutations: The Logic of Mathematical Discovery*, Cambridge University Press, Cambridge.

Langley, P., Simon, H., Bradshaw, G. and Zytkow, J. (1986) *Scientific Discovery: Computational Explorations of the Creative Process*, MIT Press, Cambridge, Mass.

Lawler, R., Du Boulay, B., Hughes, M. and Macleod, H. (1986) *Cognition and Computers*, Ellis Horwood, Chichester.

Lenat, D. (1982) The nature of heuristics. *Artifical Intelligence*, **19**(2), 189–249.

Lenat, D. (1983) Eurisko: a program that learns new heuristics and domain concepts. *Artificial Intelligence*, **21** (1) and (2), 61–98.

Medawar, P. (1969) *Induction and Intuition in Scientific Thought*, Methuen, London.

Michalski, R., Carbonell, J. and Mitchell, T. (1983) *Machine Learning: An Artificial Intelligence Approach*, Tioga Publishing Corp., Palo Alto, Calif.

Michalski, R., Carbonell, J. and Mitchell, T. (1986) *Machine Learning: An Artificial Intelligence Approach*, Vol. 2, Morgan Kaufmann Publishers, Los Altos, Calif.

Michalski, R. and Chilausky, R. L. (1980) Learning by being told and learning from examples: . . . . *Internat. J. Policy Analysis and Info. Systems*. **4**(2), 125–61.

Michie, D. (ed.) (1982) *Introductory Reading in Expert Systems*, Gordon and Breach, London.

Michie, D. (1986) *On Machine Intelligence*, Ellis Horwood, Chichester.

Michie, D. and Johnston, R. (1985) *The Creative Computer*, Penguin Books, Harmondsworth, Middx.

Miller, D. (ed.) (1987) *A Pocket Popper*, Fontana Press, Glasgow.

Minsky, M. and Papert, S. (1969) *Perceptrons: an Introduction to Computational Geometry*, MIT Press, Boston, Mass.

Mitchell, T. (1977) Version spaces: a candidate elimination approach to rule induction. *Internat. Joint Conf. on AI*, **5**, 305–10.

Mitchell, T. (1982) Generalization as search. *Artificial Intelligence*, **18**, 203–26.

Partridge, D. (1986) *AI: Applications in the Future of Software Engineering*, Ellis Horwood, Chichester.

Passmore, J. (1968) *A Hundred Years of Philosophy*, Penguin Books, Harmondsworth, Middx.

Popper, K. (1972) *Conjectures and Refutations*, 4th edn, Routledge and Kegan Paul, London.

Pylyshyn, Z. and Demopoulos, W. (eds) (1986) *Meaning and Cognitive Structure*, Ablex Publishing, Norwood, N.J.

Rosenblatt, F. (1962) *Principles of Neurodynamics*, Spartan Books, New York.

Samuel, A. (1967) Some studies in machine learning using the game of checkers II *IBM J. of R. and D.*, November, 98–113.

Schank, R. (1982) *Dynamic Memory: A Theory of Reminding and Learning in Computers and People*, Cambridge University Press, Cambridge.

Simon, H., Langley, P. and Bradshaw, G. (1981) Scientific discovery as problem solving. *Synthese*, **47**, 1–27.

Sklansky, J. and Wassel, G. (1981) *Pattern Classifiers and Trainable Machines*, Springer-Verlag, New York.

Sober, E. (ed.) (1984) *Conceptual Issues in Evolutionary Biology*, Bradford Books/MIT Press, Cambridge, Mass.

Uhr, L. (1966) *Pattern Recognition*, Wiley, New York.

Winston, P. (1984) *Artificial Intelligence*, 2nd edn, Addison-Wesley, Cambridge, Mass.

Wong, S. K. M., Ziarko, Woijciech and Ye, R. L. (1986) Comparison of rough-set and statistical methods in inductive learning. *Internat. J. Man-Machine Studies*. **24**, 53–72.

Index